Explaining Attitudes offers a timely and important challenge to the dominant conception of belief found in the work of such philosophers as Dretske and Fodor. According to this dominant view, beliefs, if they exist at all, are constituted by states of the brain. Lynne Rudder Baker rejects this view and replaces it with a quite different approach: Practical Realism. Seen from the perspective of Practical Realism, any argument that interprets beliefs as either brain states or immaterial souls rests on a false dichotomy. Practical Realism takes beliefs to be states of the whole person, rather like states of health. What a person believes is determined by what that person would do, say, and think in various circumstances. Thus beliefs and other attitudes are interwoven into an integrated, commonsense conception of reality.

Among the topics discussed in detail are intentional explanations, causal explanations, the project of naturalizing intentionality, the importance of relational properties, the use of counterfactuals to underwrite belief, the nature of objectivity, the philosophical import of the idea of "mind independence," and the relation of common sense to science.

This book will prove valuable to professional philosophers, psychologists, and cognitive scientists.

Explaining attitudes

CAMBRIDGE STUDIES IN PHILOSOPHY

General editor ERNEST SOSA

Advisory editors JONATHAN DANCY,
GILBERT HARMAN, FRANK JACKSON,
WILLIAM G. LYCAN, SYDNEY SHOEMAKER,
JUDITH THOMSON

RECENT TITLES

Explaining attitudes

A PRACTICAL APPROACH
TO THE MIND

Lynne Rudder Baker

University of Massachusetts, Amherst

CAMBRIDGE
UNIVERSITY PRESS

Published by the Press Syndicate of the University of Cambridge
The Pitt Building, Trumpington Street, Cambridge CB2 1RP
40 West 20th Street, New York, NY 10011-4211, USA
10 Stamford Road, Oakleigh, Melbourne 3166, Australia

First published 1995

Printed in the United States of America

Library of Congress Cataloging-in-Publication Data
Baker, Lynne Rudder, 1944–
Explaining attitudes: a practical approach to the mind /
Lynne Rudder Baker.
p. cm. – (Cambridge studies in philosophy)
Includes bibliographical references and index.
ISBN 0-521-42053-9. – ISBN 0-521-42190-X (pbk.)
1. Philosophy of mind. 2. Attitude (Psychology) I. Title. II. Series.
BD418.3.B35   1995
128'.2 – dc20   94-16693
                                                              CIP

A catalog record for this book is available from the British Library.

ISBN 0-521-42053-9 hardback
ISBN 0-521-42190-X paperback

To my dear husband,
Tom

Contents

Preface

For the past couple of decades, issues concerning the nature of the mind have held center stage in philosophy. Traditional philosophers of mind, philosophers of psychology, cognitive scientists, and metaphysicians have approached the mind with the conviction that the mind is the brain: Whatever mental states there are ultimately should be understood as states of an individual's brain. Typically, philosophers have seen their task as one of working out the details of this conception.

In this book, I propose an alternative approach to the mind – one compatible both with scientific study of the mind and with the assumption of materialism. Several years ago, I published a critique of the dominant assumptions about the mind, *Saving Belief: A Critique of Physicalism* (Princeton: Princeton University Press, 1987). Here I try to deepen the critique and to offer a constructive proposal that, I hope, will contribute to a different way of conceiving of the mind.

Explaining Attitudes is the outcome of several years of lecturing at colleges and universities, participating in conferences, and publishing articles in journals. So a number of the ideas have not only been market-tested (so to speak) but also transformed by the comments and criticisms of many people. I am especially indebted to Derk Pereboom for his patient and perceptive reading of multiple drafts of this book and to Gareth B. Matthews and Katherine Sonderegger for searching discussion of a wide range of philosophical issues. Also helpful have been the comments of Don Adams, Bruce Aune, Kent Bach, Alan Berger, John Connolly, Max Cresswell, Mark Crimmins, Willem deVries, Fred Dretske, Fred Feldman, Jerry A. Fodor, Jay Garfield, Edmund Gettier, Geoffrey Goddu, Don Gustafson, John Heil, Terence Horgan, Pierre Jacob, Hilary Kornblith, Billy Joe Lucas, William G. Lycan, Albert Mele, Jeffrey Poland, John Post, Annette Prieur, Russell Trenholme, J. D. Trout, Robert van Gulick, Barbara von Eckardt, and Steven Wagner.

The arguments have benefited from extended discussions when I participated in the Distinguished Visitors' program at the University of California at Riverside in 1991, the NEH Institute on Naturalism at the University of Nebraska at Lincoln in 1993, the NEH Institute on Meaning at Rutgers University in 1993, the Thirty-first Annual Philosophy Colloquium at Oberlin College in 1993, the Twenty-eighth Annual Philosophy Colloquium at the University of Cincinnati in 1992, the annual meeting of the Creighton Club in 1990, the Conference on Mental Causation at the University of Bielefeld, Germany, 1990. I also want to thank the Woodrow Wilson International Center for Scholars in Washington, D.C., for a residential fellowship for five months during 1988–9.

I revised many arguments on the basis of useful discussions when I gave talks at Princeton University, the École Polytechnique (Paris), the University of California at Davis, the University of Michigan, Virginia Commonwealth University, SUNY at Buffalo, Brandeis University, Duke University, Davidson College, the University of Connecticut at Storrs, the Ohio State University, Washington University, the University of Rochester, Western Michigan University, Union College, Manhattanville College, the University of Colorado at Boulder, the University of New Hampshire, and Harvard University.

Earlier versions of several of the arguments presented here appear elsewhere: "Content and Context," in *Logic and Language* (Philosophical Perspectives 8), ed. James E. Tomberlin (Atascadero, CA: Ridgeview Publishing Company, 1994), 17–32; "Eliminativism and an Argument from Science," *Mind and Language* 8 (1993): 180–8; "What Beliefs Are Not," in *Naturalism: A Critical Appraisal,* ed. Steven J. Wagner and Richard Warner (Notre Dame: University of Notre Dame Press, 1993), 321–37; "Metaphysics and Mental Causation," *Mental Causation,* ed. John Heil and Alfred Mele (Oxford: Clarendon Press, 1993), 75–95; "Has Content Been Naturalized?" in *Meaning in Mind: Fodor and His Critics,* ed. Barry Loewer and Georges Rey (Oxford: Basil Blackwell, 1991), 17–32; "Dretske on the Explanatory Role of Belief," *Philosophical Studies* 63 (1991): 99–111; "On a Causal Theory of Content," in *Philosophy of Mind and Action Theory, 1989* (Philosophical Perspectives 3), ed. James E. Tomberlin (Atascadero, CA: Ridgeview Publishing Company,

1989), 166–86; "Truth in Context," *Philosophical Psychology* 2 (1989): 85–94. I thank the publishers of these articles for permission to use materials from them.

Finally, I am especially grateful to Stanley Bates and Victor Nuovo, chairs of the Philosophy Department at Middlebury College, and to John Robison, head of the Philosophy Department at the University of Massachusetts at Amherst, for their long-standing support of my endeavors.

PART I

The Standard View and its problems

1

Two conceptions of the attitudes

René Descartes is famous for distinguishing between "the moral mode of knowing which suffices for the regulation of life," and "that Metaphysical mode of knowing," which is beyond all rational doubt.[1] The kind of knowledge that suffices for practical affairs is of little concern to Descartes's philosopher, who seeks knowledge that can be grasped with absolute certainty. Although the ideal of Cartesian certainty largely has been abandoned, many philosophers retain a two-tiered conception of knowledge: According to this conception, the knowledge pertaining to the "practical needs of life" is, at best, a kind of second-class truth that must either be validated by science or relegated to the dustbin of the merely heuristic.

Among philosophers who take "all traits of reality worthy of the name" to be exclusively in the hands of the sciences or, more generally, in the hands of a metaphysics that aspires to be scientific,[2] there is disagreement about the extent of scientific knowledge: Are the physical sciences the only source of genuine knowledge, as Quine holds, or should sciences that appeal to generalizations not translatable into the austere notation of theoretical physics also be recognized as sources of first-class truth, as so-called nonreductive materialists hold? Either way, according to the received two-tiered view, putative truths that resist integration into scientific theory must be understood "with a grain of salt."[3] As Wilfrid Sellars put

1 René Descartes, "Objections VII," in *The Philosophical Works of Descartes*, vol. 2, trans. Elizabeth S. Haldane and G. R. T. Ross (Cambridge: Cambridge University Press, 1979), 278.
2 W. V. O. Quine, *Word and Object* (Cambridge, MA: Harvard University Press, 1960), 228.
3 Daniel Dennett used this expression to characterize his view of attributions of belief, in "Instrumentalism Reconsidered," in *The Intentional Stance* (Cambridge, MA: MIT/Bradford, 1987), 72–3.

3

the received view so vividly, "In the dimension of describing and explaining the world, science is the measure of all things, of what is that it is, and of what is not that it is not."[4]

My ultimate aim is to expose the poverty of this received view and to propose an alternative that does not separate the knowledge needed for "the conduct of our life" from "the search after truth." According to my alternative, the knowledge that meets "the practical needs of life," whether incorporated into scientific theory or not, has its own integrity and is no less revelatory of reality – genuine reality – than is knowledge discovered by physics or any other scientific discipline.[5]

One major battleground of the controversy is inquiry into the nature of the mind – inquiry at the intersection of the philosophy of mind, the philosophy of science, and metaphysics. Although proponents of the received view agree that we have a commonsense understanding of mentality and that the commonsense understanding is indispensable for practical purposes, they grant such understanding only probationary status, pending validation by the sciences. By contrast, I want to show that the commonsense understanding of mentality, which is characterized by beliefs, desires, and intentions, requires no special validation by the sciences. While acknowledging that the study of the mind has been a fertile field of scientific study, I try to show that faulty assumptions about the nature of knowledge and reality have led to a miscasting of many of the issues hotly debated in the philosophy of mind.

Our everyday conception of mentality sparkles with notions like 'belief', 'desire', 'intention', 'hope', 'fear', 'wish', 'expectation'. We all attribute such attitudes in order to predict and explain actions, and to make sense of our own and others' lives. The attitudes are woven into the fabric of all social, legal, political, and other institutions. Nothing would be a contract or an invitation to dinner or an election or a death sentence in the absence of beliefs, desires, and intentions.[6] Without attribution of propositional attitudes, there

---

4 Wilfrid Sellars, "Empiricism and the Philosophy of Mind," in *Science, Perception and Reality* (London: Routledge and Kegan Paul, 1963), 173.

5 The quoted phrases are from René Descartes, "The Principles of Philosophy," and "Objections VII," in Haldane and Ross, *Philosophical Works,* 2:219–20, 266.

6 For discussion of the integration of attitudes into all activities of daily life, see chapters 6 and 7 of my *Saving Belief: A Critique of Physicalism* (Princeton: Princeton University Press, 1987).

would be no justifying, excusing, praising, or blaming one another. Because everyday affairs are well nigh unthinkable without the apparatus of the attitudes, questions naturally arise: What is the nature of the attitudes? Do concepts of belief and the other attitudes genuinely apply to human beings? Are attributions of attitudes literally true? Do attributions of attitudes causally explain behavior?

The attitudes have seemed to require some kind of special vindication, because they are characterized by a feature that has seemed problematic to many: intentionality. Intentionality is the ability of one thing to be *about* another thing: The sentence 'snow is white' is about snow and snow's being white; a portrait of King Henry VIII is about (or of) a particular person; *War and Peace* is about Napoleon's invasion of Russia, among other things; a belief that democracy is fragile is about democracy. The 'that' clauses, by which attitudes are attributed in English, express propositions that purport to be about one thing rather than another (hence the term, 'propositional attitudes').[7]

But how, philosophers ask, can aboutness – the capacity of one thing to represent another – be understood in purely physical terms? The worry is that, without assurance that intentional properties are understandable in terms of wholly physical properties, we will be forced either to give up the attitudes or to accept an untenable dualism.[8] Such fears give urgency to the questions just raised: Do people really have propositional attitudes, or are our attributions of attitudes just convenient devices that are literally false?

Questions like this have become the focus of intense debate. Despite considerable disagreement about the answers to these questions, there is a strong consensus on how we should go about finding the answers. This consensus is based on a particular conception of the attitudes, which I call the 'Standard View', a position to which almost all parties to the debate subscribe.[9] A first approximation of the Standard View is that the attitudes, if there are any, are (or are constituted by, or are realized in) particular brain states.

---

7 Despite the fact that some philosophers take the attitudes to be directed toward sentences rather than propositions, I am using the term 'propositional attitudes' as the more customary term of art.

8 In Chapter 7, I argue that this worry is misguided.

9 One philosopher who clearly rejects the Standard View is Frederick Stoutland, "On Not Being a Behaviourist," in *Perspectives on Human Conduct,* ed. Lars Hertzberg and Juhani Pietarinen (Leiden: E. J. Brill, 1988), 37–60.

"Beliefs as brain states" is a good slogan for the Standard View.[10] For example, if I believe that the mail has arrived, then, according to the Standard View, some particular brain state constitutes that belief. If no brain state can be said to constitute the putative belief, then I do not really have the belief.[11]

The Standard View may be thought of as "Descartes without dualism." Whereas Descartes took mental states to be states of an immaterial substance – a mind – mysteriously connected to the brain, contemporary materialists drop the notion of an immaterial mind and simply take mental states to be brain states. From a Cartesian perspective, there are only three logically possible options for understanding attitudes: Either (a) beliefs are brain states, respectable spatiotemporal entities wholly within the purview of physical sciences; or (b) there are no beliefs; or (c) beliefs are in some sense immaterial states beyond the reach of science. Because Descartes's own dualism is widely regarded as untenable, option (c) drops out and we are left with (a) and (b) as the only live possibilities. The Standard View comprises both of these forms of Cartesian materialism: Either the attitudes are brain states or the attitudes are "convenient fictions." The latter stark option is sometimes softened by being conjoined with the position that, despite the fictional status of attitudes, attributions of attitudes are not simply false but have some kind of second-class truth.[12]

As influential as it is, I believe that the Standard View is far off base. Baldly stated, I propose an account of the attitudes, which, for want of a better term, I am labeling 'Practical Realism'. According to Practical Realism, (1) concepts of belief and the other attitudes do genuinely apply to human beings, (2) attributions of attitudes are often true without qualification (i.e., not in some second-class sense), (3) attitudes causally explain behavior. However – and this is what distinguishes my position from the Standard View – (4) there is no metaphysical requirement that the attitudes be constituted by

10 I am using the phrase 'beliefs as brain states' to cover several familiar theses, which I discuss in the next section.
11 Following philosophical custom, I take belief to be the paradigmatic propositional attitude. Although I think that there are important differences among the attitudes, such differences are not my concern here.
12 Daniel C. Dennett used to take this position. See the introduction to *Brainstorms: Philosophical Essays on Mind and Psychology* (Montgomery, VT: Bradford Books, 1978). More recently, Dennett has backed away from this position. See "Real Patterns," *Journal of Philosophy* 88 (1991): 27–51.

particular brain states. And I argue for these points without supposing that the attitudes are in any sense immaterial.

The Standard View, as well as my alternative, concerns the nature of the attitudes: What is it to have a belief? According to the Standard View, to believe that, say, grass is green is at least to have a particular brain state that has the propositional content that grass is green. To say that a brain state has propositional content that p (for any proposition p) is to say that it means that p, or represents the state of affairs that p, or is about the state of affairs that p.[13] To say that beliefs are (or are constituted by) brain states is to say that for every belief token, there is a brain-state token that constitutes the belief.[14] There may not be a perfect one-to-one correlation between intuitively correct attributions of belief and brain-state tokens, according to the Standard View; but if there are beliefs, there is enough of a correlation so that any attribution of an attitude for which there fails to be a relevant brain state is to be counted as not literally true.[15] This is what I am calling the 'Standard View'. I am using the term 'Standard View' to cover a number of well-known theories (some of which may be combined in various ways):

Type-identity theories, according to which types of belief are identical with types of brain states: On type-identity theories, for any belief that p, there is a type of brain state N such that for any x, x believes that p if and only if x is in N.[16] For example, the relation between a belief that p and a brain state N is to be construed as the same as the relation between water and H_2O.[17] So, on the strongest type-identity theories, if two people share a belief, then they both

13 'P' is a stand-in for a proposition, such as the proposition that snow is white or that the building is on fire or that health insurance is expensive.
14 Since the Standard View takes a "type-token" distinction to be central to understanding belief, I shall employ it while discussing the Standard View. As noted in Part III, however, I am dubious about the usefulness of the distinction for understanding belief.
15 See Stephen Stich's "Modified Panglossian Prospect," in *From Folk Psychology to Cognitive Science: The Case against Belief* (Cambridge MA: MIT/Bradford, 1983), 221–8.
16 See David M. Armstrong, *The Nature of Mind* (Brisbane: University of Queensland Press, 1980).
17 The identification of water with H_2O is useful in philosophy even if no water sample is pure H_2O.

have the same brain state. More weakly, and more plausibly, type identity may be relativized to subjects or to physical structures: For any belief that p and any x, if x has physical structure X, then there is a type of brain state N such that x believes that p if and only if x is in a state of type N. For example, my belief that snow is white may be type-identical with one brain state and a blind person's belief that snow is white may be type-identical with a different brain state.

Token-identity theories, according to which particular belief tokens are identical with brain-state tokens:[18] On token-identity theories, for any token of a belief that p, there is a token of a brain state N with which the belief token is identical; but different tokens of the same (type of) belief that p are identical with brain-state tokens of different types.[19] Token-identity theories thus allow for "multiple realization": Different tokens of a single belief type may be identical with tokens of vastly different physical types.[20] Not only may tokens of a single belief type be identical with different types of brain states in dogs and humans, but also the monolingual English speaker and the monolingual Greek speaker may have different types of brain states that in each is the belief that Plato was a philosopher. Token identity contrasts with type identity: According to token-identity theories, each instance of a single belief is of some physical type, but not necessarily the same physical type in each instance. According to type-identity theories, all instances of the same belief are of the same physical type.

"Constitution" theories, according to which beliefs are constituted by brain states (as pebbles are constituted by molecules):[21] Al-

18 Here is an illustration of the type-token distinction: 'apples', 'apples', 'oranges'. How many words have I written? Three word tokens (spatiotemporal entities) of two word (abstract) types. If you believe that snow is white and I believe that snow is white, then we share a (type of) belief; but since (according to the Standard View) in your head there is one brain in a particular state and in my head another brain in a particular state, we have different tokens of the same type of belief. If a type-identity theory is correct, then our tokens of the same type of belief are also of the same neurophysiological type.
19 See Donald Davidson, "Mental Events," in *Essays on Actions and Events* (Oxford: Oxford University Press, 1980), 207–24.
20 See Hilary Putnam, *Philosophical Papers,* vol. 2 (Cambridge: Cambridge University Press, 1975).
21 See Robert van Gulick, "Nonreductive Materialism and the Nature of Inter-theoretical Constraint," in *Emergence or Reduction? Essays on the Prospects of Non-reductive Physicalism,* ed. Ansgar Beckermann, Hans Flohr, and Jaegwon Kim, (Berlin: Walter de Gruyter, 1992), 157–79; Richard Boyd, "Materialism without Reductionism: What Physicalism Does Not Entail," in *Readings in the Philosophy*

though both "constitution" theories and token–identity theories are considered by some to be forms of nonreductive materialism,[22] some proponents of the Standard View do not want to go so far as to say that the attitudes are identical to brain states (types or tokens), but only that beliefs are constituted by brain states. One reason to distinguish constitution from token identity, at least at the molecular level, is this: Consider a desire for ice cream on a particular occasion, and a brain state that constitutes the desire. Suppose that the brain state is constituted by molecules that you ingested while having breakfast on your first birthday. Suppose that your mother had had a choice between two jars of baby food on that day, and she had chosen to give you the one on the left. Had she chosen the jar on the right, your brain-state token would have been different from what it actually was (i.e., it would have been constituted by different molecules of the same type as those that actually constituted the desire). Nevertheless, your token desire for ice cream would be the same token desire, considered as a psychological state. So, a single token desire could have been constituted by different molecules from the ones that actually constituted it. If this is so, then the token desire for ice cream is not identical with the token brain state that constitutes the desire.[23]

A similar argument would conclude that beliefs cannot be identical with the brain-state tokens that are said to constitute them: Suppose that S acquires a belief that unemployment is down by being told that unemployment is down. And suppose there are tokens of several neural state types that could constitute the acquisition of that belief at that time – call them $b1$, $b2$, and $b3$. Now, because there was music in the background, $b2$ was tokened. The "constitution" theorist would claim that there would have been the same belief token if $b1$ or $b3$ (instead of $b2$) had been tokened at that time. Hence, according to the "constitution" theorists, the belief token is not identical with the brain-state token that constitutes the belief. In short, the "constitution" view of beliefs is weaker than the

  of Psychology, vol. 1, ed. Ned Block (Cambridge, MA: Harvard University Press, 1980), 67–106.
22 See, for example, Jerry A. Fodor, *Psychosemantics: The Problem of Meaning in the Philosophy of Mind* (Cambridge, MA: MIT/Bradford, 1987).
23 This argument, as well as a defense of nonreductive materialism, is given by Derk Pereboom and Hilary Kornblith, "The Metaphysics of Irreducibility," *Philosophical Studies* 63 (1991): 125–46.

token-identity theory. If a belief token is identical with a brain-state token, then if there had been distinct, but molecularly identical, molecules in one's brain, there would have been a different belief token. But on the "constitution" view, distinct, but molecularly identical, molecules in the brain would have constituted the same belief token.

What makes nonreductive materialism – in either the token-identity version or the "constitution" version – *nonreductive* is that it recognizes laws and explanations that are not to be explicated in terms of physics. (On the "constitution" version, not even belief tokens can be identified with brain-state tokens.) What makes nonreductive materialism *materialistic* is that it takes everything that exists to be composed only of basic physical entities.

Functionalism, according to which beliefs are functional roles occupied by brain states: On functionalist views, mental states are defined by their causes and effects.[24] What makes a mental state the belief that *p* is its relations to sensory stimulation (input), to other inner states, and to behavior (output). For example, a mental state is a belief that the glass contains water partly in virtue of its causing one to pick it up and drink its contents when one is thirsty. Although functionalists define types of mental state in terms of their functional or causal roles, they usually take the particular thing that occupies a given role (a "realizer") to be a brain state. Such versions of functionalism, which may be combined with type-identity, token-identity, or "constitution" views of brain states, are likewise versions of the Standard View.

A functionalist may identify a particular mental state with the occupant of the role (an internal state that realizes the role) or with the second-order state of having a state that occupies that role. For example, pain may be identified with a particular brain state or with the state of having a state that plays the pain role.[25] Most functionalists identify particular mental states with first-order "realizer

24 For an overview, see Lynne Rudder Baker, "Functionalism," in *The Cambridge Dictionary of Philosophy,* ed. Robert Audi (Cambridge: Cambridge University Press, forthcoming). See also William G. Lycan, *Judgement and Justification* (Cambridge: Cambridge University Press, 1988).

25 See David Lewis, "Psychophysical and Theoretical Identifications," in *Readings in the Philosophy of Psychology,* vol. 1, ed. Ned Block (Cambridge, MA: Harvard University Press, 1980), 207–15; David Lewis, "Mad Pain and Martian Pain," in *Philosophical Papers,* vol. 1 (Oxford: Oxford University Press, 1983), 122–32.

states." Realizer states are paradigmatic examples of the kind of internal states postulated by the Standard View. A functionalist however, may identify particular mental states with second-order "role states." A role state – the state of having a state that plays a certain role – is not itself an internal state. In the way that functionalists understand role states, however, this still counts as a version of the Standard View; for to be in a role state is to have some internal state that realizes that role.

Eliminative materialism, according to which beliefs, if there were any, would be brain states: On eliminative materialism, there are no brain states that can plausibly be identified with intuitively correct beliefs attributions.[26] Hence, eliminative materialists conclude, there are no beliefs. Although it remains convenient to attribute attitudes, say eliminativists, such attributions are only of practical value and not literally true.

Finally, the Standard View admits of both relational and nonrelational construals of the attitudes.[27] Say that a property F is intrinsic to x if and only if x has F and, necessarily, for any y such that y is a physical duplicate of x, y has F. Roughly, intrinsic properties are those shared by molecule-for-molecule duplicates ("twins"). On a nonrelational (or individualistic or narrow or internalist) account, whether an individual has a given attitude depends wholly on the individual's intrinsic properties.[28] On a relational (or nonindividualistic or wide or externalist) account, whether an individual has a given attitude depends in part on the individual's relation to an environment.[29] According to relational versions of the Standard

26 See Paul M. Churchland, *A Neurocomputational Perspective: The Nature of Mind and the Structure of Science* (Cambridge MA: MIT/Bradford, 1989).

27 Whether one's intrinsic states fully determine one's attitudes has been hotly debated. The debate was set off by Tyler Burge, "Individualism and the Mental," in *Studies in Metaphysics* (Midwest Studies in Philosophy 4), ed. Peter A French, Theodore E. Uehling, Jr., and Howard K. Wettstein (Minneapolis: University of Minnesota Press, 1979), 73–122. Other contributors include Fodor, *Psychosemantics,* chap. 2; Stich, *From Folk Psychology to Cognitive Science,* chap. 5; Patricia Kitcher, "Narrow Taxonomy and Wide Functionalism," *Philosophy of Science* 53 (1985): 78–97; Baker, *Saving Belief,* chaps. 2–5; Bernard W. Kobes, "Individualism and Artificial Intelligence," in *Action Theory and Philosophy of Mind, 1990* (Philosophical Perspectives 4), ed. James E. Tomberlin (Atascadero, CA: Ridgeview Publishing Company, 1990), 429–59.

28 More fine-grained distinctions among individualistic, narrow, or internalist versions do not concern us here.

29 For a relational construal of belief, see, for example, Ruth Garrett Millikan, "Biosemantics," *Journal of Philosophy* 86 (1989): 281–97, or Fred Dretske, *Ex-*

View, what makes the brain state a belief depends on the subject's environment (it is a relational property), whereas what makes a particular brain state a brain state is independent of the subject's environment (it is an intrinsic or nonrelational property). Compare: A planet may be a chunk of rock, even though what makes a particular chunk of rock a rock may be independent of the rock's environment, whereas what makes rock a planet does depend on the rock's environment. So, the Standard View can accommodate relational as well as nonrelational accounts of the attitudes.

What Standard View theories have in common is the thesis that each instance of each belief is identical with, or is constituted by, an instance of a particular brain state. Thus, any argument against the thesis that instances of belief are identical with, or are constituted by, neural tokens is an argument against every version of the Standard View. Sometimes I shall abbreviate this weakest thesis of the Standard View by omitting "or are constituted by," and simply formulate the target thesis as "Beliefs are brain states."

The Standard View is so entrenched that the literature contains few (if any) explicit arguments for it. Nevertheless, since I think that there are powerful motivations for the Standard View, I set out on three arguments for it – an argument from metaphysics, an argument from science, and an argument from causal explanation. I set these out in simpleminded detail in order to call attention to premises that are rarely articulated, and almost never defended. Proponents of the Standard View, when they argue for the basic conception of beliefs as brain states at all, tend to defend the second premise of each argument. Whether the second premises are true or not, I argue, the real culprit in each case is the first premise.

I. An argument from metaphysics

Descartes conceived of a belief as a state internal to the mind. Since, on a materialist conception, any state internal to the mind is a brain state, the Standard View follows from the Cartesian view of belief as an internal state together with materialism. Indeed, Jerry Fodor

plaining Behavior: The Place of Reasons in a World of Causes (Cambridge, MA: MIT/Bradford, 1988). For a nonrelational construal of belief, see John R. Searle, *Intentionality* (Cambridge: Cambridge University Press, 1983).

and Noam Chomsky have explicitly invoked Descartes as an intellectual ancestor.[30]

This route to the Standard View, I think, actually does descend from Descartes. According to Descartes, there are two kinds of finite substance: (immaterial) soul or mind and (material) body. Placing living organisms entirely within the realm of matter – defined as what is extended in space, and wholly explainable by physics – Descartes purged the soul or mind of any physiological role at all in functioning. Indeed, in his *Treatise of Man,* after noting that man is composed of a mind and a body, Descartes went on to describe a model of a body as

a [machine] formed intentionally by God to be as much as possible like us: Thus not only does He give it externally the shapes and colors of all the parts of our bodies; He also places inside it all the pieces required to make it walk, eat, breathe, and imitate whichever of our own functions can be imagined to proceed from mere matter and to depend entirely on the arrangement of our organs.[31]

Those of our own functions that "can be imagined to proceed from mere matter" turned out to be quite encompassing. Not only digestion and respiration, but also imagination, dreams, memory, sensation, and much bodily movement were described in terms of elementary particles in motion. Many contemporary materialists push this materialistic strain to the limit, by lopping off the Cartesian mind altogether and identifying mental states with brain states. We can derive a Cartesian thesis (Ia) from Descartes's assumptions (1) that there are only two possible kinds of finite substance, immaterial minds and material bodies; (2) that every finite attribute is an attribute of a finite substance; and (3) that beliefs (if there are such) are finite attributes. Then, coupling the Cartesian premise with a rejection of immaterial minds, we have a simple valid argument for the Standard View:

30 Jerry A. Fodor, "The Elm and the Expert: Mentalese and its Semantics" (1993 Jean Nicod Lectures); Noam Chomsky, *Cartesian Linguistics* (New York: Harper and Row, 1966).
31 René Descartes, *Treatise of Man,* French text with translation and commentary by Thomas Steele Hall (Cambridge, MA: Harvard University Press, 1972), 4. I am grateful to Gareth B. Matthews for this reference, and for discussing with me the deep issues here that are outside the scope of this book.

(Ia) Belief (if there is such a thing) is either an immaterial-mind state or a brain state.[32]

(Ib) Belief is not a state of an immaterial mind.

Therefore,

(Ic) Belief (if there is such a thing) is a brain state.

Of course, this valid argument does not establish the Standard View unless its premises are true. In Part III, I develop an alternative construal of belief that shows the Cartesian premise to express a false dichotomy – belief is neither a brain state nor an immaterial-mind state. Hence, the Argument from Metaphysics for the Standard View is unsound.

The fundamental assumption of the Argument from Metaphysics is that the attitudes must be internal states. In the presumed absence of immaterial souls, the relevant internal states are brain states, discoverable by neuroscientists.[33] Although physically realized internal states of particular organs (like brain states) are one kind of state, I use the term 'state' simpliciter much more broadly to include, for example, states of emergency and states of disgrace. Internal states, in the sense relevant to the Standard View, are spatially and temporally locatable inside a spatiotemporal entity like an organism, in a way that states of emergency and states of disgrace are not.[34] It is not controversial that to have a belief that p is to be in a state (in the broad sense that includes states of disgrace) that has propositional content that p; the controversy lies in supposing that the state in question is a physically realized internal state, such as a brain state.

---

32 Materialists hold that nothing immaterial makes any contribution at all to mentality, and hence would reject the view (associated with Thomas Nagel, e.g.) that mental states have both physical and nonphysical aspects.

33 I am obviously not stating the possibilities in full generality; for computers or Martians, the relevant physical states are not brain states at all. But since the language of the attitudes was devised for understanding people and their behavior, it applies first and foremost to human beings – if it applies to anything. To extend my arguments to intelligent beings without brains (they are organized in some other way), substitute 'physically realized internal state' for 'brain state' throughout.

34 In my broad use of 'state', I can agree that to have a belief is to be in a state that has propositional content that p; what I oppose is the requirement that a state of belief be a particular internal state.

II. An argument from science

(IIa) Science has confirmed the conception of belief as brain state.

(IIb) Any conception confirmed by science is correct.

Therefore,

(IIc) The conception of belief as brain state is correct – that is, belief (if there is such a thing) is a brain state.

Although I do not challenge the second premise, the first premise is dubious. There are two forms of the Standard View – eliminative and noneliminative. As discussed in Chapter 3, eliminative materialists do support their position by means of science. But rather than confirm or vindicate beliefs as brain states (or beliefs at all), eliminative materialists argue that, on the best theories of behavior, the internal states that are causally efficacious – brain states or syntactic or computational states that supervene on brain states – can not plausibly be identified with particular beliefs; and they conclude from this that there are no beliefs.[35] Such reasoning obviously can not confirm the Standard View; indeed, eliminative reasoning presupposes the conception of beliefs as brain states. So, in the absence of an independent argument for the Standard View, eliminative materialism per se is logically in no position to confirm or vindicate the Standard View.

Proponents of the other form of the Standard View, noneliminativists, also support their position by means of science, but they disagree with the eliminativists about what the best theories are. For example, some developmental psychologists as well as philosophers deploy theories according to which there are mental representations tokened in the brain (sometimes "sentences-in-the-brain"), which could plausibly be identified with particular beliefs

---

35 According to Stich, the behavior-explaining states are syntactic states; see his *From Folk Psychology to Cognitive Science*. According to Churchland, the behavior-explaining states are "neurocomputational" states; see his *A Neurocomputational Perspective*. See also Paul Smolensky, "On the Proper Treatment of Connectionism," *Behavioral and Brain Sciences* 11(1988): 1–74. Despite disagreement about how to interpret connectionism, the ascendant computational model of the mind, the arguments for eliminative materialism all have the form of the argument given in the text.

and hence would tend to support the Standard View. Eliminativists think the prospects of such theories are dim. Which of the kinds of scientific theories – those favored by eliminativists or those favored by noneliminativists – is more nearly correct is a scientific question, not one to be decided by philosophers. The philosophical point is this: Even to be a *candidate* for confirming the Standard View, a scientific theory would have to find a relevant neurological difference between a brain state that constitutes a belief that p and a brain state that constitutes a belief that q for any two distinct beliefs. Such a theory must be able to distinguish between a brain state that constituted, say, a belief that a soldier's following orders is a slightly mitigating factor in assessing misconduct and a belief that a soldier's following orders is a substantially mitigating factor in assessing misconduct.

My conjecture is that neither the best theory of the brain nor the best psychological theory will identify brain states that can plausibly be said to constitute particular beliefs – certainly not for all intuitively correct attributions of beliefs.[36] If that is right, then, logically, there is no way for science to vindicate the conception of beliefs as brain states. The point here, however, is that science has not so far confirmed the Standard View; and hence, the grip that the Standard View has on contemporary thinking does not rest on scientific underpinnings.

It is important to see that the Standard View is not a scientific discovery but rather a metaphysical conception of the attitudes. Neuroscientists may be able to answer the question on which philosophers are placing bets: Are there particular brain states that can plausibly be said to constitute particular beliefs? But they cannot determine whether beliefs should be thought of as brain states in the first place. If the best theories did not allow identification of particular brain states with particular beliefs, one could either draw the eliminativist conclusion that there are no beliefs or reject the Stan-

36 Some nonreductive materialists would continue to endorse belief as long as cognitive psychology developed a belief-desire theory that could be integrated into the physical sciences, whether particular brain states could be found to constitute particular belief tokens or not. But a cognitive psychology that did not identify particular brain-state tokens as constituting particular belief tokens could hardly be said to confirm the conception of belief as brain state. For that Standard View conception would just be a metaphysical add-on that would play no role in the psychology. (I argue that the Standard View is not needed for materialism.)

16

dard View that beliefs are brain states. Since I give independent reasons to reject the Standard View, and since I argue that commonsense psychology is cognitively significant apart from integration into any overarching scientific theory, I would not be an eliminative materialist no matter what the outcome of science.

III. An argument from causal explanation

Traditionally, beliefs and the other attitudes are taken to guide behavior. The most compelling motivation for those proponents of the Standard View who acknowledge belief, I believe, stems from a particular conception of causal explanation: Genuine causal explanations must appeal to physical states or entities. The causes of behavior are internal to the agent. The only internal states that plausibly can explain behavior are brain states. So, if beliefs are candidates for causally explaining behavior, they must be brain states. Here, then, is a central argument that I want to refute:

(IIIa) Unless beliefs were brain states, they could not causally explain behavior.

(IIIb) Beliefs can causally explain behavior.

Therefore,

(IIIc) Beliefs are brain states.

As I argue, belief explanations are causal explanations. So, I heartily endorse (IIIb): Beliefs can causally explain behavior.[37] However, I think that (IIIa) is a source of metaphysical mischief. A major task of Part II is to show that the conception of causal explanation that supports (IIIa) is inadequate, and inadequate for reasons unrelated to attributions of belief. On a better general view of causal explanation, (IIIa) is seen to be false. (See Chapter 5 for a detailed argument.) Hence, the Argument from Causal Explanation is unsound.

Premise (IIIa) is an extremely rich philosophical thesis. It is a modal claim ("Unless beliefs *were* . . ., they *could not* . . ."). If the premise were merely a truth-functional conditional, then, on the assumptions that beliefs do causally explain behavior, and beliefs

---

37 Eliminative materialists, who deny that there are beliefs, dissent from (IIIb).

17

are in fact brain states, (IIIa) would be true – even if there were no connection between the causal explanatoriness of belief and beliefs' being brain states. So, (IIIa) must support counterfactuals: In nearby worlds in which beliefs causally explain behavior, they are brain states (or, more generally, physically realized internal states). Thus, the conclusion of the argument against (IIIa) in Chapter 5 is that even if beliefs are brain states in the actual world, they need not be brain states in order to be causally explanatory. It is not in virtue of being brain states (or physically realized internal states at all) that beliefs are explanatory.

Philosophers sometimes distinguish "the order of knowing" from "the order of being." The Argument from Causal Explanation concerns the order of knowing. This argument aims to give grounds for the Standard View: Since beliefs causally explain behavior, they are brain states. From a Standard View perspective on the order of being, however, the inference may go the other way: Since, according to the Standard View, beliefs are brain states, they are causally explanatory. The relation between these two lines of inference is parallel to the relation between a representative realist's two lines of inference: Since we have representations of Fs in certain circumstances, then there are Fs (the order of knowing); and since there are Fs, we have representations of Fs in certain circumstances (the order of being). Although there is no conflict between these lines of inference in either case, the order-of-being inferences would give no reason to believe that beliefs are brain states (or, for that matter, that there are Fs). For the order-of-being inference takes the conception of belief as brain state as a premise. No inference *from* a conception of beliefs as brain states could provide reason to endorse the Standard View in the first place.

Of course, there may be arguments for the Standard View, unthought of by me, in addition to the Argument from Metaphysics, the Argument from Science, and the Argument from Causal Explanation. When they are produced, I shall consider them. But in the meanwhile, in Part I, I also challenge the Standard View directly – both "internally," by showing that it leads to seemingly insoluble difficulties on its own terms, and "externally," by uncovering and criticizing metaphysical assumptions on which it rests. The weaknesses of the Standard View in turn motivate a non-Cartesian alternative, one that avoids both relativism and immaterialism.

The alternative that I propose differs from the Standard View in method as well as in substance. The Standard View is a theory-based theory: It emerges from the metaphysics of materialism. Some proponents of the Standard View begin with an overarching picture of how things must be, and then they consider how what we take to be the case fits in to the big picture; whatever fails to fit is deemed illusory.[38] I want to propose a practice-based theory: It emerges from consideration of successful cognitive practices – in everyday life as well as in science. Instead of holding views on the attitudes to be accountable to scientific or metaphysical *theories* untethered to actual practices, I hold views on the attitudes accountable to views of successful explanatory *practice* in everyday life as well as in science. Some proponents of the Standard View would agree with my emphasis on practice but would confine attention to scientific practice.[39] These proponents of the Standard View, however, have a particular *theory* of science, according to which all sciences must be integrated into physical science.[40] In any case, whether they defend materialism or assume its truth, all proponents of the Standard View require that any account of the propositional attitudes conform to a comprehensive metaphysical theory to which they have prior commitment.

The central methodological contrast between Practical Realism and the Standard View is this. According to the Standard View, scientific or metaphysical theory always trumps practice: Apparent knowledge derived from reflection on practice must either be validated by theory or discarded. By contrast, Practical Realism does not start from any comprehensive theory, but rather from investigation of successful cognitive practices in everyday life as well as in science. From the more pragmatic perspective, theory and practice

---

38 For example, Hartry Field takes adequacy to materialism to be a constraint on theorizing. See his "Mental Representation," *Erkenntnis* 13 (1978): 9–61.

39 For example, see Stich, *From Folk Psychology to Cognitive Science,* and Fodor, *Psychosemantics.* Some may reject the Standard View and yet take metaphysics to be informed by science. Indeed, they may be willing to give up materialism on the basis of causal-explanatory practice in psychology. See, for example, Tyler Burge, "Mind–Body Causation and Explanatory Practice," in *Mental Causation,* ed. John Heil and Alfred Mele (Oxford: Clarendon Press, 1993), 97–120.

40 For example, see Jerry A. Fodor and Ernest LePore, *Holism* (Oxford: Blackwell, 1992), 17.

must be brought into reflective equilibrium: Knowledge derived from reflection on practice has its own integrity. Although practice-based claims, like any others, are defeasible and hence correctable, their epistemic legitimacy derives from successful use in practice, not from their relations to any overarching theory.

My understanding of practice includes explanatory practices of everyday life as well as of science. Although I do not think that there is a sharp divide between science and everyday life, or between theoretical knowledge and practical knowledge, there are important differences. Science consists of paradigm-governed research programs, the pursuit of which requires special training, and which aims at increasing systematization of knowledge. By contrast, knowledge of everyday life requires no special training, and it aims not at increasing systematization of knowledge, but at human flourishing. The knowledge required for such flourishing may or may not be validated by science. I argue that commonsense psychology and, more generally, the cognitive deliverances of everyday life – from how to maintain good relations with colleagues to what to do when the lights go out – need no validation from science.

Methodologically, then, Practical Realism differs from the Standard View in two important ways: First, it looks to everyday practices as sources of knowledge, apart from connections between (putative) commonsense knowledge and any metaphysical or scientific theory. Second, with respect to propositional attitudes, it does not begin with an assumption that beliefs are internal states, either of a brain or of an immaterial mind. Instead, it counsels that to understand beliefs, look to see to what uses we put them.

Practical Realism is a metaphysical view based on practice. When I call the alternative to the Standard View 'Practical Realism', I am using the term 'practical' not to denote a theory of truth or meaning but to denote a method in metaphysics. My procedure is to consider what we use beliefs and other attitudes to do, and then to ask: How should we understand the attitudes if they are to play their roles in our successful explanatory practices – in science and in everyday life? Ordinary explanatory practices provide data for theorizing; philosophy should try to comprehend things that actually matter to people outside of the study. Although my approach is pragmatic, my goal is metaphysical. The nature of the attitudes is best revealed by their operation in our practices.

20

According to Practical Realism, practice has metaphysical as well as methodological import: We should take as genuine the ontological commitments of our practices. The existence of many things is partly dependent on practices. It is not just that A's telling B that she ought to look for another job *causes* B to suspect that she will not get tenure; but the very *content* of the suspicion – that she will not get tenure – depends on our practices. In the absence of our academic employment practices, there could be no beliefs or suspicions about tenure at all. Practices are implicated in much of what is real, not just in our knowledge about it. Ontologically speaking, Practical Realism recognizes persons with intentional states, medium-sized objects, natural and artifactual, conventions and institutions – everything presupposed by successful explanatory practices in science and in everyday life. (See Chapter 8.)

If Practical Realism is correct, beliefs are not theoretical entities, like electrons; they are not spatiotemporal entities or internal states at all. Since the term 'belief' is just a nominalization of 'believes that', S has a belief if and only if there is some proposition p such that S believes that p. Whether S believes that p depends solely on what S would do, say, and think in various circumstances. Although S may not always manifest beliefs in behavior, there must be some circumstances in which S's belief makes a difference to what S would do, say, or think. It is important that what S does, says, or thinks may be specified by ordinary descriptions of actions, such as 'return the phone call', 'register to vote', 'pay a fine', 'mail the check', 'insult the director', and so on. The Practical Realist view of belief is this: S believes that p if and only if there are certain counterfactuals true of $S,$ where content of the counterfactuals may be intentionally characterized.[41] (Hence, Practical Realism is not behavioristic.) The Practical Realist claim is not that facts about beliefs are nothing over and above facts about counterfactuals, but rather that the nature of belief is revealed by counterfactuals about the believer. A person believes that foxes have tails if and only if relevant (intentionally specified) counterfactuals are true – independently of how the brain is organized. According to Practical Realism, it may be the case that only those with a certain kind of brain

---

41 To convert this "formal mode" appeal to counterfactuals to the "material mode," one may speak instead of dispositions, provided that dispositions are construed relationally and intentionally.

have beliefs, but it is a category mistake to suppose that beliefs are constituted by particular brain states. (See Chapter 6.)

"But, surely," a proponent of the Standard View may respond incredulously, "to have the relevant counterfactuals true of one is to be in a certain state; and in the presumed absence of immaterial souls, the relevant state must be a brain state." This inference is faulty. For what is required for the relevant counterfactuals to be true is not any particular internal state, but a state in an extended sense: My "state" in virtue of which it is true that I would lend you money for lunch if you asked me depends on my being embedded in a certain social and linguistic environment. There is no good reason to identify such a state with a particular state of one's brain. Similarly for belief states: The reality of belief does not depend on the term 'belief"s denoting a kind of spatiotemporal entity or of a particular internal state. One's state of believing that p depends on global properties (including relational properties, and properties about what would happen in various counterfactual circumstances) of whole organisms.

In short, what I am calling 'Practical Realism' is *practical,* because it holds metaphysical theories accountable to successful practice in ordinary affairs as well as in science; it is *realistic* because it affirms the unvarnished truth of the language that partially constitutes successful practice. This commonsense realism should be distinguished from the kind of metaphysical realism, associated with the Standard View, based on a distinction between what is mind-independent and what is mind-dependent.[42] There is as much a fact of the matter about whether one has had tea with the queen as about whether one has brown eyes, and as much a fact of the matter about whether one has been indicted as about whether one is six feet tall. There is nothing subjective about the fact that one has had tea with the queen or about the fact that one has been indicted. Anyone can be mistaken about these matters: There is a clear difference between being right and thinking that one is right about whether so-and-so (even oneself!) has had tea with the queen. Such facts are not a matter of "opinion," nor is it "up for grabs" whether they obtain. Admittedly, they depend on social practices, but they are no less

42 For a vigorous defense of the kind of Metaphysical Realism that I reject, see Michael Devitt, *Realism and Truth* (Princeton: Princeton University Press, 1984). There may be other kinds of metaphysical realism – about, say, theological matters – on which I take no stand here.

real for all that – regardless of any "grounding" in mind-independent reality. (See Chapter 8 for further discussion.)

Let me outline some ways in which Practical Realism contrasts with the Standard View:

1. On the Standard View, a person *has* a belief that *p* if and only if the person has a particular brain state that *is* (or *constitutes*) a belief that *p;* there are beliefs if and only if there are internal spatiotemporal particulars that satisfy the open sentence '*x* is (or constitutes) a belief that *p.*' According to Practical Realism, believing that *p* is an irreducible fact about a person. A person has a belief that *p* if and only if there is a range of circumstances in which, given various other attitudes, the person would perform a range of intentional actions, understood broadly enough to include covert speech acts.[43]

2. On the Standard View, beliefs are subpersonal: It is in virtue of having an organ in a particular state that one has a belief. According to Practical Realism, it is not in virtue of having any particular brain state that a person has a belief; rather, it is in virtue of there being a certain set of counterfactuals true of a person that she has a belief, without regard to the state of any organ.

3. On the Standard View, the explanatory power of the attitudes rests on a matchup, one by one, of attributions of attitudes with particular brain states ("distributed" or not). According to Practical Realism, the explanatory power of the attitudes rests solely on the fact that they have predictable consequences: by manipulating attitudes, one can manipulate behavior – without regard for any hypotheses about brain states.

4. On the Standard View, we must wait for science to tell us what beliefs are (and whether there are any at all). According to Practical Realism, understanding our cognitive practices tells us what beliefs are, and the reliability of those practices in the sciences as in everyday affairs assures us that there are beliefs.

What justifies our confidence in the attitudes is their explanatory power, which as I show in Part II, does not derive from identification of attitudes with brain states. Part of my strategy is to show that *nonpsychological* causal explanations in general do not require that explanatory properties be physically realized internal states;

43 An important qualification to this as a sufficient condition for having a belief that *p* is discussed in Chapter 6. Obviously, this is not a definition. Therefore, it is not circular; it is only nonreductive.

and, some philosophers to the contrary notwithstanding, there is no compelling reason to require that explanatory properties cited by *psychological* causal explanations be physically realized internal states either.

Practical Realists join proponents of the Standard View in taking explanation of behavior to be a key to understanding the mind. Proponents of the Standard View who endorse eliminative materialism concur, but take explanations in terms of belief not to be genuine explanations. Other proponents of the Standard View, along with Practical Realists, take beliefs to be causally explanatory. So, let me say how I use terms like 'belief explanation', and give a preliminary argument for the causal explanatoriness of such explanations. (In Part II, I argue that – contrary to the Standard View – being constituted by brain states is not a requirement for beliefs to be causally explanatory.)

Commonsense-psychological explanations comprise a motley. Some everyday explanations cite intentions ('She took her books because she intended to catch up on her schoolwork over the vacation'); others cite desires ('He started jogging because he wanted to lose weight'); others cite beliefs ('She went to the rally because she believed that the president would speak'); still others cite combinations ('He tiptoed because he believed that the baby was asleep and he did not want to disturb her'). Others make no explicit mention of propositional attitudes at all ('He went to the movies because he was lonely'). Although belief, desire, and intention have held center stage, a broad range of attitudes figure in commonsense-psychological explanations: hope, expectation, fear, yearning, and so on.

As shorthand, I shall use the term 'belief explanations' for any of these commonsense-psychological explanations, whether they actually mention beliefs or not. On this usage, 'She went back to the office at midnight because she intended to shred the documents' is a belief explanation, and so is 'She went back to the office at midnight because she was afraid that the documents would be subpoenaed the next day'. What characterizes belief explanations is that they purport to explain ordinary actions in terms of attributions of propositional attitudes to agents.

24

Although I want to defeat the Argument from Causal Explanation for the Standard View, I am in full agreement with the second premise: Beliefs causally explain behavior. In this section, I try to show that we have good reason to agree with many proponents of the Standard View that belief explanations are causal explanations. But first, let me make some terminological points about how I understand explanations, more or less pretheoretically.

1. I take the notion of an explanation to have epistemic import. This is not to say that explanations (or correct explanations) are confined to what we now have at hand, or even to what we can now envisage. But, in the sense that concerns me here, I would not count something as an explanation if it is unknowable in principle, or if it would remain undiscovered at the idealized Peircean "end of inquiry."

2. By *explanation,* I (generally) mean 'good explanation' or 'correct explanation'. There is a well-known ambiguity in the term 'explanation'. In one sense, appeal to phlogiston furnished an explanation of combustion, although a mistaken explanation; in another sense, appeal to phlogiston provided no explanation at all since there is no such thing as phlogiston. Since I want to contrast belief explanations with phlogiston explanations, I generally use 'explanation' to mean 'correct explanation'. When there seems a possibility of confusion, I use 'putative explanation' to indicate that I am talking about a putatively correct explanation, which may or may not actually be correct. So, explanations must be both knowable and true.

3. An *explanandum* is what an explanation explains. Explananda may be thought of as facts, propositions, states of affairs, or in Kim's terms, events as things'-having-properties-at-times, or in Davidson's terms events-described-in-certain-ways. I use the word 'phenomenon' as a cover term for any such explananda.

4. By *intentional explanation,* I mean an explanation that mentions an intentional property, where a property is intentional if and only if: Either it is the property of having a propositional attitude or it is a property that presupposes that there are propositional attitudes. So, belief explanations are intentional explanations.

5. By *nonpsychological intentional explanation,* I mean an intentional explanation that does not cite any individual's psychological or mental states. Thus, most social, legal, economic, political, and aesthetic explanations are nonpsychological intentional explana-

tions – in contrast to belief explanations, which are psychological intentional explanations.

Are belief explanations causal explanations? Typically, a causal explanation cites a state of affairs or event or condition that brings about the phenomenon to be explained, where the explaining condition obtains before (or at the same time as) the phenomenon to be explained. Although I do not clinch the argument for the causal explanatoriness of belief until Chapter 5, I can give two reasons at the outset to suppose that belief explanations are causal explanations: (1) Philosophers who deny that belief explanations are causal explanations typically make assumptions about the character of causal explanation that do not accord with actual explanatory practice either in the sciences or in everyday life, and (2) we clearly treat belief explanations as causal explanations.

1. Some philosophers deny that belief explanations are causal explanations. I consider three such philosophers who are otherwise dissimilar. First, Kathleen Wilkes construes belief explanations instrumentalistically. Here is Wilkes's example: Suppose that we explain Joe's stumbling at the top of the stairs by saying that he thought that there was another step there. Wilkes asks rhetorically: "Who, though, would want to say, and above all what would it mean to say, that there 'really is' such a thought in his head?"[44] She takes it that beliefs and desires do not causally explain actions because they are not entities in the head. However, only one under the spell of the Standard View would suppose that Joe's *really* having the relevant belief – or for the belief to be causally explanatory – requires his brain to be in some particular state. Again, there is an enormous class of causal explanations to which internal states are in general irrelevant. Moreover, Wilkes's grounds for denying that belief explanations are causal explanations indicate that she is assuming that if beliefs causally explain behavior, they must be brain states. This claim is (IIIa) – the premise in the Argument from Causal Explanation that I intend to refute. Hence, Wilkes's instrumental account of belief explanations rests on assumptions about causal explanation that should be rejected.

A second philosopher who presents a case for denying that attitudes explain behavior causally is Jaegwon Kim, whose account

44 Kathleen Wilkes, *"Nemo Psychologus Nisi Physiologus,"* Inquiry 29 (1986): 175.

takes belief explanations to be normative – and, hence, on his view, to be noncausal. Underlying belief explanations is a Desire-Belief-Action Principle:

(DBA) If a person desires that *p,* and believes that doing *A* will secure *p,* then ceteris paribus he will do *A.*

Kim interprets this as a "normative principle that tells us the conditions under which a given action is rationalizable as an appropriate thing to do." Explanations in terms of such principles justify actions; they are "not causal-predictive."[45] According to Kim, belief explanations concern our reflectively making sense of ourselves. I agree. But such self-understanding, when accurate, does not preclude the explanations' being causal. Kim thinks otherwise. He draws a sharp line between causal-predictive explanations and rationalizing explanations. Rationalizing explanations are not "aimed at acquiring knowledge of the causal mechanisms leading from our desires and beliefs to actions" (318). True again, but many, perhaps most, causal explanations, I argue, do not aim at acquiring knowledge of causal mechanisms; so, the fact that belief explanations do not aim at "acquiring knowledge of causal mechanisms leading from our desires and beliefs to actions" does not prevent them from being causal explanations.

Finally, a philosopher of a wholly different stripe who denied that belief explanations are causal explanations was Gilbert Ryle. Ryle argued that "to explain an action as done from a specified motive or inclination [he put 'believes' in the same family as motive words] is not to describe the action as the effect of a specified cause. Motives are not happenings and are not therefore of the right type to be causes."[46] However, as I argue in Part II, causal explanations often cite conditions or states of affairs that are not "happenings" in Ryle's sense.[47]

Although I think that Ryle would endorse (IIIa) – the first premise of the Argument from Causal Explanation for the Standard

---

45 Jaegwon Kim, "Self-Understanding and Rationalizing Explanations," *Philosophia Naturalis* 21 (1984): 314, 316.
46 Gilbert Ryle, *The Concept of Mind* (New York: Barnes and Noble, 1949), 113, 134.
47 The locus classicus of arguments that belief explanations are causal explanations is Donald Davidson's "Actions, Reasons and Causes," in *Essays on Actions and Events* (Oxford: Clarendon Press, 1980), 3–20.

View – Ryle had no truck with the notion that beliefs are brain states. With respect to the Argument from Causal Explanation, Ryleans would convert the argument from a *modus ponens* to a *modus tollens*. That is, Ryleans may agree with proponents of the Standard View that if beliefs did causally explain behavior, then they would be brain states, but deny that attitudes are brain states; and hence they would conclude that belief explanations do not causally explain behavior. I take issue with both the Ryleans and the proponents of the Standard View. Against Ryleans, but with proponents of the Standard View, I hold that belief explanations are causal explanations; against proponents of the Standard View, but with Ryleans, I hold that attitudes are not particular internal states. Both the Ryleans and the proponents of the Standard View are working with defective assumptions about the character of causal explanation – namely, that attitudes must be particular internal states in order to be causally explanatory.

2. We treat belief explanations as causal explanations. We spend countless billions of dollars on advertising campaigns, drug education programs, mass mailings about global warming and baby seals, and much more in an effort to change people's beliefs and so to affect their behavior. These expensive endeavors would be senseless if we did not think that beliefs and other attitudes were causally explanatory. And general disapproval of people's beliefs about the inferiority of various groups of people stems from taking there to be a causal-explanatory relation between, say, racist beliefs and racist behavior. We respond to each other – for example, start up or break off friendships – on the basis of belief explanations as causal explanations of behavior. If we did not take belief explanations to be causal explanations, it would be unconscionable to convict people of perjury or fraud. (Jean Harris, convicted of killing her lover, spent years in prison, partly on the basis of a belief explanation. Apparently, the jury took Mrs. Harris's attitudes toward her victim and his younger lover to be causally relevant to her killing her lover; otherwise, I would wager, it would not have convicted her.) It is clear that we regard belief explanations as causal explanations in all parts of life.

Although not conclusive, these two points constitute substantial reason for construing belief explanations as causal explanations. In Chapter 5, I propose a test for causally explanatory properties generally – a test that beliefs and other attitudes obviously pass.

My goals are both metaphysical and methodological. Metaphysically, I hope to give an account of the attitudes that does justice to their role in explanatory practice, and that shows them to be interwoven into, and ineliminable from, a global commonsense framework without which there would be no recognizably human affairs. Methodologically, I depart from the mainstream in contemporary philosophy in two ways: First, rather than approaching the attitudes with metaphysical assumptions about materialism or science, I look to cognitive practices, everyday as well as scientific, for clues to what is real. Second, as a guide to actual explanatory practice, I consider a huge class of explanations that have not received much philosophical attention: social, legal, political, economic explanations. Such nonpsychological causal explanations with intentional presuppositions provide a basis for a unified understanding of causal explanation, in which belief explanations find a natural home.

Part I focuses critically on the Standard View of the attitudes, the view of beliefs (if there are any) as brain states. The Standard View sets a number of tasks for its noneliminative proponents, and Chapter 2, "Content and Causation," examines work of three noneliminative philosophers who aim to work out the Standard View – William G. Lycan, Jerry A. Fodor, and Fred Dretske. These attempts to assign content to internal states (with or without a "language of thought" hypothesis) in such a way that beliefs can be causally explanatory turn out to be unsuccessful. The upshot is that the Standard View generates problems that it lacks the resources to solve.

Chapter 3, "The Myth of Folk Psychology," examines an assumption common to eliminative and noneliminative proponents of the Standard View: that commonsense psychology in terms of belief explanations is a kind of would-be scientific theory, susceptible to overthrow by a more mature scientific theory, as Ptolemaic astronomy was overthrown by Copernican astronomy. The assumption, which is crucial to arguments for eliminative materialism, misconstrues the nature and function of commonsense psychology. Thus, Part I shows that the Standard View, in both its eliminative and noneliminative guises, has serious internal difficulties.

29

Part II is a transition from the Standard View to Practical Realism. A major motivation for the Standard View, as I have said, stems from the Argument from Causal Explanation. In Chapter 4, "On Standards of Explanatory Adequacy," I argue that the conception of causal explanation endorsed by proponents of the Standard View is in general misguided – without any special reference to the attitudes. In particular, the constraints imposed on causal explanation serve to exclude almost every *nonpsychological* explanation in the social sciences that has ever been accepted as a causal explanation. In Chapter 5, "How Beliefs Explain," I propose a test for causal explanations in general; not only does the test allow explanations from the physical and social sciences to be causal explanations, but also it deems belief explanations to be causal explanations. Furthermore, Chapter 5 offers a new argument for the irreplaceability of belief explanations by physical-counterpart explanations – an argument that shows that even if beliefs actually were brain states, it would not be by dint of their being brain states that they are causally explanatory. Part II thus prepares the way for an alternative to the Standard View by showing the Argument from Causal Explanation to be unsound, and thereby undercutting a central motivation for the Standard View.

Part III develops Practical Realism. Chapter 6, "Belief without Reification," sets out the alternative account of belief and contrasts it with the Standard View. Chapter 7, "Mind and Metaphysics," dispels metaphysical worries about Practical Realism: that it does not "naturalize" intentionality, that unreified belief is unsuitable for scientific psychology, that Practical Realism is incompatible with materialism, and that Practical Realism is no genuine realism at all.

Finally, in Chapter 8, "Practical Realism Writ Large," I argue that there is a single integrated commonsense conception of reality, according to which the world is populated with ordinary things like medium-sized objects (natural and artifactual) and persons with intentional states. Belief explanations, and commonsense psychology generally, are abstracted from this comprehensive conception of reality, in which the distinction between what is intentional and what is nonintentional fades in importance. While not denying the coherence of a distinction between what is mind-independent (i.e., what can exist in a world without minds) and what is not, I do deny the metaphysical significance and utility of the distinction; in particular, the distinction does not mark off what is genuinely real from what stands in need of grounding, or is of no reality at all. This repudiation of a central assumption underlying the Standard View leads to a different conception of objectivity, according to which deliverances of common sense may be objective.

My first aim is to show how attitudes can causally explain behavior without appealing to the Standard View and without courting untenable dualism. My broader aim is to use the unification of psychological and nonpsychological causal explanations to suggest a comprehensive, nondualistic metaphysics – a metaphysics of practice – to replace the metaphysics of the Standard View, which calls into question the practices that make it possible. Far from providing a firm foundation, metaphysics cut off from what can be known by nonmetaphysical inquiry seems to me to be slippery ground indeed. A metaphysical account of, say, causation that rules out (or is inapplicable to) almost every putative causal explanation ever offered or accepted seems to me to be like a wheel in a machine that does not move anything else. Such accounts are in sore need of a "reality check."

Contemporary philosophy of mind is haunted by Descartes's ghost. It is difficult to see what else – other than fear that an immaterial soul might slip in – could be driving the philosophical concern to show how belief can be a physically respectable internal state. Wittgenstein once complained that philosophers suffer from a one-sided diet. Nowhere are the effects of that deficiency more acute than in the philosophy of mind, with its craving for the respectability of the physical sciences and its fear of poisoning by immaterialism. If we expand our diet, I hope, we can overcome both the craving and the fear of poisoning.

2

Content and causation

Proponents of the Standard View who countenance beliefs – non-eliminativists – have the task of showing how beliefs may be scientifically respectable internal states suitable for causal explanation. Since beliefs are identified by content, the task is to show how content may be assigned to internal physical states in such a way that beliefs can be causally explanatory. Although assignment of content to brain states is a purely technical problem – and as a result, this chapter is a fairly technical discussion – it is a problem whose solution is required if there are beliefs as construed by the Standard View. Eliminative materialism, discussed in Chapter 3, is not faced with these problems since it does not recognize beliefs anyway; but the problem of content and causation is an urgent one for noneliminative proponents of the Standard View.

Without trying to survey all the recent work on content, I consider three different approaches to the problem of assigning content to internal states. Two appeal to a language-of-thought hypothesis. The first, proposed by William G. Lycan, tries to show that brain states are syntactically structured entities; the second, proposed by Jerry A. Fodor, looks to a new kind of semantic property – narrow content – to be causally explanatory. The third approach, Fred Dretske's, offers an account of belief as indication, without appeal to a language of thought. I argue that none of these theories is satisfactory: They all have technical (but interesting) difficulties that seem insoluble. All the views under consideration here share the Standard View assumption that beliefs must be physically realized internal states in order to have a causal-explanatory role in behavior. That assumption – the first premise in the Argument from Causal Explanation for the Standard View – is the target of Chapters 4 and 5.

Because I use thought experiments here, let me defend my method at the beginning. In this chapter, I am concerned with various theories of the contents of beliefs. Theories have modal, or counterfactual, force: They purport to tell us not just what in fact has been the case or will be the case, but also what would be the case if certain conditions were to obtain. They tell us not only the conditions under which a person is in a state of a certain type, but they entail that if anyone *were* in those conditions, then she *would be* in a state of that type. In the thought experiments that follow, I imagine that two people are in the same conditions that the theory deems relevant, and I ask whether they are in the same state of the relevant type.

To isolate the features that the theories claim to be relevant, and to avoid extraneous issues, I hold constant features irrelevant to the theory – at the cost of empirical improbability. But the fact that it is empirically improbable, for example, that two people are ever in exactly the same (theory-relevant) conditions simply does not matter. What does matter is this: The thought experiments do not rip the concepts out of the contexts in which they have application; I am not supposing that it makes sense to ask, say, whether it is now five o'clock on the sun.[1] Rather, I am imagining the kinds of ordinary situations in which the concepts in question are designed to apply. Then, bracketing irrelevant features of the individuals in those situations, I ask: Do the dictates of the various theories accord with the core ways in which we actually apply the concepts in question?[2] Since we do not have, for example, multiple subjects in the same brain states available for testing, we cannot actually control the conditions the theories take to be relevant to belief. In that case, it is difficult to see how better to test theories of belief than by imagining the theory-relevant conditions to be satisfied in ordinary situations, where there is no violation of known law or even abrogation of custom or convention. There is nothing unfamiliar about the situations envisaged by the thought experiments.

SYNTAX AND THE PROBLEM OF THE PARAMETER

Many philosophers hold that propositional objects of belief (expressed in 'that' clauses of attributions) have constituent structure. If someone believes that snow is white and believes that snow is

---

1 Wittgenstein emphasized the senselessness of asking such questions.
2 We may change application of a concept under pressure from a theory (e.g., we may begin to take nine-month-old fetuses to be persons on the basis of biological theory); but central cases are resistant to such pressures. Unless we were to give

cold, she has two beliefs with an element in common – a concept of snow. A number of philosophers of mind think that mental states themselves, not just their propositional objects, also have constituent structure. On the hypothesis of a language of thought, belief states have syntactic structure.[3] Psychological processes are causal processes on sentencelike entities, individuated syntactically. The idea is that syntax is, as William G. Lycan says, "psychologically real," that is, syntax is physically realized by structures in the brain. Because syntax is assumed to be fully determined by, or to be supervenient on, brain structure, syntactic properties are thought to be able to be causally explanatory.[4]

Since the language-of-thought hypothesis seems made to order to explain linguistic behavior, I focus on utterances as caused by brain states with syntactic structure. Let me make a simplifying assumption: Suppose that we identify certain utterances as 'standard' in the following way: They are sincere, assertive utterances that p that are causally explained by a belief that p and a desire to assert that p.[5] Call the belief that p that causes a standard utterance that p the 'related belief'. This assumption may be grossly implausible, but, as we shall see, even sticking with standard utterances, matters are not simple.

How is the syntactic structure of a belief to be determined? One prominent suggestion that is reasonably well worked out is Lycan's: Associated with every sentence is a "semantic representation," which displays the logical form of the sentence and which can serve as input for syntactic transformations. For each belief, say, that snow is white, there is a neural sentence that gives the logical form of the sentence 'snow is white'. Now suppose that someone issues a standard utterance of 'I am tired now'. What is the appropriate syntax to attribute to the related belief? One obvious suggestion is that the syntax has parameters for the indexical ele-

---

up applying the concept of a person altogether, we would continue to apply it to healthy adult human beings in the face of any new biological theory.

3 See, for example, Jerry A. Fodor, "Why There Still Has to Be a Language of Thought," in *Psychosemantics: The Problem of Meaning in the Philosophy of Mind* (Cambridge MA: MIT/Bradford, 1987), 135–54.

4 Note that this is an inference from "the order of being."

5 It is noteworthy – although the literature does not suggest it – that it is highly unusual to cite a belief that p as causally explaining an assertion that p. Unless one doubts the speaker's sincerity or linguistic competence, or doubts the truth of p, we just assume that one believes what one asserts.

ments. So, we must allow for indexical and other contextual elements to be provided for in the syntax of beliefs.

Call features of context that affect the truth conditions of a sentence or belief 'semantically relevant features'. In public language, a hearer's appreciation of context may contribute to the causal relevance of an utterance. For example, suppose that Jill's shouting to Jack, "There's a charging bull," causes Jack to jump a fence. The utterance has its effect partly in virtue of its meaning and partly in virtue of the context in which it occurs: Jack understands Jill's utterance; as an English speaker, he knows what it means, and being aware of the circumstances, he knows how to respond. With the language of thought, however, the situation is different. If Jack's jumping the fence is caused by his belief that there's a charging bull – a belief that he may have acquired by understanding Jill's warning – the belief has its effect (of getting Jack out of the way of the bull) solely in virtue of the syntax of the internal sentence. (As Lycan says, concurring with Harman, "I do not 'understand' my own language of thought in the same sense in which I understand a natural language".[6]) In the language of thought, those features of context that can make a difference in behavior must be explicitly represented in the brain. There is not a similar constraint on the representation of the logical forms of sentences in public languages, where salient features of context may be taken for granted.[7]

Since the causal efficacy of sentences in the language of thought, on this view, is wholly determined by brain states of the agent, every element whose presence or absence can affect behavior must be represented in the brain. So, whether or not public language requires that every semantically relevant feature be represented in logical form, the function of the syntax of the language of thought in causing behavior requires that every semantically relevant feature be explicitly represented in logical form and physically encoded in the brain.

So, the syntactic structure of any belief must have a "slot" (a parameter or a variable) for each semantically relevant feature. For example, in the case of "I am tired now," the syntactic structure of the belief must have parameters for speaker and for time. Obviously, there are many other contextual elements that must be syn-

6 William G. Lycan, *Logical Form in Natural Language* (Cambridge, MA: MIT/Bradford, 1984), 237.
7 This was pointed out to me by Max Cresswell.

tactically represented in the brain state. For example, there are all sorts of hidden parameters in ordinary discourse ("I gave it to the woman on the left" – on the left of what?). The belief that standardly would cause assertion of "I gave it to the woman on the left" must have a "slot" for the hidden parameter to be filled in by whatever the woman was to the left of.[8]

For this picture to serve its purpose of showing how syntactically structured brain belief states cause behavior, it must impose two constraints on the syntactic structure of beliefs:

(A) Syntactically distinct beliefs have physically distinct realizations in the brain.

(B) A belief with n parameters is syntactically distinct from a belief with $n + 1$ parameters.

(A) is simply the requirement that syntax is to be physically represented in the brain. (B) may seem more controversial: After all, semantical indexes are not always marked in surface sentences; so why must they be marked in neural entities? Regardless of how we think of the semantics of public language, semantical indexes would still have to be marked in the language of thought if the language of thought is to play its causal role in producing behavior (as proponents of the Standard View construe causal role). The neural entity is supposed to be a syntactically structured inner cause: It must be able to cause behavior in virtue of its syntactic properties. Anything that can make a difference to behavior must be represented syntactically in the brain. Differences in number of parameters are differences in number of semantically relevant features; this kind of difference in truth condition can make a difference in behavior, and hence must be reflected in different physical realizations in the brain.

Unfortunately, (A) and (B) lead straight to trouble. The problem arises for any term that some people take to be relational, and others take to be nonrelational; terms of morals and manners come readily to mind. It also arises for terms, like 'tall', which apply to objects only relative to some implicit reference class; again, semantically relevant features that may remain implicit in a public language must be made explicit in the language of thought. I shall illustrate the general difficulty by an example from science since we

8 These ideas are taken from *Logical Form in Natural Language*.

agree on its correct truth conditions, but I emphasize that the problem is not confined to theoretical contexts. Consider various standard utterances (all true and correctly believed to be true) of the following English sentence.[9]

> (s) An event on the sun is not simultaneous with anyone's seeing it.

The first utterance is by a nineteenth-century Newtonian physicist; the second utterance is by a twentieth-century Einsteinian physicist. Do the related beliefs, realized in the brains of the speakers, have the same syntactic structure or not?

(YES): Suppose so. If one assumes that Einstein's theory, with a frame-of-reference parameter for simultaneity, gives the actual truth conditions of (s), then the Einsteinian's related belief must represent all the semantically relevant features of (s) and the internal sentence must have a frame-of-reference parameter. So, if the Newtonian's belief has the same syntactic structure as the Einsteinian's, the Newtonian's related belief must also have a frame-of-reference parameter. Question: How did a frame-of-reference parameter get into the Newtonian's head?

In the unlikely event that we could answer that question, more are waiting in the wings. Since the Newtonian would deny that simultaneity was relative to inertial frame, must we conclude that the Newtonian did not understand Newtonian physics? What about Newton himself? Must we say that, in maintaining absolute simultaneity, he did not know what he was talking about? What are *we* saying when we say, "Newton believed that simultaneity was absolute"? And when Aristotle said, "Those things are called *simultaneous* without qualification and most strictly which come into being at the same time" (*Categories,* 14b25), did he have a frame of reference parameter in his head?

On the current alternative of saying that all the standard utterances of (s) have the same truth conditions, which are given by relativity theory, there is no way even to entertain the possibility of absolute simultaneity. For if all standard utterances of (s) have a frame-of-reference parameter, then it is difficult to see how even to

9 This and other criticisms of Lycan's version of the language of thought hypothesis may be found in greater detail in my "Truth in Context," *Philosophical Perspectives* 2 (1989): 85–94.

formulate truth conditions for an assertion of absolute simultaneity. If we assume that an expression used in a counterfactual utterance has the same meaning that it does in a standard utterance, the following becomes unintelligible (on the current alternative): "If Newton had been right, then simultaneity would have been absolute" (= 'it would have been the case that simultaneity is absolute').

Moreover, if the correct truth conditions for (s) are already encoded in Newton's brain, then the correct theories are already represented in our brains before they are 'discovered'. In that case, to find out about the physical world, we should not do physics, but psychology and linguistics. Thus, it seems hopeless to suppose that the beliefs related to standard utterances of (s) of the Newtonian and Einsteinian physicists are brain states with the same syntactic structure. So, turn to the other alternative.

(NO): Suppose that the physically realized beliefs related to the Newtonian's and Einsteinian's standard utterances of (s) have different syntactic structures. Then, presumably, the Einsteinian's brain state has a frame-of-reference parameter that the Newtonian's lacks. In that case, 'simultaneous' would be ambiguous. Of course, on some radical conceptions of theory change, it *is* ambiguous. Let us investigate the implications of ambiguity for the language-of-thought hypothesis.

To bring out the difficulty, I shall set up an example in a way that highlights exactly the relevant points. Suppose that the Newtonian and Einsteinian each has a daughter and a son; it happens that the daughters, who have been brought up in restricted environments, have been subjected to exactly the same kinds of sensory stimulation over their lifetimes, and that at the time we encounter them, their brains are in the same state. Suppose that both parents, emitting exactly the same noises, tell their respective daughters that it takes time for light to get to Earth from the sun, and hence that (s). Now, suppose that, in each scene, the brother arrives, and each daughter (flushed with new knowledge) issues a standard utterance of (s).

On the current alternative, brain states that are the beliefs related to Newtonian and Einsteinian physicists' respective standard utterances of (s) differ in truth condition: The Einsteinian's, but not the Newtonian's, brain state has a frame-of-reference parameter. If we also assume that their daughters' similar beliefs inherit their parents' truth conditions (otherwise, it would be miraculous that anyone ever learned a language), then at least one of the constraints (A) or (B), is violated. Since the daughters' brains were in the same states and they had the same physiological histories, and the information about simultaneity was transmitted by means of physically identical sounds, they do not now have different physical realizations in their brains; so by (A), their brain states are syntactically the same. But since, by assumption (NO), one brain state has a frame-of-reference parameter but the other doesn't, their beliefs have syntactic structures with different numbers of parameters; hence, by (B), their brain states are syntactically distinct. Hence, (A) and (B) lead to contradiction.

Lycan has replied to this by holding, at least tentatively, that "'simultaneous' remains a two-place predicate for ordinary people but has become a three-place predicate for the *cognoscenti*."[10] Then, since neither daughter knows physics, "presumably neither has the three-place predicate on board." So, according to Lycan's tentative reply, the beliefs that produce standard utterances of (s) in the two girls do have the same syntactic structure. On the other hand, according to Lycan's theory, syntactic structures realized in the brain encode the truth conditions of the belief. If, however, 'simultaneous' is a two-place predicate for both daughters, then the girls' standard utterances of (s) do not have the correct truth conditions of (s): For, as we now know, simultaneity is relative to frame, and hence 'simultaneous' is in fact a three-place predicate. Thus, Lycan's tentative reply seems to entail that the girls' standard utterances of (s) have truth conditions that in fact they do not have.

Moreover, suppose that, as Lycan's reply suggests, the surface sentence, 'An event on the sun is not simultaneous with anyone's seeing it', is ambiguous: Underlying utterances of it are two logical forms with two different truth conditions. It is difficult to see how to understand the ambiguity. Contrast a typical case of ambiguity – for example, 'I put my money in the bank'. The ambiguity in such typical cases arises from the fact that an occurrence of a surface expression like $b\hat{\ }a\hat{\ }n\hat{\ }k$ may really be either of two different words: 'Bank' may refer to a financial institution or to the ground beside some river or stream. But 'simultaneity' is not like 'bank': There is only one physical phenomenon of simultaneity, and it is relative to frame. So, if we assume that 'p' is true if and only if p is the case,

10 William G. Lycan, "Reply to Baker," *Philosophical Psychology* 2 (1989): 97.

there is only one set of truth conditions for utterances of (s), and in it 'simultaneous' is a three-place predicate. 'Simultaneous' thus should not be taken as ambiguous. If each daughter represents 'simultaneous' by a two-place predicate, then neither daughter represents the truth conditions of (s) – in violation of Lycan's theory.[11]

Finally, any strategy that takes different people's standard utterances of (s) to have different truth conditions inherits all the difficulties attending the thesis in the philosophy of science that theories are incommensurable – and then compounds them by supposing that the incommensurable relations between theories must be reflected in the physical structures of the brain. On the current alternative, the Newtonian says nothing false when she says, "Simultaneity is not relative to a frame of reference." For the Newtonian's utterance has different truth conditions from the Einsteinian's; on the current alternative, the Newtonian's utterance is true if and only if simultaneity construed as a two-place relation is not relative to frame; so, the Newtonian's utterance is true. Moreover, on the assumption that their utterances of (s) have different truth conditions, the Einsteinian and the Newtonian don't disagree when one says, "Simultaneity is absolute," and the other says, "Simultaneity is relative." Lycan's reply seems to subject his view to all the counterintuitive consequences of the "incommensurability" view of theory change.

Therefore, it seems that either answer to the question – Do standard utterances of (s) by both Newtonians and Einsteinians have the same truth conditions? – comes to grief when we assume that syntax is "psychologically real." So, I think that the language-of-thought hypothesis is afflicted with what we might call 'the problem of the parameter.'[12]

Actually, to use an example like 'simultaneity' underestimates the problem of the parameter for the language-of-thought hypothesis. For, as already suggested, the problem of the parameter may be generated by any hidden parameter: Consider (putative) representa-

11 Perhaps one would want to relativize truth conditions to individuals: Conditions under which (s) is true for one may not be the same as the conditions under which (s) is true for another. Not only is this an implausible construal of truth conditions of a public language, but also it is not available to realists like Lycan.
12 The example has implications beyond the language-of-thought hypothesis. First, it suggests that there are syntactic as well as semantic issues of theory change; second, it suggests that any theory of meaning based on syntactic primitives is at least liable to the problem of the parameter.

tions of 'slurping soup is impolite' in the heads of an absolutist and a relativist. In the scientific case, theories provide accounts of which features are the semantically relevant ones. But in most ordinary contexts, things are not so tidy. We have no general theory of semantically relevant features of standard utterances, nor will we until we solve the frame problem.[13]

And until we do solve the frame problem, it seems to me that we have no theory whatsoever, only a relabeling of the problem. To say, as Lycan does, that all contextual elements are handled via an all-purpose assignment function is not to say anything informative without some account of what features are semantically relevant in general. Without such an account, the only available specification of the assignment function is that it takes as arguments all the different parameters realized in the brain and returns as values all and only semantically relevant features of the context, whatever they may be.

Note that I am not talking here about empirical questions of how the brain functions to encode the requisite parameters, nor am I asking for mechanisms that show how the brain computes the values for the assignment function. I am asking the prior question of what parameters need to be encoded (by whatever mechanisms). For the language-of-thought proposal to work, we need a context-free theory of context, but I see no such theory in the offing.[14] Lycan remains unmoved: "Our present or even future inability to specify a context does not matter to the thesis that a determinate assignment function exists."[15] Perhaps; but in view of the difficulties presented here, I see no good reason to think that there is a function (in the mathematical sense) from particular brain states to the semantically relevant features of utterances.

In any case, the problem of the parameter would seem to afflict any account of beliefs as syntactically structured brain states. Since any language-of-thought hypothesis assumes that syntax is physi-

13 The frame problem is how to get a machine to update knowledge of a changing situation by "noticing" salient features and ignoring others. For example, knocking the support out from under a box causes it to change position but not to change color. See Hubert L. Dreyfus, *What Computers Can't Do,* rev. ed. (New York: Harper and Row, 1979) and John Haugeland, *Artificial Intelligence: The Very Idea* (Cambridge, MA: MIT/Bradford, 1985).
14 Since I do not believe that we will ever have a context-free theory of context, I am prepared to live with a measure of context dependence – in the evaluation of counterfactuals, for example.
15 Lycan, "Reply to Baker," 99.

cally realized in brains and any such hypothesis must accommodate semantically relevant features of context in some way, the problem of the parameter is not peculiar to Lycan's view. Rather, any view that takes the syntax of internal sentences to cause behavior must have some way to specify the syntactical features of the language of thought that avoids these difficulties. These examples show that we can not simply assume that it makes sense to think of the brain as organized in terms of states that generally realize syntactic properties.

THE DEAD END OF NARROW CONTENT

Beliefs are ordinarily attributed in English by sentences with embedded 'that' clauses – for example, 'Jones believes that rock-climbing is dangerous'. Such sentences identify beliefs by what have come to be called 'broad contents'. Since broad contents individuate beliefs in part by reference to the believer's environment, beliefs are *relational* mental states: The conditions for having a belief, say, that water is wet or that arthritis is painful, depend not only on the intrinsic properties of the believer, but also on the nature of the believer's physical and social environment.[16]

Assuming that beliefs individuated by 'that' clauses (or by broad contents) are relational, I am here concerned with the causal-explanatory status of belief states. Are beliefs (or the properties that individuate them) causally explanatory?[17] Are relational properties ever causally explanatory? Some philosophers – prominently, Jerry A. Fodor – acknowledge the causal relevance of relational properties generally, but take beliefs individuated by broad content to be metaphysically unsuitable for purposes of causal explanation.[18] I

16 Tyler Burge is largely responsible for the widespread agreement that (*de dicto*) beliefs as ordinarily attributed are relational. See his "Individualism and the Mental," in *Studies in Metaphysics* (Midwest Studies in Philosophy, 4), ed. Peter A. French, Theodore E. Uehling, Jr., and Howard K. Wettstein (Minneapolis: University of Minnesota, 1979), 73–122.
17 I follow Fodor and speak sometimes of states and sometimes of their individuating properties as causally explanatory.
18 See *Psychosemantics* and "A Modal Argument for Narrow Content," *Journal of Philosophy* 88 (1991): 5–26. Hereafter, references to this article appear in the text as "MANC," followed by a page number. In "The Elm and the Expert: Mentalese and Its Semantics" (1993 Jean Nicod Lectures), Fodor gives up his theory of narrow content. My arguments here remain important, however, in that they show that denial of the causal explanatoriness of broad content leads to denial of

want to challenge this position, by arguing that broad contents are causally explanatory, and that if Fodor's argument were to cast doubt on the claim that broad contents are causally explanatory, then it would cast doubt equally on the claim that any relational property is causally explanatory.

Explanatory properties, according to Fodor, are taxonomic, that is, they are projected by the laws of some science; and since the sciences aim at causal explanations, Fodor holds, taxonomy in the sciences is by causal powers.[19] Fodor argues that broad contents do not contribute in the relevant way to an individual's causal powers, and hence that they can not be taxonomic in psychology. Nonetheless, he upholds the explanatory status of other relational properties; indeed, Fodor says, "Taxonomy by relational properties is ubiquitous in the sciences" (MANC, 12). Thus, Fodor defends the conjunction of (A) and (B):

(A) Relational properties that individuate belief states are not taxonomic in psychology.

(B) Some relational properties are taxonomic in the special sciences.

I try to show here that (A) and (B) do not sit comfortably on the same bench. Fodor's arguments, I urge, either fail to disqualify broad contents as taxonomic, or else disqualify all relational properties as taxonomic. I am not going to claim that broad contents must be taxonomic in psychology, only that the metaphysical considerations against their being taxonomic are faulty.[20] Logically and metaphysically speaking, as broad contents go, so go relational properties generally – Fodor's claims to the contrary notwithstanding.

the causal explanatoriness of relational properties generally. In Chapter 6, I criticize Fodor's latest proposal.

19 Sometimes Fodor speaks of causal powers as properties (as in "a cause property might fail to count as a causal power in virtue of its responsibility for one effect property, but still might constitute a causal power in virtue of its responsibility for some other effect property"); and sometimes he speaks of causal powers as the things that have such properties (as in "We have seen that twater thoughts and water thoughts are not different causal powers"). For my purposes, I think that I can overlook this ambiguity. MANC, 12, 25.

20 For a different argument, see Robert van Gulick, "Metaphysical Arguments for Internalism and Why They Don't Work" in *ReRepresentation: Readings in the Philosophy of Mental Representation,* ed. Stuart Silvers (Dordrecht, Holland: Kluwer Academic Publishers, 1989), 151–9.

Fodor's argument for (A) in MANC is part of an argument that intentional psychology individuates states with respect to narrow content, where narrow contents are nonrelational. Narrow content supervenes on the subject's intrinsic properties, without regard to the subject's environment. The skeleton of Fodor's new argument for narrow content is this:

(1) All scientific taxonomies individuate states with respect to their causal powers.

(2) Intentional psychology individuates states with respect to intentional content.

(3) Difference in broad content does not suffice for (relevant) difference in causal powers.

Therefore,

(4) Intentional psychology individuates states with respect to narrow content.

Fodor's latest argument consists mainly of a new defense of (3), in which Fodor proposes a necessary condition (what I shall call the "no-conceptual-connection" test) for a difference to count as a difference in causal power, and then claims that broad contents fail it.

Fodor formulates two tests – the no-conceptual-connection test and the cross-context test – for determining when a property is a causal power and hence may be taxonomic in some science. More precisely, the tests are to show when the difference between having a particular property and not having it is a difference in causal power, in virtue of the responsibility of the property for properties of the subject's behavior. Since Fodor holds that taxonomic properties in psychology must make a difference to the subject's actual or possible behavior, only properties whose possession makes a difference to the bearer's causal powers can be taxonomic. Fodor argues that broad contents can not be taxonomic in psychology, because they fail the no-conceptual-connection test, but that other relational properties, like the property of being a planet, can be taxonomic in other sciences, because they pass both tests. I argue that the only principled way that Fodor has to rule out broad contents as taxonomic would also rule out other relational properties, like that of being a planet, as taxonomic. In particular, broad contents actually pass Fodor's no-conceptual-connection test in the relevant way; and any interpretation of the cross-context test which would disqualify belief individuated by broad content as taxonomic would also disqualify relational properties generally as taxonomic.

The no-conceptual-connection test

I want to show that broad contents in fact do satisfy Fodor's necessary condition for a difference to count as a difference in causal power, in virtue of its responsibility for a difference in behavior.[21] Hence, the argument for (3) collapses.

Fodor offers a schema in terms of which he casts his argument. Consider a situation in which there is a pair of causes C_1, C_2, and their effects E_1, E_2, such that

C_1 differs from C_2 in that C_1 has cause property CP_1 where C_2 has cause property CP_2.
E_1 differs from E_2 in that E_1 has effect property EP_1 and E_2 has effect property EP_2.
The difference between C_1 and C_2 is responsible for the difference between E_1 and E_2 in the sense that, if C_1 had had CP_2 rather than CP_1, then E_1 would have EP_2 rather than EP_1; and if C_2 had had CP_1 rather than CP_2, E_2 would have had EP_1 rather than EP_2. (MANC, 9)

I shall follow Fodor and think of the schema "sometimes as relating events and sometimes as relating event types" (MANC, 9). Now, asks Fodor, which instances of the schema "are cases where the difference between having CP_1 and having CP_2 is a difference in causal power in virtue of its responsibility for the difference between E_1 and E_2?" More briefly, when is the difference between CP_1 and CP_2 a difference in causal power? Fodor's answer: when the difference in cause properties is not conceptually connected to the difference in effect properties.[22] Fodor initially states this requirement by saying that the difference between CP_1 and CP_2 is a difference in causal power

only when it is not a conceptual truth that causes which differ in that one has CP_1 where the other has CP_2 have effects that differ in that one has EP_1 where the other has EP_2. (MANC, 19)

---

21 Fodor is specifically concerned with properties' being causal powers in virtue of their responsibility for the properties of their bearers' behavior, but I shall leave this qualification implicit in most of what follows.
22 I do not explore complexities (and perplexities) surrounding the notion of conceptual connection here. The argument to follow applies to any account that takes conceptual truth to be a species of necessary truth.

This necessary condition is supposed to rule out broad contents as causal powers because, although the difference between having water thoughts and having twin-water thoughts is responsible for the difference in intentional properties of behavior (e.g., drilling for water versus drilling for twin water), it is a conceptual truth that thoughts that differ only in being water or twin-water thoughts have effects that differ only in being water drillings or being twin-water drillings.

The necessary condition is then revised to take care of an objection posed by Stephen Stich. Suppose, for example, that water is Bush's favorite drink. Then, it is not a conceptual truth that beliefs that differ in that one is about Bush's favorite drink and the other is about twin water have effects that differ in that one is a water behavior and the other a twin-water behavior. Yet, Fodor does not want to count the difference between being about Bush's favorite drink and being about twin water as a difference in causal powers. So, he must amend his necessary condition on causal powers to rule out such a case.

Although Fodor never actually formulates the patched-up version of the necessary condition, he adds the requirement that the following not be conceptually necessary:

If B [e.g., being concerned with Bush's favorite drink] is a property that water behaviors have, then if my thoughts are water thoughts, then my behaviors have B.

If B is the property of being concerned with Bush's favorite drink, then this instance of the conditional is, as Fodor wants, conceptually necessary: There is a conceptual connection between water thoughts and water behaviors, and there is no possible world in which being concerned with Bush's favorite drink is a property of water behaviors, and Fodor's thoughts are water thoughts, yet Fodor's behaviors fail to be concerned with Bush's favorite drink.

To see that not all conditionals of this form are conceptually necessary truths, Fodor says, suppose that thinking about topology causes headaches and compare the following conditional:

If B [e.g., being painful] is a property of headaches, then if S's thought is about topology, S's mental state is painful.

This conditional, though true, is not a conceptually necessary truth. The "headache" conditional is only a contingent truth, because it is a contingent truth (if it is a truth at all) that topology thoughts cause headaches. In some other world, headaches have B (the property of being painful), S has topology thoughts, yet S's mental state lacks B – because in that world topology thoughts do not cause headaches.[23]

Putting these conditions together, we have the following as a necessary condition on causal powers: Suppose that C_1, C_2, CP_1, CP_2, E_1, E_2, EP_1, and EP_2 satisfy Fodor's schema. Then:

(FCP)   Two cause-properties, CP_1 and CP_2, are different causal powers only if neither (i) nor (ii) is a conceptual truth:

    (i) Causes C_1 and C_2, which differ in that C_1 has CP_1 and C_2 has CP_2, have effects, E_1 and E_2, which differ in that E_1 has EP_1 and E_2 has EP_2; and

    (ii) If B is a property that events with EP_1 have, then if C_1 has CP_1, then E_1 has B.[24]

Fodor believes that broad contents fail to satisfy this necessary condition for being causal powers. I believe, however, that Fodor has too narrow a view of the difference that difference in broad content can make. I want to show that differences in broad content unaccompanied by physiological differences make a causal difference in behavior that satisfies Fodor's necessary condition(s) on causal powers. So, let us consider an example.

In English, the word 'jade' denotes both jadeite and nephrite, which differ in structure. Although they are similar in appearance, jadeite, which is found mainly in Burma and in Central America, is much more valuable than nephrite, which is found all over the world. Despite the fact that knowledgeable people are aware of these differences, 'jade' in English still refers not only to jadeite but

---

23 I am paraphrasing Fodor here. I believe that this point raises deep questions about (Fodor's conception) of the nature of causal laws. In "Making Mind Matter More," *Philosophical Topics* 17 (1989): 63, Fodor says that he is "hard put to see how anybody could seriously object" to the "idea that hedged (including intentional) laws necessitate their consequents when their ceteris paribus clauses are discharged." Fodor's conception of causal law there warrants close attention, which I can not give here.

24 Since Fodor himself never actually formulates his amended condition, I can only guess at how clause (ii) should go. Clause (ii) as stated needs further work; however, since I do not see how better formulation of (ii) could block my counterexample, I do not undertake to improve it here. Ultimately, it is up to the proponent of the "no-conceptual-connection" test to formulate the condition that is supposed to block counterexamples.

to nephrite as well. As (spoof) proof, let me cite *Webster's Unabridged Dictionary,* which gives the following as a definition of 'nephrite': "the less valuable of two varieties of jade, compact in structure and varying in color from white to dark green."

Now suppose that there is another community, in which all the differences between jadeite and nephrite are also well known by the experts and by the informed jewelry-buying public. But in the other community, the word that sounds like 'jade' denotes only jadeite. 'Jade' is as inapplicable to nephrite in the other community as 'gold' is to iron pyrite in our community. The less valuable nephrite is called something else and is not in the extension of 'jade'. The truth conditions of the sentences 'There are jade stones', then differ in the two communities. In English, 'There are jade stones' is true if there are either jadeite or nephrite stones. In the other community, 'There are jade stones' is true if there are jadeite stones.

Consider another possible world that has in it both our English-speaking community and the other community (or their counterparts), and suppose that there are two microphysical duplicates, Ann and Jan, in that other world. Ann lives in the English-speaking community, and Jan in the other community. Although both use (what sounds like) 'jade' in various correct sentences in their respective communities, neither is a jewelry buyer, and neither knows that there are two similar kinds of tough green stones. So, when Ann has thoughts about jadeite or nephrite, Jan has thoughts about jadeite.

Now suppose that Ann and Jan both appear as contestants, in their respective communities, on qualitatively identical quiz shows. For the grand prize, each has to identify a stone. (The stones are qualitatively identical pieces of nephrite.) Each quiz show host says: "Here's a lovely green stone. Can you identify it?" To this, Ann and Jan give acoustically identical replies: "The stone is jade." Now Ann has given a winning answer; in Ann's community, nephrite is a variety of what is called 'jade'. Jan, however, has given a losing answer; in Jan's community, nephrite is not a variety of what is called 'jade'. At this point – when Ann hears the audience applaud and Jan hears the audience groan – the physical descriptions of the contestants part ways; Ann and Jan cease to be duplicates.

Now put this story into Fodor's schema. Ann tokens neurophysiological type *T,* which has the property of being a belief with the same truth condition as the English sentence, "The stone is jadeite or nephrite," and which causes emission of a sound of acoustical type U that has the property of being a winning answer. Jan tokens neurophysiological type T, which has the property of being a belief with the same truth conditions as the English sentence, "The stone is jadeite," and which causes emission of a sound of acoustical type U that has the property of being a losing answer. Schematically:

(C_1) a state realized by neurophysiological type T

(C_2) a state realized by neurophysiological type T

(CP_1) being a belief with the same truth condition as the English sentence "The stone is jadeite or nephrite."

(CP_2) being a belief with the same truth condition as the English sentence "The stone is jadeite."

(E_1) emission of a sound of acoustical type U

(E_2) emission of a sound of acoustical type U

(EP_1) being a winning answer

(EP_2) being a losing answer

The beliefs, (C_1) and (C_2), have different cause properties, (CP_1) and (CP_2), and the answers, (E_1) and (E_2), have different effect properties, (EP_1) and (EP_2). Furthermore, if (C_1) had had the truth conditions that (C_2) had, then (E_1) would have been a losing (rather than a winning) answer. Fodor proposes to block broad contents as causal powers if the relevant instances of (i) and (ii) in (FCP) are conceptual truths. To see that they are not conceptual truths, let (i') and (ii') illustrate relevant instances of (i) and (ii):

(i') Two states realized by neurophysiological states of type T, which differ in truth conditions (as described), have effects (acoustically identical sounds), which differ in that one is a winning answer and the other is a losing answer.

(ii') If being a winning answer is a property of winning answers, then if a state realized by neurophysiological state of type T has the property of being a belief with the same truth conditions as the English sentence, 'The stone is jadeite or nephrite', then the emitting of a sound of acoustical type U is a winning answer.

(i') and (ii') are, of course, true; but, obviously, they are not conceptually necessary truths. There is no conceptual connection between having certain truth conditions and being a winning answer. (ii') is parallel to Fodor's "headache" conditional; the "headache" conditional is only contingently true, because in other worlds, topology thoughts do not cause headaches, and the conditional is false in such worlds. (ii') is only contingently true, because in other worlds, a belief with the given truth conditions may not produce a winning answer. If Ann and Jan had been presented with the same stones and asked the same questions in some context other than a quiz show, then their answers would not have had the properties, respectively, of winning and losing.

Although in the example, being a winning answer and being a losing answer are different "effect properties," notice that they, in turn, are causally efficacious and that they produce very different results. (E_1) elicits cheers from the studio audience; (E_2) elicits groans from the studio audience. (E_1) leads to Ann's taking away the grand prize; (E_2) leads to Jan's going away empty-handed. When Ann's husband suspiciously questions Ann about how she suddenly acquired such wealth, Ann can cite this *as a cause:* "I gave the winning answer." The winning answer allows Ann to retire while the losing answer forces Jan to return to a dreary job. Such differences in subsequent effects indicate that the quiz show episodes are parts of *causal* processes.

Someone may object that psychologists are not concerned with the difference between being a winning answer and being a losing answer. To this objection, I have a twofold reply. First, there may well be contexts in which the difference between winning and losing answers is exactly what a psychologist is interested in. (You may seek out such a psychologist to treat your underachieving child, who oddly produces wrong answers when you suspect that he knows better.) We can not say a priori under what kinds of descriptions psychologists will explain behavior. Second, even if psychology never countenanced properties like 'being a winning answer,' that fact would be irrelevant to my point. For Fodor's condition is perfectly general; it does not apply exclusively to psychology. My point is that Fodor gave a necessary condition for properties to be explanatory, and he claimed that broad contents do not satisfy this condition (the no-conceptual-connection test). And I provided a counterexample to show that, in fact, broad contents do satisfy it. Hence, Fodor's no-conceptual-connection test can not rule out differences in broad contents as causally explanatory differences, regardless of what counts as behavior in psychology.

Here, then, is what I claim for the "jadeite" example: Differences in broad content, unaccompanied by neurophysiological differences, causally explain differences in behavior that are not conceptually connected to the broad contents that explain them. Fodor may insist that such differences in broad content as I have described fail to be differences in causal powers in his sense; in that case, I would reply that causally explanatory properties need not be causal powers in his sense. (I do not care about the term 'causal powers', which seems to flop around anyway.) On the other hand, if we simply agree to call causally explanatory properties "causal powers," I do not believe that Fodor's conditions have ruled out broad contents as causal powers. Thus, I do not believe that Fodor has given reason to think that differences in broad content, unaccompanied by neurophysiological differences, fail to be causally explanatory. Fodor's necessary condition on causal powers, in terms of conceptual connections between cause and effect properties, does not preclude differences in broad contents as differences in causal powers. I now want to show that broad contents are as worthy as nonpsychological relational properties to be causally explanatory.

The cross-context test

The no-conceptual-connection test is not the only weapon against broad content in Fodor's arsenal. In addition to passing that test, explanatory properties must also pass the cross-context test. To see whether causal powers are the same or different, we must compare the individuals "*across* contexts rather than *within* contexts" (MANC, 8). The idea of the cross-context test is that two individuals have the same causal powers if and only if, in the same context, they have the same effects. To see whether a relational property makes a difference to causal powers, consider two individuals who are similar except that one has the relational property in question and the other lacks it. Now, according to Fodor, the property makes a difference to causal powers only if the individuals have different effects when considered "across contexts."

Before examining the cross-context test, note that Fodor himself no longer puts stock in the cross-context test to rule out broad contents as explanatory. Indeed, in order to motivate the no-conceptual-connection test, Fodor says that broad contents *do* survive the cross-context test:

> Whatever the context of utterance, my utterance is a water request and his utterance is a twater request. So our behaviors remain relevantly different under these intentional descriptions *even by the across-context test*. It is this residual difference between the behaviors – their cross-context difference under certain intentional descriptions – which is the challenge to individualism and local supervenience. (MANC, 8–9; emphasis in original)

Fodor seems to be admitting here that – without the aid of the no-conceptual-connection test, which we have seen to be no help – the cross-context test does not disqualify differences in truth condition alone as differences in causal powers, in virtue of the effects of such differences on the properties of behavior. Nonetheless, the cross-context test deserves consideration. In particular, does my counter-example pass the cross-context test?

The difficulty with the cross-context test is that Fodor never explicitly formulates it, and his comments about it suggest more than one interpretation. I offer several interpretations of the cross-context test – all the interpretations for which I find evidence in Fodor – and argue with respect to each one of them either that broad contents pass it or that other relational properties like being a planet fail it (or both). If that is right, then the cross-context test can not rule out broad contents as taxonomic without also ruling out nonpsychological relational properties in good standing.

Here is an initially plausible way to interpret the cross-context test:

(CCT₁) Property P is causally explanatory only if its possession makes a difference to the causal powers of its possessor, where x and y have the same causal powers if and only if: If x had been substituted for y, then x (in y's context) would have had all the same effects that y did have.

(CCT₁) would disqualify all relational properties – such as being a planet – as causal powers. Fodor says that being a planet is a relational property in good standing, and that this property could "distinguish molecularly identical chunks of rock," and that being a planet constitutes a causal power in good standing (MANC, 12). Let R_1 be a planet revolving around a star and R_2 be a nonplanetary microphysical duplicate held (for a time at least) in an elliptical orbit by the distribution of matter in the universe. Now substitute R_1 for R_2 and vice versa. Since R_2 is a microphysical duplicate of R_1, when R_2 is substituted for R_1, R_2 will orbit around R_1's star, and hence will be a planet when put in R_1's environment. So, if R_2 is substituted for R_1, R_2's effects have all the same properties that R_1's effects did have. Hence, on (CCT$_1$), R_1 and R_2 have the same causal powers, and the difference between being a planet and not being a planet fails to be a difference in causal power. So, on (CCT$_1$), the property of being a planet does not pass the cross-context test.

No relational property can pass the cross-context test as interpreted via (CCT$_1$) for the simple reason that (CCT$_1$) amounts to a requirement (or stipulation) that properties that suffice for a difference in causal powers be nonrelational. Indeed, (CCT$_1$) is almost a paraphrase of Stephen Stich's replacement argument for his "Autonomy Principle," the point of which is to confine explanatory properties to those that supervene on the current intrinsic properties of their bearers.[25] And, as Fodor points out, the property of being a planet does not supervene on the current intrinsic properties of its bearer. Thus, if we use (CCT$_1$) to interpret the cross-context test, then no relational properties are taxonomic. Since Fodor says that "taxonomy by relational properties is ubiquitous in the sciences," (CCT$_1$) does not yield the correct interpretation of the cross-context test.

So, let us try another interpretation. In discussing the cross-context test in "A Modal Argument for Narrow Content," Fodor comments in a footnote: "One applies the cross-context test by asking whether Ann would have the same effects as Jan does have if Ann were to interact with the same things . . . with which Jan does interact" (MANC, 8). This suggests interpreting the cross-context test by means of (CCT$_2$):

(CCT$_2$) Property P is causally explanatory only if its possession makes a difference to the causal powers of its possessor,

25 Stephen P. Stich, *From Folk Psychology to Cognitive Science: The Case against Belief* (Cambridge MA: MIT/Bradford, 1983).

where x and y have the same causal powers if and only if: If x had interacted with the same things that y did in fact interact with, then x would have had all the same effects that y in fact did have.

If we interpret the cross-context test on the basis of (CCT$_2$), a difference in truth conditions suffices for a difference in causal powers, but the difference between being a planet and not being a planet does not suffice for being a difference in causal powers.

The case of broad contents: Ann and Jan also differ in causal powers if the original story is amended slightly. Suppose that Ann and Jan had never interacted with either jadeite or nephrite, and that both learned what sounds like 'jade' in their respective languages from teachers who had never interacted with either jadeite or nephrite either. Indeed, the teachers themselves could be microphysical duplicates. (If this seems implausible, take the original story and suppose that Ann and Jan have microphysically identical children to whom Ann and Jan teach what each calls 'jade' in her respective language – before the quiz show, while Ann and Jan are still duplicates.) The physical identities of the individuals with whom Ann and Jan interacted are irrelevant to the intentional and semantic properties that Ann and Jan acquire. So, given (CCT$_2$), the cross-context test does not block the counterexample.

The case of the property of being a planet: Again, let R_1 be a planet revolving around a star and R_2 be a nonplanetary microphysical duplicate held in an elliptical orbit by the distribution of matter in the universe. Then, if we assume gravitational pull to be an interaction, if R_2 had interacted with everything that R_1 in fact interacted with, R_2 would be revolving around the star and thus would be a planet; and if R_1 had interacted with everything that R_2 in fact interacted with, R_1 would not be revolving around a star and hence would not be a planet. Hence, on (CCT$_2$), the difference between being a planet and not being a planet fails to be a difference in causal powers.

So, (CCT$_2$) can not provide the interpretation of the cross-context test that suits Fodor's purposes: For (CCT$_2$) both allows the counterexample to go through and disqualifies differences in nonintentional relational properties like that of being a planet as differences in causal powers.

Here is a final attempt to interpret the cross-context test. In

54

introducing the cross-context test, Fodor gives an example in *Psychosemantics:* "Roughly, our biceps have the *same* causal powers if the following is true: For any thing x and any context C, if you can lift x in C, then so can I; and if I can lift x in C, then so can you."[26] This suggests interpreting the cross-context test by means of (CCT_3):

(CCT_3) Property P is causally explanatory only if its possession makes a difference to the causal powers of its possessor, where x and y have the same powers if and only if: There is no context C such that x has an effect in C that y in C does not have.

If we interpret the cross-context test on the basis of (CCT_3), Ann and Jan clearly have different causal powers. Here is a relevant context: Let the quiz show be part of the international Quiz Show Olympics, in which multilingual translators determine what each contestant says – what answer she gives. The contestants enter identical isolation booths and simultaneously have identical auditory sensations, but because of the differences in languages, they are not asked the same question. (Perhaps instead of a human translator, there is only a machine translator. The program of the machine includes, for each contestant, specification of the language that she speaks; so, each contestant's vocal emissions are automatically treated as being in her native language.) Physically speaking, there is a single context: a room with a translation device and two isolation booths and appropriately placed mirrors, so that the visual sensations of the contestants are also alike. In this context, the property of being a winning answer is one that Ann's behavior has and Jan's behavior lacks. Assuming that the quiz show's translators are competent and alert, Ann's is the winning answer, and Jan's the losing answer – as in the original story. So, given (CCT_3), the cross-context test does not block the counterexample.

Although I think that this is an adequate response to (CCT_3), let me elaborate a bit by posing a possible objection. The objection is that we should allow Ann and Jan to differ only in the truth conditions of their mental states, not in any other way that quiz show judges can detect.[27] This objection amounts to an ad hoc stipula-

26 Fodor, *Psychosemantics,* 35.
27 Paul Boghossian made a similar objection in conversation. I formulated the response that I give later in part in correspondence with Pierre Jacob.

tion. Typically, in Olympic competitions, the knowledge of national identities of the participants is highlighted, not bracketed. In any case, a counterexample may assume whatever is necessary for there to be a difference in truth conditions in what sounds like 'The stone is jade' in each language, and there must be other differences between the communities in order for the mental states of Ann and Jan to differ in truth conditions. The other differences will likely include intentional differences. If so, then I am free to exploit such differences as are required for Ann's and Jan's mental states to differ in truth condition. I need only claim that Ann's and Jan's local contexts are physically similar, not that there are no other differences elsewhere in the communities.[28]

In sum, I can not find an interpretation of the cross-context test that blocks my counterexample without also ruling out uncontroversial relational properties (like being a planet) as unsuitable for scientific taxonomy. The moral is that broad contents are on a par with other relational properties, whose usefulness in science cannot be ruled out on a priori grounds.

BELIEFS AS STRUCTURING CAUSES

Beliefs are individuated by meaning or content, typically identified by 'that' clauses of attributions of belief in English. It is now generally agreed that semantic properties like meaning or content – properties in virtue of which states have truth conditions – are relational properties. If we assume, with the Standard View, that beliefs are internal states, this recognition poses the problem of showing how relational semantic properties of an internal state can be causally relevant to behavior. Content, or a state's having content, must help explain the behavior produced by the brain state. Otherwise, contents, and the beliefs that they individuate, are simply epiphenomenal.[29]

The prima facie problem is this: According to the Standard View, meaning or content is a relational property of internal states,

---

28 Note that Ann's and Jan's communities are in the same possible world; so there is no question of whether their "whole worlds" are physical duplicates.
29 In "Anomalous Monism and the Problem of Explanatory Force," *Philosophical Review* 98 (1989): 153–88, Louise Antony has argued that Davidson's view of reasons as causes fails to account for the explanatory power of reasons.

but the causally efficacious properties of internal states are nonrelational. What actually causes one's finger to move (and the trigger to be pulled), for example, is intrinsic properties of brain states. If this is right, how can relational properties have any kind of causal or explanatory role in behavior? Fred Dretske tries to meet this challenge by showing how meaning, though a relational property of internal states, can still have a causal role in behavior. Dretske's account, like other naturalistic accounts of meaning for internal states, is two-tiered. At the ground level, meaning is linked directly to the (nonintentional, nonsemantic) physical world; then, with those naturalistic credentials in hand, other kinds of meaning may have social and linguistic components. Since I do not think Dretske (or anybody else) has furnished an "upper level" account of meaning, I focus solely on Dretske's ground-level account.

Dretske distinguishes between two kinds of causes: triggering causes and structuring causes. Suppose that a terrorist hooked up a car bomb to the ignition of a certain general's car; the general turned the key to start his car and thereby detonated the bomb. The triggering cause, which actually brought about the detonation of the bomb, was the general's turning the key in the ignition; but the structuring cause, which is responsible for there being a key-turn detonation process in the first place, was the terrorist's planting the bomb. The structuring cause (the terrorist's attaching the bomb to the ignition) may well be the causal explanation that authorities seek. The triggering cause sets in motion a process at a particular time; the structuring cause is whatever is causally responsible for the process to be in place.

Dretske finds a causal role for belief as structuring cause of behavior.[30] Suppose that an internal token of type C (where being of type C supervenes on intrinsic properties of the brain), causes a token of bodily motion type M on a certain occasion. Then the token of C is a triggering cause: Given the background conditions in which a $C \rightarrow M$ process is (in some sense) realized in the brain, the

---

30 Even if Dretske's account is successful in showing how meaning can have a structuring causal role in behavior, it still cannot explain any actual tokening of a behavioral process. Particular actions (such as shooting an intruder) would not be explained by showing how beliefs had a role in the shooter's being structured in such a way that when a certain internal event occurred, it caused a certain bodily movement.

token of C brought about the token of M. But the behavior has another kind of cause as well: The structuring cause is what brought it about that the $C{\to}M$ process is structured the way that it is.

Dretske builds up his account from the basic relation of indication.[31] The idea is to give a nonintentional and nonsemantic account of what an internal state means or represents (its content) in terms of what it indicates.[32] Indication is a relation between token events: Token event b of type B indicates a token event a of type A if and only if (i) a caused b and (ii) there is reliable covariation between type-B events and type-A events. If a B-token indicates an A, then we may say that 'A' is the natural meaning of the B-token. Obviously, indication or natural meaning is insufficient for representation. For there is no representation without the possibility of misrepresentation, and there is no possibility of "misindication." So, an indication theorist must move from indication (or natural meaning) to something that allows for error. Dretske does this by defining a new relation: *having the function of indicating* something. C may have the function of indicating F even if, on occasion, a token of C fails to indicate F – for example, the token of C is caused by something that is not F.

What is needed, and what Dretske supplies, is a naturalistic, ground-level account of how a natural indicator of F acquires the function of indicating F. Let C be a natural indicator of F. Then C acquires the function of indicating F if: (1) C is "recruited" (by a learning process) as a cause of M, where M is a bodily movement, and (2) C is so recruited because C indicates F. The recruitment structures a $C{\to}M$ process, so that, after the learning period, tokens of C cause tokens of M. Since it is because C indicates F that C is recruited as a cause of M, C's indicating F is (in Dretske's terms) a structuring cause of the behavior M. C then has the function of

---

31 Fred Dretske, *Explaining Behavior: Reasons in a World of Causes* (Cambridge MA: MIT/Bradford, 1988). In *Explaining Behavior,* Dretske identifies behavior with the causal process $C{\to}\ M;$ however, in "Mental Events As Structuring Causes," in *Mental Causation,* ed. John Heil and Alfred Mele (Oxford: Clarendon Press, 1993), 121–36, he applies his view to the more standard conception of behavior as simply the resulting M, not the whole causal process.

32 Although Dretske is (knowingly) casual about the type-token distinction, sometimes the distinction is important to his theory. For example, Dretske defines 'indication' as a relation between tokens; but his theory requires indication to be a relation between types. Talk of a state's structuring a $C{\to}M$ behavioral process likewise is to be understood as the state's structuring a *type* of process.

indicating F when the fact that C indicates F becomes a structuring cause of some behavior. Finally C's meaning or representing F is understood in terms of C's having the function to indicate F, where C acquired that function via a naturalistic learning process.

Now suppose that, after a $C{\to}M$ process is established by a learning process, a token of C occurs and produces the bodily motion M. Then, on Dretske's view, meaning has a causal role in the production of M, in virtue of the fact that C's indicating F is a structuring cause of the $C{\to}M$ process. I believe that my remarks, though compact, accurately represent the structure of Dretske's view.[33] What I wish now to show is that it is thoroughly circular.

On the account just given, a state has meaning in the first place in virtue of its structuring a $C{\to}M$ process.

> (a) A mental state C has meaning in virtue of its having a structuring causal role in a $C{\to}M$ behavioral process.

However, Dretske's goal is to show "how ordinary explanations, explanations couched in terms of an agent's *reasons*, explain."[34] Like other physicalists, Dretske takes explanatory role to be causal role. That is, Dretske's goal is to show how having meaning gives a state a structuring causal (and hence explanatory) role in behavior. If this is the goal, then Dretske is committed to the following:

> (b) A mental state C has a structuring causal role in a $C{\to}M$ behavioral process in virtue of its having meaning.[35]

(a) and (b) form a tight circle.[36] The circle is apparent in Dretske's characterization of beliefs as "those representations whose causal role in the production of output is determined by their mean-

---

33 I give a more detailed account in "Dretske on the Explanatory Role of Belief," *Philosophical Studies* 63 (1991): 99–111. See also Dretske's "How Beliefs Explain: A Reply to Baker," ibid., 113–17.

34 Dretske, *Explaining Behavior*, 52.

35 For the moment, I am omitting quantifiers for ease of exposition. The intended reading of (a) is this: For any C, if C has meaning, there is a $C{\to}M$ process in which C has a structuring causal role, and in virtue of which C has meaning. The intended reading of (b) is this: For any C, if there is a $C{\to}M$ process in which C has a structuring causal role, then C has that role in virtue of having meaning. In the more technical discussion, I consider alternative readings.

36 It may be thought that Dretske is giving a logical analysis of 'having meaning', in which case (a) and (b) may be tautologous rather than circular. I believe, however, that Dretske aims to give an informative account of "the place of reasons in a world of causes."

ing or content – by the way they represent what they represent."[37] If, as the account has it, meaning is itself determined by (structuring) causal role, then that same (structuring) causal role cannot in turn be determined by meaning.

Dretske objects that the account "isn't circular because the causal roles meanings are supposed to explain aren't the causal roles from which meanings are derived."[38] Now both the causal roles that meanings are supposed to explain and the causal roles from which meanings are derived are structuring causal roles in behavioral processes. It may seem that Dretske is saying that there is no circle because C has two distinct causal roles in a single $C \rightarrow M$ process. But on Dretske's theory, there is only one structuring causal role per behavioral process. Once the $C \rightarrow M$ process has been structured, a token of C becomes a triggering cause of the behavior; there is no more structuring to be done. Dretske says that C's meaning F is now a structuring cause of $C \rightarrow M$; but if C's meaning F is *now* a structuring cause of $C \rightarrow M$, it is so in virtue of the fact that C's *past* indicatings of F structured the $C \rightarrow M$ process: C's structuring causal contribution was completed in the past. So, there is no "logical space" for C's having two structuring causal roles.

Perhaps Dretske is distinguishing between two kinds of behavioral processes in which C has a structuring causal role: one behavioral process in virtue of which C's structuring causal role gives C meaning, and a different behavioral process in virtue of which C's having meaning is causally explanatory. That is, perhaps Dretske's reply to my argument is this:

(Reply) For any behavioral process, $C \rightarrow M$, C's meaning F causally explains $C \rightarrow M$ if and only if there is some *other* behavioral process, $C \rightarrow N$, such that C-tokens' past indicatings of F are the structuring cause of $C \rightarrow N$.

Of course, I agree that (a) and (b) do not really form a circle if a state C has meaning in virtue of its causal role in one behavioral process, but it has a causal role in some other kind of behavior in virtue of having meaning.

But (Reply) cannot be satisfactory. For it severs the behavior that C's meaning F causally explains from the behavior in which C had

37 Dretske, *Explaining Behavior*, 52.
38 Dretske, "How Beliefs Explain: A Reply to Baker," 113.

a structuring causal role. In that case, the theory crumbles; for there is no provision for showing how C's meaning F has a causal role in *one* type of behavioral process in virtue of the fact that C's indicating F is a structuring cause of a *different* type of behavioral process. Unless the same behavior can be at issue in both (a) and (b), we would lose the explanatory link between the fact that C is a structuring cause and the fact that C's meaning has a causal role in behavior.

In the second place, (Reply) gives meaning an ubiquitous causal role: It follows from (Reply) that, for any state C that has meaning at all, the meaning of C causally explains all of C's behavioral effects. To put it another way, (Reply) has no room for a distinction between (i) cases in which C's meaning F causally explains behavior and (ii) cases in which C means F, but C's meaning does not causally explain the behavior C produces. For example, suppose that in the past, C's indicatings of danger structured certain avoidance behavior, so that C has come to mean 'danger'. Suppose that on some occasion a C triggers some other behavior – say a blink of an eye, which is not structured by C's past indicatings of danger. According to (Reply), C's meaning danger causally explains the blink. This is intuitively wrong. Thus, I think that, although (Reply) avoids the circle, it undermines Dretske's strategy for giving a causal role to meaning.

What Dretske is trying to show is that C's meaning something can give C a causal role in behavior. If meaning something were solely a matter of indicating something, there would be no problem: C would mean 'F' in virtue of the fact that C indicates F, and meaning 'F' would have a (structuring) causal role if C were recruited to cause M. But indicating F is not enough for meaning 'F.' Meaning 'F' requires *having the function of indicating F;* but by definition C does not have the function of indicating F unless C is already a structuring cause of some behavior.

So, here is the problem: Dretske takes meaning to be a structuring cause of behavior – whence the causal role of belief. C's meaning 'F' (at the ground level) is identified with C's having the function of indicating F. C's having the function of indicating F depends on the fact that C's indicating F is a structuring cause of the $C \rightarrow M$ process. Therefore, Dretske cannot – without circularity – take meaning, or the fact that a state has meaning, to be the structuring cause of $C \rightarrow M$ (or of the behavioral output M). For the structuring

61

of the $C \rightarrow M$ process is a precondition of C's having meaning. The circularity slips in because meaning is implicitly identified both with C's indicating F (meaning as structuring cause) and with C's having the function of indicating F (meaning as representing F).

There is a way out of the circle, but only at the cost of giving up the explanatory or causal role of belief. The circle is generated, as we have seen, by a slide from the notion of C's indicating F to the notion of C's having the function of indicating F. It is only the former that is (noncircularly) a structuring cause of behavior; but it is only the latter that gives C a meaning: 'F' becomes the (non-natural) meaning of C in virtue of C's acquiring the function of indicating F.[39] So, the circle may be broken by consistently taking C's indicating F (not C's having the function of indicating F) both to be a structuring cause of behavior and to be a relation that *underlies* meaning or representation. But to say that a single relation is both a structuring cause and underlies meaning gives no causal role whatever to meaning. Meaning, on this noncircular rendition, remains wholly epiphenomenal.

Therefore, I believe that the most detailed attempt to provide an explanatory role for belief, construed as an internal state, does not succeed. For either it is circular or it accords the meaning of internal states no causal role at all. Although I cannot be sure, I believe that other naturalistic accounts of meaning, if developed in the detail of Dretske's, would fall to similar arguments.

---

39 In his recent "Mental Events As Structuring Causes," Dretske ignores the crucial distinction between indicating F and having the function of indicating F – noting only that a token of a type earlier tokens of which were indicators of F may misrepresent something as an F (135n). But the account of meaning *requires* the distinction between indicating F and having the function of indicating F, as Dretske acknowledges in *Explaining Behavior*. For example, assuming that tree rings indicate the age of a tree, suppose that bizarre weather conditions produced tree rings on a certain tree that did not correspond to age. Such tree rings would not be *in error*. They would not misrepresent the age of the tree in the sense relevant to misrepresenting a cow as a horse on a dark night. Even if there is generally a correlation between tree rings and the age of trees, failure of the correlation in a particular case would not be a mistake. In order for the unusual tree rings to misrepresent, they would have to have *the function of indicating* the age of the tree. Indication is not enough for misrepresentation; and as Dretske agrees, there is no representation without the possibility of misrepresentation. Ignoring the distinction between indicating F and having the function of indicating F obscures the circle, but does not eliminate it.

One of the aims of this book is to give relational properties their metaphysical due. Often, it is in virtue of relational properties that something is the kind of thing that it is (e.g., a planet, or a husband).[40] And as many have argued, it is in virtue of relational properties that one has a belief that p. But what is a relational property?

We are accustomed to thinking of relational properties as expressed by two-place predicates of the form 'Rxy' and thinking of nonrelational properties as expressed by one-place predicates of the form 'Fx'. But this is not the relevant contrast at all. For many one-place predicates express relational properties. Obvious cases (such as 'Sally is a sister') are easily converted into two-place predicates: 'Sally is a sister of x'. But other cases are less obvious: 'This bill is counterfeit'; 'Jones has tenure'; 'Michael Jordan was a basketball player'. It is unclear even how to express these relational properties as two-place predicates.

Let us understand relational properties broadly. Say that R is a relational property if and only if: x's having R entails that there is some y distinct from x. In the language of possible worlds: R is a relational property if and only if for any world w and individual x, if x has R in w, then there is a y in w such that y is distinct from x. So, being counterfeit, having tenure, and being a basketball player are relational properties. There is a growing consensus, to which I am a party, that the property of having a belief that water is wet is likewise a relational property.[41] For in a world in which S is the sole inhabitant (e.g., there is no water, or twater, or anything other than S), S does not have that belief. Predicates of the form 'believes that p' express relational properties for any p which could not be an object of S's belief in a world in which S is the sole inhabitant.

Say that a property P supervenes on local microstructure if and only if: Necessarily, if x has P and y lacks P, then there is a microphysical difference between x and y. Now relational properties expressed by predicates of the form 'Fx' (such as 'has tenure' or 'is a

40 More radically – although I cannot argue for this here – sometimes it is in virtue of relational properties that something is the individual that it is.
41 Standard View accounts of belief in terms of relational properties are called "externalist" accounts.

planet') do not supervene on local microstructure. So, if one holds with Fodor that taxonomy in the sciences is by causal powers, and that relational properties can be taxonomic, then one is logically barred from taking causal powers to supervene on local microstructure. Suppose that Fodor is right – as I think that he is – when he says:

> Taxonomy by relational properties is ubiquitous in the sciences, and it is not in dispute that properties like being a meteor or being a planet – properties which could, notice, distinguish molecularly identical chunks of rock – constitute causal powers. (MANC, 12)

Then, he should retract what in *Psychosemantics* he calls his "metaphysical point" about science: "Causal powers supervene on local microstructure."[42] However, abandoning that thesis in general would kick the motivation out from under the project of showing that a difference in broad content is not a difference in causal power in virtue of its responsibility for the properties of one's behavior. For if causal powers generally do not supervene on local microstructure, why must mental causal powers supervene on local microstructure?

Here, I think, is Fodor's rationale for holding mental causal powers to be locally supervenient: Mental causal powers are properties invoked by nonbasic laws. Nonbasic laws must be implemented by mechanisms that connect the satisfaction of the antecedents to the satisfaction of the consequents. In the case of psychological laws, the only plausible implementing mechanisms, claims Fodor, are neurological, and neurological properties supervene on local microstructure.

But to conclude from this that psychological properties must supervene on local microstructure is a non sequitur.[43] If we take implementing mechanisms to be chains of individual events, Fodor may be seen as claiming that for each sequence of individual events

---

42 Fodor, *Psychosemantics*, 44. In "Must Psychology Be Individualistic?" *Philosophical Review* 100 (1991): 179–204, Frances Egan has argued that this metaphysical point is false.

43 Fodor may now agree with this point. In his post-*Psychosemantics* writing, he has placed increasing emphasis on implementing mechanisms and has not coupled his "implementing mechanism" thesis with the claim that psychological states supervene on neural states. See Chapter 6 for further discussion and criticism of Fodor's claim that psychological laws must be implemented by computational mechanisms that supervene on neural processes.

subsumed by a psychological law, there is a sequence of individual events subsumed by neurological laws. But, as Burge has argued, this claim entails nothing about the individuation of event types.[44] For the following are consistent (whether true or not): (1) Neurological properties supervene on local microstructure; (2) psychological laws are "implemented" by neurological mechanisms; (3) properties projected by psychological laws do not supervene on neurological properties; nor do psychological property instantiations supervene on neurological property instantiations. From the fact (if it is a fact) that neurological mechanisms "implement" psychological laws, it does not follow that the neurological properties of any individual event fix the psychological properties of any individual event. Psychological properties may fail to supervene on neurological properties because individuation of psychological states is more sensitive to the subject's environment than is individuation of neurological states.

Indeed, in general, properties of a higher-level process do not supervene on properties of mechanisms that implement the higher-level process. To take a commonsense example, consider a presidential press conference carried live on television. The political property of being a televised presidential press conference does not supervene on the intrinsic properties of implementing mechanisms. A microphysically duplicate mechanism may implement something quite different from a presidential press conference. Or consider the mechanism by which the automatic-teller machine gives me money from my checking account. The same mechanism could be used to implement an entirely different process; it could, for instance, give me green pieces of paper (functionally equivalent to "pink slips") whose numbers tell me which employees to lay off. There are endless examples like these. The moral is that the intrinsic properties implementing mechanisms do not generally fix the properties of the processes that they implement. So, the fact (if it is a fact) that neural mechanisms implement psychological laws would provide no motivation for narrow taxonomy in psychology.

---

44 This general line of thought is advanced by Tyler Burge, "Individualism and Psychology," *Philosophical Review* 95 (1986): 3–46. A similar argument is developed in "Individuation and Causation in Psychology," *Pacific Philosophical Quarterly* 70 (1989): 303–22.

To begin to dislodge the Standard View, I have presented three attempts to work out a Standard View conception of belief that would give beliefs a causal-explanatory role in behavior. All three, I have tried to show, come to grief. Although my arguments do not prove that no Standard View account of belief can ever succeed, they should give pause: The range of views discussed is broad, and problems encountered are deep. Alongside those proponents of the Standard View who undertake to show how beliefs can be constituted by particular brain states are eliminative materialists, who, reading neuroscience as casting doubt on the thesis that beliefs are constituted by particular brain states, give up on belief altogether. After trying to cut the ground out from under eliminative materialism in the next chapter, I argue in Part II that the causal explanatoriness of belief does not require that they be identical with or constituted by particular brain states at all.

3

The myth of folk psychology

Proponents of the Standard View divide into two camps: non-eliminativists, who set about showing how brain states can be beliefs, and eliminative materialists, who doubt that brain states can be coherently identified with particular beliefs, and·hence deny that there are beliefs or other attitudes. By denying that there are any beliefs, eliminativists bypass the problems discussed in Chapter 2. The arguments for eliminative materialism, however, all depend on construing commonsense psychology as a kind of folk theory – dubbed 'folk psychology' – in competition with scientific psychology. Although I do not dispute anything eliminativists say about the scientific psychology that they envisage, I think that they are seriously mistaken about the nature and function of commonsense psychology: It is not a folk theory in competition with science.

The arguments for eliminative materialism proceed from a premise with which I am in sympathy to a conclusion I reject. From the premise

> (S) Beliefs and other attitudes (attributed by 'that' clauses) will not be vindicated by a serious scientific psychology.[1]

the eliminative materialist concludes:

> (EM) There are no beliefs or other attitudes.

The truth of (S) depends upon the fate of a particular research program in psychology. If sentential theories, according to which beliefs are syntactically structured entities tokened in the brain, were supplanted by, say, certain kinds of neurophysiological or

---

1 The literature suggests that there are several grades of vindication of common sense: (1) a scientific psychology that quantified over beliefs, and so on, (2) some weaker reduction of some of common sense to scientific psychology, (3) Stich's "modified Panglossian prospect." I discuss these alternatives in *Saving Belief: A Critique of Physicalism* (Princeton: Princeton University Press, 1987). For purposes here, we need not settle what should count as vindication.

connectionist theories, which generalize over nothing describable as beliefs, then (S) would be established. For purposes of this chapter, I do not dispute (S). But (S) is not eliminative materialism: A mind-body dualist – even Descartes himself – could endorse (S). Eliminative materialism is much stronger than (S); it concerns, not just the fate of a particular research program in psychology, but rather the truth and/or legitimacy *tout court* of ordinary attributions of beliefs in terms of 'that' clauses.

Clearly, (S) by itself does not entail (EM). An additional premise is needed. Call the additional premise (M) – 'Metaphysical' or for 'Missing':[2]

> (M) If there are beliefs and other attitudes, then they will be vindicated by a serious scientific psychology.

Enter the idea of folk psychology. Eliminative materialists simply assume (M) because they take beliefs and other attitudes to be constitutive of a kind of folk theory. Like any other theory, folk-psychological theory would be subject to replacement by a better theory. Now, if it were to be replaced, and if the scientific theory that replaced it posited no states that could be coherently identified as belief states, then – the argument goes – we would have to conclude that there are no beliefs. After all, if beliefs are theoretical posits of a false theory and the correct theory does not invoke beliefs, then we may have no more reason to suppose that there are beliefs than that there are humors.[3]

Eliminative materialists, along with some (but not all) other proponents of the Standard View, thus take that part of the commonsense conception of reality used to describe, explain, and predict people's behavior to be a would-be scientific theory: folk psychology.[4] Since I do not think that commonsense psychology is a would-

---

2 In "How to Be Realistic about Folk Psychology," *Philosophical Perspectives* 1 (1988): 69–82, George Graham and Terence Horgan make a similar point.

3 For a discussion of putative deficiencies in the commonsense conception as a scientific theory, see Paul M. Churchland's "Eliminative Materialism and Propositional Attitudes," *Journal of Philosophy* 78 (1981): 67–90. For a discussion of the putative implications of scientific psychology for commonsense psychology, see Stephen P. Stich, *From Folk Psychology to Cognitive Science: The Case against Belief* (Cambridge MA: MIT/Bradford, 1983), 9–10.

4 For explicit statements of this construal of folk psychology, see Patricia S. Churchland, *Neurophilosophy: Toward a Unified Science of the Mind/Brain* (Cambridge MA: MIT/Bradford, 1986), 299, and Terence Horgan and James Woodward, "Folk Psychology Is Here to Stay," *Philosophical Review* 94 (1985): 197. For

be theory, or is a rival of scientific theories, I shall argue that there is no such thing as folk psychology (construed as a would-be scientific theory).[5]

To sum up: (M), or some other premise of equal scope, is required to make the eliminative materialists' argument even valid.[6] (M) is underwritten by the thesis that common sense is a theory (or perhaps a set of theories). Eliminative materialists, if they argue for a premise like (M) at all, proceed by arguing that commonsense psychology is a theory. So let us consider the arguments for the conclusion that common sense is a theory – "folk psychology" – ripe for replacement (or vindication) by a scientific psychology.

WHAT'S THE PROBLEM?

Given the weight carried by the claim that common sense is a theory, eliminative materialists say remarkably little about what does, or does not, constitute a theory. It is even less clear what makes something a *folk* theory. Patricia Churchland mentions that folk-theoretical generalizations have "a cracker-barrel quality," but it is difficult to discern such in the proffered examples – for example, in the impetus theory of motion, the best scientific theory of its day.[7] I am not asking for a definition here, only for some intuitive

alternative views, see Daniel C. Dennett, *The International Stance* (Cambridge MA: MIT/Bradford, 1987), 52; Adam Morton, *Frames of Mind* (Oxford: Oxford University Press, 1980); Robert M. Gordon, "The Simulation Theory: Objections and Misconceptions," *Mind and Language* 7 (1992): 11–34; Alvin I. Goldman, "The Psychology of Folk Psychology," *Behavioral and Brain Sciences* 16 (1993): 15–28.

5 Not everyone uses the term 'folk psychology' to imply that our commonsense conception is a theory. See George Graham, "The Origins of Folk Psychology," *Inquiry* 30 (1987): 357–79, and Graham and Horgan, "How to Be Realistic about Folk Psychology," 69–82. Also K. V. Wilkes, in "Pragmatics in Science and Theory in Common Sense," *Inquiry* 27 (1984): 339–61, argues that "lay psychology" or "commonsense psychology" is not a theory.

6 For discussion of a similar argument, see Lynne Rudder Baker, "Eliminativism and an Argument from Science," *Mind and Language* 8 (1993): 180–8.

7 *Neurophilosophy,* 301. After noting that folk generalizations have a cracker-barrel quality, Churchland adds that "this does not in the least imply that they are simple-minded." Or as Paul M. Churchland says: "What needs pointing out is that the 'laws' of folk theories are *in general* sloppy, vague, and festooned with qualifications and ceteris paribus clauses" ("Folk Psychology and the Explanation of Human Behavior," *Proceedings of the Aristotelian Society,* suppl. vol. 62 [1988]: 215; emphasis in original). For discussion of the impetus theory, see *Neurophilosophy,* 289ff.

sense of what a folk theory is supposed to be that would allow most of the cited examples to be folk theories. Indeed, it is not even clear what the examples are supposed to be. Exactly what are folk biology, folk chemistry, folk thermodynamics, folk mechanics?[8] Until we have some idea of the difference between being a folk theory and being a genuine scientific theory, calling commonsense psychology a "*folk* theory" is irrelevant – other than as a persuasive device.

The real question is whether commonsense psychology is a would-be theory, or a set of theories, at all.[9] No one has been more explicit in construing commonsense psychology as a would-be theory in competition with mature scientific theories than Paul Churchland. Churchland argues that "the network of principles and assumptions constitutive of our commonsense conceptual framework can be seen to be as speculative and as artificial as any overtly theoretical system."[10]

What is an "overtly theoretical system"? We use the term 'theory' in many different ways, most of which are not relevant to the discussion here. We have number theory, the theory of the Forms, conspiracy theories, theories of evil, and so on. There is an accepted sense of 'theory', according to which a theory is any set of sentences used to predict and explain; in that sense, I take it as obvious that common sense *is* a theory. But that is not the sense of 'theory' at issue here. For from the mere fact that common sense is used for explanatory purposes, nothing follows about the relation between common sense and physics, or between common sense and scientific psychology. The issue that concerns me is the relation between

8 "Folk Psychology and the Explanation of Human Behavior," 209. (Is there such a thing as folk philosophy – represented by Aristotle? Chisholm? Eric Hoffer?)

9 Indeed, Patricia Churchland defines eliminative materialism in part by the claim that folk psychology is a theory (*Neurophilosophy*, 396). This has the interesting consequence that if there is no such theory as "folk psychology," eliminative materialism is false – without any scientific investigation at all. Also, since in my usage 'folk psychology' is defined as a theory, Patricia Churchland is here using the term 'folk psychology' in the neutral way that I use the term 'commonsense conception'.

10 Paul M. Churchland, *Scientific Realism and the Plasticity of Mind* (Cambridge: Cambridge University Press, 1979), 2. Churchland also says that "the common-sense conception of reality is a loosely integrated patchwork of subtheories rather than a unified monolith" (42). My arguments apply whether the claim is that the commonsense conception is one theory or many, as long as the commonsense conception is taken to be exhaustively theoretical.

common sense and theories recognized as scientific. (Indeed, in some sense, what I am doing here is theoretical: I offer an account of common sense, according to which the target of my "theory" – common sense – is not itself a primitive version of mature scientific theory.)

If one insists on using 'theory' to refer to any set of claims used to explain and predict, then the question that I am raising can be recast as a question of whether commonsense psychological explanations in terms of attitudes can be replaced wholesale by explanations in terms of concepts employed by the sciences that do not presuppose phenomena like believing, desiring, and intending. However, since eliminative materialists couch the issue as whether common sense is a theory (or a set of theories), I continue to pose the question like this: Is common sense a theory or a set of theories?

The question of what a theory is leads to complex and controversial issues, to which I can not begin to do justice here. Fortunately, for purposes at hand, only a certain feature of certain theories is relevant to the issue of the status of common sense. A Quinean view of theories brings to the fore the crucial issue I want to discuss, namely, whether commonsense psychology is subject to replacement or falsification in toto by scientific advances, as Ptolemaic astronomy and the phlogiston theory of combustion were replaced or falsified in toto. Quine's mention of "the shift whereby Kepler superseded Ptolemy, or Einstein Newton, or Darwin Aristotle"[11] both illustrates what sorts of things are theories (e.g., Newtonian mechanics) and alludes to the fact that theories are subject to being totally displaced by better theories. For purposes here, I take Quine's examples to be paradigms of theories, and I take the hallmark of a theory in the relevant sense to be susceptibility to wholesale replacement.[12]

11 W. V. O. Quine, "Two Dogmas of Empiricism," in *From a Logical Point of View* (New York: Harper and Row Torchbook, 1963), 43.
12 There has been much discussion in developmental psychology about whether commonsensical understanding of the mind is "theoretical." In these discussions, the term 'theory' is often used in ways irrelevant to the question of the replaceability of commonsense psychology. For example, revisability is not clearly distinguished from outright replacement. For another, experts' knowledge of chess or medical diagnosis or dowsing is just assumed to be theoretical; in this sense of 'theory,' the consummate hostess should be said to have a theory of dinner parties. For detailed discussion of these and other issues, see Alison Gopnik, "How We Know Our Minds: The Illusion of First-Person Knowledge of

What is wholesale replacement? First, let me characterize replacement relative to a community. Let A and B be sets of distinct sentences such that there is no "smooth reduction" or pairwise translation from one to the other. Suppose that A is used by some community in order to accomplish certain purposes. Then B *replaces A in some community* only if (1) the community stops using A; (2) the community starts using B; and (3) the community uses B to do what it used A to do in the past. On this very general characterization of replacement, Spanish may replace English; sign language may replace spoken language. (Furthermore, the activities whose identity and meaning depend on language go the way of the language that gives them point. For example, if we stopped using American-football sentences, then American football would disappear. Without football sentences, there would be no football rules, and without the rules of football, nothing would count as a tackle or a touchdown. But nothing is to prevent us from ceasing to play football.)

Let us say that something is a *theory* in the relevant sense only if we can elicit from it a reasonably comprehensive set of sentences that meet the following conditions: (1) Sentences in the set purport to describe, explain, and predict phenomena in a certain domain, and (2) they are subject to replacement in the relevant community – typically, a disciplinary community that certifies the epistemic credentials of the sentences.

When we speak of a commonsense conception, the relevant community is a whole linguistic community. If theories were to replace common sense, then sets of sentences (whose epistemic credentials are certified by disciplinary communities) would replace all reasonably comprehensive sets of sentences containing commonsense terms in a linguistic community. To say that commonsense psychology is irreplaceable is to say that not all reasonably comprehensive sets of sentences in which commonsense psychological terms occur can be replaced by theories that are themselves replaceable.

There are several points to mention here. First, I am not giving a sufficient condition for something to be a theory. Second, the condition for being a theory is given in terms of *eliciting* a set of sentences in order to avoid assuming that theories are propositional or

Intentionality," *Behavioral and Brain Sciences* 16 (1993): 1–14; and Alvin I. Goldman, "The Psychology of Folk Psychology," ibid., 15–28, followed by commentary.

linguistic entities; if theories are propositional or linguistic entities, then the relevant set of sentences will be entailed by the theory. Third, to require the set of sentences to be "reasonably comprehensive" is quite vague, but the set can not be the theory itself (even if theories are sets of sentences). For if theories are replaceable by better theories, then the replaced and replacing theories must have some overlap insofar as they apply to the same domain; since A and B are to be sets of distinct sentences, they must be proper subsets of the replaced and replacing theories.

Even with these caveats, the notion of replacement remains vague. For example, what counts as a community's doing with one set of sentences what it previously did with a set of distinct sentences in the past? Since my interest is not in definition per se, however, I shall not attempt further refinement of the notion of replacement, and hope that it is clear enough for the purpose at hand. At any rate, I believe that our understanding of the idea of replacement derives largely from historical cases such as Quine offers.

The central question, then, is this: Are commonsense explanations in terms of attitudes replaceable by scientific explanations that do not presuppose attitudes? To answer "yes" is to construe commonsense psychology as "folk psychology." Now this central question is begged if, at the outset, one conflates common sense with some particular scientific theory. For example, Ramsey, Stich, and Garon (RSG) assume, without argument, that the properties posited by traditional cognitive, artificial intelligence (AI) models – properties like functional discreteness – just *are* the properties of commonsense belief. They simply make the unsupported assertion that "common sense psychology seems to presuppose that there is generally some answer to the question of whether a particular belief or memory played a causal role in a specific cognitive episode."[13] Then, arguing that connectionist models posit properties incompatible with such functional discreteness, RSG conclude that if connectionism is correct, then so is eliminativism about beliefs and other attitudes. This is rather like identifying properties posited by

13 William Ramsey, Stephen Stich, and Joseph Garon, "Connectionism, Eliminativism and the Future of Folk Psychology," (Philosophical Perspectives 4) in *Action Theory and Philosophy of Mind, 1990,* ed. James E. Tomberlin, (Atascadero, CA: Ridgeview Publishing Company, 1990), 499–533. Hereafter, 'RSG'. The quotation is from p. 513.

the impetus theory with commonsense properties of motion, and then arguing that since Newtonian mechanics posits properties incompatible with impetus, if Newtonian mechanics is correct, then so is eliminativism about motion. Clearly, even if commonsense psychology were a theory, it would not follow that properties such as functional discreteness posited by traditional cognitive models are the properties posited by commonsense psychology.[14] The relevant question concerns the status of common sense (which antedates the advent of AI by millennia), not the status of properties posited by traditional cognitive AI models.

The question of the theoretical status of commonsense psychology is not just a technical issue: The controversy about "folk psychology" has extensive ramifications. For, as I argue in Chapter 8, commonsense psychology is only an abstraction from a comprehensive commonsense metaphysics, according to which the world is populated with persons and medium-sized objects. While the psychological aspects of common sense have been controversial, the rest of the commonsense framework has received scant attention (since Eddington, at least). There is, however, no neat division internal to the commonsense framework that has psychological-intentional concepts on one side and nonpsychological-nonintentional concepts on the other. Many commonsense claims that are *not* psychological have intentional presuppositions: 'You can't get married without a license' or 'Stop signs are red'. The properties of being a stop sign, and of getting married are clearly intentional: Nothing is a stop sign – or a marriage – in a world without attitudes.

This suggests – rightly, I think – that the part of common sense that pertains to persons is on a par with other parts of common sense vis-à-vis developments in science. A psychology that did not employ concepts (like belief) from the framework of commonsense psychology would threaten the conception of persons neither more nor less than a physics that employed no concepts of medium-sized objects would threaten mundane truths like 'Upholstered chairs are

14 RSG give examples of commonsense psychological explanations in which belief that *p* is distinguished from belief that *q* as having a causal role in a bit of behavior. They are correct that commonsense psychology makes such a distinction; but it is another matter to suppose that such a distinction requires functional discreteness in their sense. The distinction is easily handled in terms of counterfactuals. (See Parts II and III.)

more comfortable than church pews'. Persons are as safe as tables and chairs.[15]

Indeed, this "relative consistency proof" receives unintended support, I believe, even from those who take common sense to be theoretical. For example, the RSG argument for the conclusion, "If connectionism is correct, so is eliminativism concerning attitudes," has an exact analogue leading to the conclusion, "If quantum physics is correct, so is eliminativism concerning medium-sized objects." As I mentioned, RSG take classical AI models as a stand-in for common sense, and argue as if what is at issue is only the relation between classical AI models and connectionist models. To make their argument even relevant to the issue of common sense – as opposed merely to the competition between classical AI and connectionism – I am taking it to apply to common sense construed as a theory.[16] Then, their argument has this form:

(1) Common sense is a theory that posits entities of kind K.

(2) Entities of kind K have a property P.

(3) Theory T posits entities "deeply and fundamentally different from" entities with property P.

(4) The commonsense theory and theory T "are competing at the same explanatory level. If one is right, the other is wrong."

(5) If two theories are "competing at the same explanatory level," and one is a superior theory, and the superior theory posits entities "deeply and fundamentally different from" the entities posited by the other theory, then the entities posited by the other theory do not exist.

15 The issue here concerns sameness of significance of the posits of science for persons and medium-sized objects. It is compatible with my point to hold that persons (or concepts pertaining to them) raise special philosophical problems.
16 Note that we would still have the "relative consistency proof" if we took the theory mentioned in the first premise to be classical AI, instead of common sense concerning attitudes; the analogue for medium-sized objects would be classical mechanics. Interestingly, RSG cite with approval Paul Smolensky's explicit comparison between traditional AI – connectionism and classical mechanics – quantum mechanics, but they do not draw what seems to me the obvious conclusion. See the next note.

75

Therefore,

(6) If theory T is correct, then there are no entities of kind K.[17]

Put in this schematic way, the parallel between the RSG argument against attitudes and a similar argument against medium-sized objects is apparent. In the RSG argument, entities of kind K are propositional attitudes, property P is functional discreteness, theory T is connectionism.[18] In the analogue, entities of kind K are medium-sized objects, property P is the property of having a definite spatiotemporal location, theory T is quantum mechanics. Thus, if the RSG argument works against the attitudes, it should work equally against trees and houses.

RSG may object to this analogy on the grounds that a change to connectionist models would be "ontologically radical," in that "the posits of the new theory strike us as deeply and fundamentally different from those of the old theory.[19] But this is irrelevant as long as the change to quantum mechanics was also ontologically radical. Is the difference between posits of quantum mechanics and properties attributed to pencils and planets any less radical than the difference between posits of connectionism and properties attributed to persons? RSG give no reason to think so.[20]

17 RSG, 502, 503, 512, 500–1. Some may find premise (4) to be obviously false in the quantum mechanics case, but RSG apparently do not think so. Without dissent, they cite Smolensky, who "suggests that connectionist models stand to traditional cognitive models (like semantic networks) in much the same way that quantum mechanics stands to classical mechanics. In each case, the newer theory is deeper, more general, and more accurate over a broader range of phenomena. But *in each case* the new theory and the old are competing at the same explanatory level. If one is right, the other must be wrong." RSG, 511–12; my emphasis.

Although this argument is the closest that I can come to finding a valid argument in the RSG text, adding quantifiers is a nontrivial task. What is the general underlying principle? Perhaps it is this: For any theory T, if T posits entities of kind K, and T is correct, then there are entities of kind K. But if we take (1) as "If common sense is a correct theory, then there are entities of kind K," then the argument requires denying the antecedent and is thus invalid. But if we take (1) as a biconditional, then it is false – even if common sense is a theory. For even if common sense were an incorrect theory, there could be another theory that is correct and posits entities of kind K. (Gareth B. Matthews pointed out this difficulty.)

18 In Part III, I argue that propositional attitudes are not entities in any ordinary sense.

19 RSG, 502.

20 For what it is worth, the conceptual changes in quantum mechanics strike me as maximally radical. See N. David Mermin, "Quantum Mysteries for Anyone," *Journal of Philosophy* 78 (1981): 397–408.

I am only noting the parallel between the RSG argument against attitudes and its analogue against medium-sized objects. Obviously, I am endorsing neither. Indeed, I think that the first and fourth premises are false, since common sense is not a theory, and attitudes are not on a par with theoretical posits. Moreover, RSG's justification for the second premise is vitiated by their failure to distinguish between properties posited by traditional cognitive models (like functional discreteness) and properties posited by common sense (nothing so determinate as functional discreteness). In any case, the point remains this: Claims about attitudes are as safe as claims about medium-sized objects. Although I shall focus on eliminative materialism, what is ultimately at issue is not just the fate of commonsense psychology, but the fate of the whole framework of reality in terms of persons and medium-sized objects.

To anticipate: I endorse Quine's view of theories and his metaphor of the web of belief as well. Where I disagree with Quine is in his view that there is no more to the web of belief than theories in this sense; for I argue that the commonsense conception of reality is also part of the web, yet is not wholesale replaceable by a theory or by anything else that lacks categories for medium-sized objects or for persons with attitudes with propositional content. My position is not that the commonsense conception is knowable a priori but, rather, that it is required to serve our (nonoptional) interests in getting along in the world.

ASSESSMENT OF ARGUMENTS FOR "FOLK PSYCHOLOGY"

Sticking with a Quinean view of theories, I consider three lines of argument for the thesis that common sense is a theory: The first concerns putative empirical failures and revisability of commonsense psychology; the second, the meanings of the terms of commonsense psychology; the third, the nature of its explanatory generalizations.

Empirical failure and revisability

Sometimes it is claimed that commonsense psychology is a theory because it is subject to empirical failure. Although empirical research is clearly relevant to various aspects of common sense, I think that the empirical case against commonsense psychology has been both misdescribed and overstated.

The case against commonsense psychology is misdescribed when philosophers suppose common sense to aim to explain internal mechanisms (like the construction of three-dimensional visual images from two-dimensional arrays), and then criticize it for failing to do so.[21] Now, if commonsense psychology were a research program aimed at explaining internal mechanisms, then even its diehard defenders would have to admit it to be a failure. But it is an error to suppose that commonsense psychology – with us at least since Homer – is meant to apply to underlying mechanisms in the first place. Faulting commonsense psychology for failing to explain internal mechanisms is like faulting a cookbook for failing to explain digestion. They are just different kettles of fish.

Paul Churchland does not recognize this point, I believe, because he simply assumes that commonsense psychology is a research program and argues that, as a research program, it is a failure. But to use the term 'folk psychology' to refer indifferently to commonsense psychology and to a research program, as Churchland does, is to use it equivocally. On the one hand, if 'folk psychology' refers to a particular research program (for example, classical AI) in competition with connectionism, then "folk psychology" is not the commonsense psychology learned at mother's knee. Failure of "folk psychology" in this sense would not put the attitudes at risk; it would only falsify sentences-in-the-brain models of the attitudes. On the other hand, if 'folk psychology' refers to our ordinary practices of attributions of attitudes, then connectionism (or any other theory of internal mechanisms) no more threatens "folk psychology" than quantum mechanics threatens our commonsense understanding of traffic jams.[22] So, the empirical case against commonsense psychology has been misdescribed.

The empirical case against commonsense psychology is overstated when philosophers take particular neurophysiological dis-

---

21 "Eliminative Materialism and Propositional Attitudes," 73. In "Folk Psychology Is Here to Stay," 200, Horgan and Woodward also criticize Churchland's objection.

22 These points are taken from my review of Paul M. Churchland's A *Neurocomputational Perspective: The Nature of Mind and the Structure of Science* (Cambridge MA: MIT/Bradford, 1989). The review appeared in *Philosophical Review* 101 (1992): 906–8.

coveries to reveal the would-be scientific status of common sense. Even if the discovery of blindsight, for example, did force us to "revise our conception of what sort of state awareness is,"[23] as Patricia Churchland has claimed, it would hardly follow that our ideas of awareness constitute a would-be scientific theory.[24] From the mere fact that claims about awareness are revisable on the basis of scientific discoveries, we can draw no conclusion about the wholesale replaceability of anything.

Of course, I agree that common sense has ample room for novelty, from whatever source. For example, change in – or refinement of – commonsense psychology may be prompted by creative genius (e.g., Sophocles) as well as by theoretical innovations (e.g., Freud's theory of the unconscious) and empirical findings (e.g., discovery of patterns of inferential error). So, my remarks do not imply that common sense is impervious to the results of empirical theories: Think of Nisbet and Ross, Kahnemann, Slovic and Tversky, but note that their hypotheses are couched in terms of commonsense psychology that appeals to beliefs and other attitudes,[25] and hence are in no position to show that it is in error in any wholesale fashion.[26] Common sense may be revisable without being wholesale replaceable by a scientific theory with a different conceptual apparatus.

The opposing idea – that if commonsense psychology is revisable at all, it is wholesale replaceable – has been fostered by the image of Neurath's ship at sea, repairable plank by plank. On Quine's view, pressure from anywhere in the web can lead to theory replacement. Quine defends his point on historical grounds: Theory change in the past has resembled rebuilding a ship at sea.[27]

---

23 *Neurophilosophy*, 224–8.
24 In fact, I think that Churchland's claim that blindsight forces revision of our conception of awareness is vitiated by her mistaken assumption that our concept of awareness entails that "someone experiences something if and only if he is aware that he has experienced it." *Neurophilosophy*, 227.
25 Richard Nisbett and Lee Ross, *Human Inference: Strategies and Shortcomings of Social Judgment* (Englewood Cliffs, NJ: Prentice-Hall, 1980); Daniel Kahnemann, Paul Slovic, and Amos Tversky, *Judgment under Uncertainty: Heuristics and Biases* (Cambridge: Cambridge University Press, 1982).
26 Oddly enough, Stich cites attribution theory, which explicitly presupposes commonsense concepts, as empirical evidence that the commonsense conception is false in toto. See *From Folk Psychology to Cognitive Science*, 231–2.
27 W. V. O. Quine, *Word and Object* (Cambridge, MA: MIT, 1960), 3–5. Quine lifts the ship metaphor from its context·in Neurath's essay. Neurath says, "Vague

This historical point about theory change, however, ("the shift whereby Kepler superseded Ptolemy"), does not touch the question of whether common sense is a theory in the first place.

Although Quine's point is historical, others may want to use the metaphor of Neurath's ship to make a logical point. This would be a mistake. For the inference from "any plank of commonsense psychology is replaceable" to "all planks of commonsense psychology are replaceable" may conceal a fallacy of composition. Any plank may be leaky; but we should not conclude that they all may be leaky. After all, the ship floats. Compare: Each participant in the lottery has a greater than zero probability of losing, but it does not follow that there is a greater than zero probability that they all will lose. Similarly, each tenet of common sense has a greater than zero probability of being false, but it does not follow that there is a greater than zero probability that they all are false.

So, from the fact that commonsense psychology is revisable, we should not conclude that it is wholesale replaceable. In contrast to the cases of theory change, we have no historical examples of any society's ever having abandoned the commonsense conception of persons with intentional states. Under the circumstances, it seems just idle to insist that common sense "may have to go." I conclude that the eliminativists' arguments about the alleged empirical failures and revisability of common sense have not shown commonsense psychology to be susceptible to wholesale scientific disconfirmation, in which case these arguments lend no support to (M).

The meanings of commonsense terms

Now turn to the second line of argument for the view that commonsense psychology is a theory. According to it, common sense is taken to be a theory because the semantics of the terms of commonsense psychology is no different from the semantics of theoretical terms in science. The Churchlands say that commonsense terms, like theoretical terms generally, derive their meanings from their places in networks of generalizations. To learn the meanings

linguistic conglomerations always remain in one way or another as components of the ship. If vagueness is diminished at one point, it may well be increased at another." ("Protocol Sentences," in *Logical Positivism,* ed. A. J. Ayer, [New York: Free Press, 1959], 201.) On these matters, I have benefited from discussion with Derk Pereboom and Hilary Kornblith.

of terms of commonsense psychology is thus to learn the relevant generalizations. As Patricia Churchland sees it, all terms are learned in the same way: "Just as learning the word 'dog' involves learning generalizations about dogs, so learning words such as 'is in pain' involves learning such things as that hunger, a bang on the thumb with a hammer, . . . and sustaining a cut all cause pains." It "is in virtue of such generalizations that the embedded categories are implicitly defined."[28]

Granting the analogy between the semantics of 'is a dog' and 'is in pain', and granting that the meanings of both expressions derive from their places in networks of generalizations, we still may not think that either is a part of a theory. Not every network of generalizations constitutes a theory in the sense of being wholesale replaceable by a scientific theory: The term 'is a sonnet' is learned via its place in a network of generalizations. One learns the term 'is a sonnet' by learning such things as that sonnets have fourteen lines, that they sometimes are declarations of love or depictions of nature, that Shakespeare wrote a lot of famous ones, and so on. But these facts do not make sonnets part of a theory subject to falsification or replacement by a scientific theory. Would anyone suppose that science may reveal that there are no sonnets?

There are endless obvious examples here: One learns the term 'is bankrupt' by learning such things as that solvency is preferable to bankruptcy, that creditors stop pursuing bankrupt people, that bankrupt people have difficulty getting mortgages. Again, the fact that 'is bankrupt' derives its meaning from its place in a network of generalizations does not imply that 'is bankrupt' is part of a theory replaceable by a better scientific theory. Likewise, the fact that 'is in pain' is learned by learning relevant generalizations no more makes 'pain' part of a would-be scientific theory than do the facts that 'grade point average', 'treason', 'quarterback', and 'modern art' are learned by learning relevant generalizations make them parts of scientific theories, replaceable by better theories. So, the argument to the conclusion that 'is a dog' and 'is in pain' are parts of replaceable theories, depends on a non sequitur.

According to Patricia Churchland, whether a term is theoretical "is a matter of its being semantically embedded in a network of

<hr>

28 *Neurophilosophy,* 307.

corrigible assumptions."[29] But if all that is meant by taking terms to be theoretical is just a rejection of denotational semantics, then the term 'theory' is being used idiosyncratically with no more connection to science than to baseball.[30] Blanket use of the term 'theory-laden' has obscured the difference between a terms's dependence on a particular scientific theory (e.g., 'phlogiston', 'electron') and a term's dependence on practices and generalizations that have no special link to science (e.g., 'movie star', 'junk bond'). But once we distinguish the different ways that terms may be theory-laden, and see that the meanings of most so-called theory-laden terms have nothing to do with scientific theories, it is hard to see how the semantic argument for the scientific replaceability of common sense gets any bite.

Commonsense explanatory generalizations

The third line of reasoning leading to the conclusion that commonsense psychology is a would-be theory concerns the nature of explanation. Sometimes, Paul Churchland sounds as if the fact that we use common sense to describe and explain is enough by itself to make it a theory. For example, speaking of commonsense psychology, he says: "It is a framework of concepts, roughly adequate to the demands of everyday life, with which the humble adept comprehends, explains, predicts, and manipulates a certain domain of phenomena. It is, in short, a folk *theory*."[31]

But in this sense of 'theory', generalizations about baseball constitute a theory: The players, umpires, and fans have a framework of concepts ('double-play', 'home run', 'error', 'strike', and so on) with which they comprehend, explain, predict, and manipulate a domain of phenomena. Yet, very few would think that baseball "might be shown to be radically defective by sheerly empirical findings." To be used to comprehend, predict, explain, and manipulate just does not suffice to make something a theory in any sense

29 Patricia S. Churchland, "Reply to Wilkes," *Inquiry* 29 (1986): 252–9.
30 And if the term 'theory' is so appropriated, then we shall need another term to mark the contrast between 'foe', 'food', and 'fun' (which appear in generalizations confirmable by anybody) on the one hand, and 'quark', 'nucleus', and 'atomic number' (which appear in generalizations confirmable only by those with special training) on the other.
31 Paul M. Churchland, *A Neurocomputational Perspective: The Nature of Mind and the Structure of Science* (Cambridge MA: MIT/Bradford, 1989), 111; emphasis in original.

relevant to the debate about the status of common sense. For it is not obvious – indeed, it is just what is at issue – that anything that is used to comprehend, explain, predict and manipulate "may be rejected in its entirety."[32] Nevertheless, Churchland claims that commonsense psychology is constituted by explanatory generalizations and that this fact suffices to make common sense a "theory."[33]

Let us look at Churchland's psychological generalizations of folk psychology and compare them with equally explanatory non-psychological generalizations of common sense. Churchland's examples include:

1. A person who suffers severe bodily damage will feel pain.
2. A person who suffers a sudden sharp pain will wince.
3. A person denied food for any length will feel hunger.

Commonsense explanations of human behavior are similar to commonsense explanations of medium-sized objects.[34] Compare Churchland's list of psychological causal generalizations with the following list of nonpsychological (but equally commonsensical) explanatory generalizations:[35]

1. A porcelain vase will break if dropped on a cement floor.
2. Butter melts when left in the sun.
3. A person's nose will bleed if struck sharply.

The nonpsychological generalizations also appear in ordinary causal explanations, and they also support counterfactuals. The Churchlands would grant the similarities between the psychological and nonpsychological generalizations, and perhaps even accept

---

32 This and the preceding quotation are from *A Neurocomputational Perspective*, 111.
33 Although in *A Neurocomputational Perspective*, Churchland withdraws his support for covering law models of explanation, he continues to argue that our "self-understanding" is a theory on the grounds that the commonsense conception consists of "genuine causal/explanatory 'laws.'" This is somewhat surprising, since on his novel PDP model of explanation, it is unclear what role Churchland now thinks that laws have in explanation at all. But I cannot pause to consider that issue here.
34 Others have made similar comparisons; for example, both Dennett ("Three Kinds of Intentional Psychology," in *The Intentional Stance*, 48) and Charles Chastain ("Comments," in reply to my "Cognitive Suicide," in *Contents of Thought* [Tucson: University of Arizona Press, 1988], 18–26) compare "folk psychology" with "folk physics."
35 Again, this is not to suggest that there is a neat bifurcation into the psychological and the nonpsychological, or that that distinction cuts nature at the joints. Many commonsense generalizations just would not fit: Power corrupts; vacations are relaxing; user-friendly software sells well; ruthless people tend to have few friends.

the "relative consistency proof," but go on to insist that both kinds of generalizations are up for grabs.

There is an important disanalogy between commonsense and theoretical generalizations in terms of their justification, however. Our *grounds* for gross generalizations about medium-sized objects (e.g., porcelain objects break when dropped on concrete) no more stem from physics than do the grounds for gross generalizations about persons (e.g., people relish the downfall of bullies) stem from scientific psychology. I am not suggesting that the commonsense generalizations are knowable a priori: No one would suppose that 'noses bleed when struck sharply' is knowable a priori. Rather, such generalizations are confirmed and disconfirmed in the course of ordinary life, and are warranted as long as they reliably enable us to accomplish our aims – regardless of the ultimate outcome of science. When David went out to slay Goliath, he did not need to wait for a mature physics to be justified in selecting stones instead of twigs for his slingshot. The justification available to David was as complete as it would be today: Knowledge of quantum mechanics would neither add to his grounds nor undermine them.

Nonpsychological generalizations – such as that rocks make better battlefield projectiles than twigs – are confirmed in prescientific everyday life and have nothing to fear from developments in science: No discovery in microphysics would falsify the generalization about battlefield projectiles. Whether matter is continuous or atomic, whether there are n or $n + 2$ kinds of quarks, and so on, are simply irrelevant to the truth of the generalization about the superiority of rocks to twigs on the battlefield. Similarly, psychological generalizations – such as that a person who suffers a sudden sharp pain will wince – are confirmed in prescientific everyday life. (Likewise, no discovery in neuroscience would falsify the generalization about wincing.) Thus, assuming with the Churchlands that commonsense psychological and nonpsychological generalizations are in the same explanatory boat, we need not take either kind to be theoretical in the relevant sense.

This completes my discussion of the main lines of positive argument that commonsense psychology is a theory. I conclude that the direct arguments that aim to show that commonsense psychology is a would-be theory – arguments about alleged empirical failure and revisability, about meanings of terms, and about explanatory generalizations – are unsuccessful, and hence do not establish (M). Nevertheless, many philosophers, even those who are not eliminative materialists, endorse (M) and the idea that common sense is a would-be theory. Why? I believe that such philosophers, perhaps a majority, have an overarching metaphysical commitment, from which (M) simply falls out.

METAPHYSICAL MOTIVATION FOR THE "THEORY" VIEW OF COMMON SENSE

The overarching metaphysical commitment that has (M) as a special case is captured nicely by the aphorism I quoted in Chapter 1: "In the dimension of describing and explaining the world, science is the measure of all things, of what is that it is, and of what is not that it is not."[36] Let me formulate the commitment as the following thesis:

(MT) Reality, insofar as it is knowable, is knowable exclusively by means of science.[37]

Now even in the absence of convincing arguments that common-sense psychology is a would-be scientific theory, (MT) would justify (M) and make the argument for eliminative materialism at least valid. However, an initial difficulty is to tie down the idea of science so that (MT) is neither trivial nor prima facie implausible, yet still yields (M). If we take 'science' to apply to any activity that aims at true descriptions and explanations – in short, to any activity that aims at knowledge – then (MT) is vacuous. If we take 'science' to apply only to partially interpreted calculi, then (MT) is too narrow to be plausible. If we take 'science' to apply to the method of conjecture and refutation, then (MT) will lend no support to (M); for predictions of behavior on the basis of attitudes are constantly borne out – independently of scientific psychology. (Regardless of the fate of, say, connectionism, I would still have good grounds for predicting that you will meet me at the airport if you told me that you would.) If (MT) is to support (M), then 'science' must apply to

---

36 Wilfrid Sellars, "Empiricism and the Philosophy of Mind," in *Science, Perception and Reality* (London: Routledge and Kegan Paul, 1963), 173.
37 Hilary Kornblith suggested this formulation. I also discuss (MT) in "Eliminativism and an Argument from Science," *Mind and Language* 8 (1993): 180–8.

actual disciplines (like physics) that produce systematic descriptions and explanations.

Notice how strong (MT) is, if it is interpreted in a way to support (M). First, it is much stronger than old-fashioned scientific realism, according to which theoretical entities like quarks are assigned ontological status. The thesis (MT) is not just that science reveals the truth, but that science reveals *all* the truth that can be known. One may be an old-fashioned scientific realist as opposed to an instrumentalist – for example, one may still suppose that there are quarks – without being committed to the thesis. (Putnam, I think, would be in this position.)[38] Second, (MT) is independent of rejection of foundationalism, or rejection of a neutral observation language. For one may deny that there is a comprehensive observation-theory distinction and thus deny that there is a neutral observation language, without being committed to the thesis. (The later Wittgenstein, I believe, would be in this position.)[39] Third, (MT) is independent of mere materialism. For (MT) concerns not the constitution, but the organization, of reality. One may endorse materialism, in the sense that there is nothing other than matter and the void, or in the sense that everything globally supervenes on the physical, without being committed to (MT). (Davidson, I believe, would be in this position.)[40] So (MT) is not required by a healthy respect for science: One may deny (MT) and still be a materialist, an antifoundationalist, and a traditional scientific realist.

Why would philosophers hold such a strong view as (MT)? The only remotely plausible argument that I know of is an inductive argument from the history of science. I have never seen the argument stated carefully, and I am not confident about how to state it myself. Here, however, is a stab:

The history of science is the history of progressive expansion of the domains of science. Time and again, phenomena previously

---

38 Putnam has said: "If a scientific realist is one who believes, among other things, that all knowledge worthy of the name is part of science, then I am not a scientific realist." See "What is Realism?" in *Scientific Realism,* ed. Jarrett Leplin, (Berkeley: University of California Press, 1984), 141.
39 See Wittgenstein's *Philosophical Investigations,* 3rd ed., trans. G. E. M. Anscombe (New York: Macmillan, 1958), passim.
40 According to Davidson's "anomalous monism," mental events, which are physical events described in a certain vocabulary, are not governed by strict laws. See, for example, his "Mental Events," in *Essays on Actions and Events* (Oxford: Clarendon Press, 1980), 207–25.

thought beyond the reach of science have been found to have scientific explanations. For example, Galileo paved the way for a scientific explanation of the heavens, Darwin for a scientific explanation of life, Freud for a scientific explanation of the human psyche. So, [the argument goes] we have good inductive reason to think that every phenomenon will ultimately be in the domain of some science, and any putative phenomenon that resists incorporation into science in the long run is to be deemed illusory. In that case, whatever is knowable is knowable exclusively by means of science.

My reply: The conclusion of this argument for (MT) far outstrips what is warranted by the premises. Consider portraits – are they real? According to (MT), either nothing has ever been a portrait or portraits are knowable by some science. The expression 'portraits are knowable by some science' may be understood in either of two ways: (i) portraits qua portraits are knowable by science, or (ii) portraits qua physical objects are knowable by science.[41] (i) is too strong, and (ii) is too weak. Hence, given (MT), we should conclude – at least until someone comes up with a better interpretation of the thesis – that there are no portraits. Such a result is, I think, a reductio ad absurdum of (MT).

Let me show why (MT) leads to the conclusion that there are no portraits. On the one hand, to say (i) – that portraits qua portraits are knowable by science – is to say that the property of being a portrait is taxonomic in some science. But it seems unlikely that there will be a science of portraits, in any constrained sense of 'science'. On the other hand, to say (ii) – that portraits qua physical objects are knowable by science – is, roughly, to say this: "Although we do not have and probably never will have a science of portraits, portraits are physical objects and all physical objects are in the domain of physics. Thus, we can know portraits by means of physics."

But interpretation (ii) will not stand as warrant for concluding *that there are portraits*. For application of the interpretive strategy that yields (ii) would equally show that witches qua physical objects are knowable by science: "Although we do not have and probably never will have a science of witches, witches are physical objects and all physical objects are in the domain of physics." If interpreta-

---

41 For related points, see the discussion of the idea of mind independence in Chapter 8.

tion (ii) vindicates portraits, the parallel interpretation vindicates witches; but I assume that no one would consider this reasoning a vindication of witches. The difficulty is that interpretation (ii) is an instance of a general schema, 'Fs qua physical objects are knowable by science'. But satisfaction of this schema cannot be what establishes the existence of Fs; for the question of whether there are Fs is prior to the question of whether Fs satisfy this schema. For example, to say that physics vindicates portraits but not witches (since there are no witches) requires that one antecedently assume that there are portraits and there are no witches; in that case, the "vindication" of portraits is completed before instantiating the schema that yields interpretation (ii). So, interpretation (ii) cannot not vindicate portraits or anything else.

To sum up: Interpretation (ii) of 'knowable by science' fails as too broad; but on interpretation (i), portraits are not knowable by science inasmuch as the property of being a portrait is not taxonomic in any current or foreseeable science. Since on neither interpretation (i) nor (ii) are portraits knowable by any current or foreseeable science, application of (MT) leads to the conclusion that there really are no portraits, or at the least that we should suspend judgment about portraits. But such a conclusion is ridiculous! The argument for (MT) is based wholly on the past successes of science; but the past successes of science provide no reason at all to deny the existence of portraits of George Washington, or even to suspend judgment.

The multitude of commonsense examples like that of being a portrait weakens considerably the inductive argument for (MT). Moreover, there is an inductive counterargument that goes against (MT): Scientific advances have always taken place against a background of extrascientific assumptions, the making of which presupposes phenomena that show no sign of ever being incorporated into scientific theory, for example, phenomena characterized as experiments, nonfraudulent results, hypotheses. It is difficult to see how science could proceed at all if nothing really were a hypothesis, no results ever nonfraudulent, nobody ever really performed an experiment. Yet, we have no science of hypotheses and so on. Such phenomena, no doubt, are vindicated because they are required by science and science is successful. But what (MT) claims is not just that science reveals reality, but that all knowable reality is revealed by science. The fact that our commitment to there being hypotheses, nonfraudulent results, and experiments is vindicated by the success of science provides no reason whatever to think that science is our *only* successful cognitive enterprise.

Moreover, I can think of no argument for the thesis that science is the guardian of all knowable truth that does not include a claim like this as a premise: Science alone has increased our knowledge of reality in the past. But such a premise is questionable, I believe, for two reasons.

1. Law, literature, art, and music are leading sources of insight into human reality. It is embarrassingly obvious to mention that commonsense psychology, accessible to those without specialized training, has been well explored and expanded by Confucius, Augustine, Shakespeare, Jane Austen, T. S. Eliot, and countless others. One endorsing the exclusivity of science must hold either that these writers did not contribute to what we know, or that they were "really" doing science. Since neither alternative has a shred of plausibility, the premise that truth belongs to science alone seems false.

2. The second difficulty with the premise concerns the unclarity about what should be counted in the history of science. Should the term 'science' apply to Democritus's atomism, Plato's cosmology, Pythagoras's mysticism – all of which were equally unempirical? If the term is applied to anything that developed into science, then the Hermetic tradition of magic, central to Renaissance Neo-Platonism, should be considered as science.[42] But if this form of Zoroastrianism is a science, then what fails to be a science? On the one hand, the less constrained the term 'science', the more vacuous the premise of the inductive argument for (MT); on the other hand, the more constrained the term 'science', the less likely the premise is to support the strong conclusion (MT).

If, as I have argued, the direct arguments that commonsense psychology is a theory are unsuccessful, and the argument for the underlying metaphysical thesis (MT) rests on a dubious premise, then perhaps we should entertain the possibility that commonsense psychology is not a would-be theory at all. Practical Realism aims

---

42 Frances Yates, "The Rosicrucian Enlightenment" in *The Rosicrucian Enlightenment* (London: Routledge and Kegan Paul, 1972), 220. She also stresses "the importance of the Renaissance hermetic tradition as the immediate antecedent of the emergence of science." See "The Hermetic Tradition in Renaissance Science," in *Art, Science and History in the Renaissance,* ed. Charles S. Singleton (Baltimore: Johns Hopkins University Press, 1967), 270.

to provide an alternative that does justice both to common sense and to science at the same time. By contrast, I believe that the Standard View outlook that leads to (MT) runs a serious risk of declaring nonexistent anything that anyone has ever cared about.

CONCLUSION

Folk psychology is a myth because it misrepresents our common-sense psychology for explaining intentional behavior: Folk psychology wrongly takes common sense to be a would-be scientific theory that either must be incorporated into, or superseded by, mature scientific theory. Like many another myth, however, folk psychology serves the purposes of its champions. For taking commonsense psychology to be a theory that rivals scientific theories puts the fate of common sense in the hands of scientific psychology, and thus provides the motivation for eliminative materialism. But if folk psychology is a myth, so is eliminative materialism.

Let me review the line of argument. To make their argument valid,[43] eliminative materialists need a metaphysical premise like this:

(M) If there are beliefs and other attitudes, then they will be vindicated by a serious scientific psychology.

(M) is supported by the claim that commonsense psychology in terms of attitudes is folk psychology – a would-be scientific theory, or a rival of scientific theories. I have rebutted three kinds of arguments that commonsense psychology is a theory in wholesale competition with scientific theories. Then I have discussed a metaphysical assumption (MT) underlying the view that commonsense psychology is a theory, an assumption shared by both eliminativists and noneliminativists, and suggested that the inductive argument for it is, at best, inconclusive. If I am correct here, however, the Standard View rests on a mistaken assumption about the nature of common sense. If we construe theories as scientific theories subject to wholesale replacement, common sense is not a roughly correct theory, as reductionists think; nor is it a radically incorrect theory, as eliminativists think. It is not a theory at all.

43 Whether the argument is sound is another question.

90

PART II

Explanation in theory and practice

4

On standards of explanatory adequacy

The Standard View seems to many to be so obviously correct that mere criticism may not dislodge it. Although I argue in Part I that both eliminativist and noneliminativist versions of the Standard View are beset with difficulties, I want to push farther. In Part II, I want to undercut a central motivation for the Standard View, namely, that the role of beliefs in causal explanation requires that beliefs be brain states. As is pointed out in Chapter 2, noneliminativists typically are concerned to vindicate the causal-explanatory role of belief. Even eliminativists, who deny that there are any beliefs at all, agree that belief explanations purport (albeit wrongly, they contend) to be causal explanations. If we rule out appeal to "immaterial" causes, it may seem that if beliefs have a causal-explanatory role in behavior, then they must of necessity be physically realized internal states of believers – in short, they must be brain states.

This claim – that the causal explanatoriness of belief requires that beliefs be brain states – and, with it, the motivation for the Standard View rest on a hopelessly anemic conception of causal explanation. In this chapter, I want to expose the shortcomings of the conception of causal explanation that underlies the claim. Why does the claim seem plausible? The answer, I think, is that philosophers impose certain constraints on causally explanatory properties. I examine a series of possible constraints and then argue that each of them would either exclude (or be silent about) a huge class of *nonpsychological* explanations. Then, I urge that any acceptable standard of explanatory adequacy should admit explanations from this class as adequate.

On some conceptions of explanation, all of the explanations that are actually offered and accepted are incomplete: The full explanation of any phenomenon, on such views, is beyond human comprehension – perhaps it involves the whole light cone of the past. Such conceptions sever the notion of explanation from anything that could serve our explanatory interests. Since my concern is with explanations that can serve explanatory purposes, I confine attention to explanations that are in principle knowable and expressible in a public language.

The proposals for standards of explanatory adequacy that I consider place metaphysical constraints on the kinds of properties that can be explanatory. Although I do not want to get into exegetical intricacies, the proposed standards are at least loosely associated with writings of Jaegwon Kim, Stephen Stich, Jerry Fodor, and Donald Davidson, respectively. Even though these philosophers have not explicitly formulated conditions of adequacy on explanation in so many words, the seeds for each of the proposed standards may be found in the writings of these and other philosophers. If the philosophers from whose writings the constraints are elicited would not deploy them as standards of explanatory adequacy, but rather as defining properties of explanations, so much the better. My aim in this chapter is to eliminate reasons for thinking that attitudes must be brain states if they are to be causally explanatory. For this purpose, the distinction between not being an adequate explanation and not being an explanation at all is unimportant: The interest here is in with whether classes of putative explanations are adequate causal explanations.

First, I set out briefly four proposed standards of causal-explanatory adequacy; then I give some putative causal explanations that are representative of an enormous class of explanations that has been neglected by analytic philosophers.

1. Consider a conception of explanation based on causal realism. Here is Kim's view of explanation of individual events, which, for Kim, are roughly states of affairs or objects' having properties.[1]

---

1 Jaegwon Kim, "Events as Property Exemplifications" in *Action Theory*, ed. Myles Brand and Douglas Walton (Dordrecht: Reidel, 1980), 159–77.

The proposition that event c occurred explains the proposition that event e occurred only if there is an objective relation between c and e, which meets at least this condition: "That it is instantiated does not entail anything about the existence or nonexistence of any intentional psychological state – in particular, an epistemological or doxastic state – except, of course, when it is instantiated by such states."[2]

There is an ambiguity here: Must the relation be independent of the existence of all intentional psychological states everywhere, or just of particular psychological states (such as that someone believes that a causal relation obtains)? Kim further explicates the notion of objectivity by remarking that a relation is not objective if it "depend[s] crucially on what goes on within our body of knowledge and belief."[3] To be independent of what goes on "within our body of knowledge and belief" is presumably to be independent of the existence of all intentional states, not just of some particular intentional states. So, here is the first proposed standard of adequacy:

(K) A causal explanation is adequate only if instances of the putatively explanatory properties enter into an objective relation with the instance of the property to be explained, where an objective relation is one that can be instantiated in a world without intentional states (unless the relata are intentional psychological states).

2. Now turn to perhaps the most familiar and controversial standard of adequacy, one associated with Stephen Stich and at one time with Jerry Fodor. It is motivated by Stich's well-known "replacement argument." The argument (or rather the intuition) is that, at least for purposes of scientific psychology, an exact physical duplicate of an organism would behave in exactly the same way as the original organism in all circumstances. (It is clear that Stich takes all causal explanation to be scientific explanation.)[4] Purely historical or environmental differences between organisms must be irrelevant to

2 Jaegwon Kim, "Explanatory Realism, Causal Realism, and Explanatory Exclusion," in *Realism and Antirealism* (Midwest Studies in Philosophy 12), ed. Peter A. French, Theodore E. Uehling, Jr., and Howard K. Wettstein (Minneapolis: University of Minnesota Press, 1988), 226.
3 "Realism and Explanatory Exclusion," 227.
4 See Stephen F. Stich, *From Folk Psychology to Cognitive Science: The Case against Belief* (Cambridge, MA: MIT/Bradford, 1983), 245.

causal explanation of behavior. This leads to the second proposed standard of explanatory adequacy:

> (S) A causal explanation is adequate only if the putatively explanatory properties supervene on the current intrinsic physical properties of their bearer.

3. A subtly different standard may be elicited from writings of Jerry Fodor. Genuine causal explanations of phenomena are what are provided by the various sciences, and causally explanatory properties are properties that individuate entities in terms of their causal powers; so an entity's property p is not a genuine explanatory property of the entity's behavior unless its possession affects the causal powers of its bearer – that is, unless the bearer can have different effects in virtue of having that property.[5] Fodor's remark that "you can't affect the causal powers of a person's mental states without affecting his physiology"[6] is a special case of the general view: Possession of a property affects causal powers, and hence is explanatory, only if it affects the physical constitution of its bearer.[7] This can be converted into a standard of adequacy on explanations:

> (F) A causal explanation is adequate only if possession of the putatively explanatory properties affects the physical constitution of their bearers.

Notice that (F) and (S) are not coextensional: (S), at least stated in its bald form, would preclude all explanations attributing relational

5 In "A Modal Argument for Narrow Content," *Journal of Philosophy* 88 (1991):5–26, Fodor relativizes cause properties to their responsibility for particular effect properties: "The point I am wanting to emphasize is that a cause property might fail to count as a causal power in virtue of its responsibility for one effect property, but still might constitute a causal power in virtue of its responsibility for some other effect property" (12–13). I am ignoring this qualification.
  There has been significant discussion (by, e.g., Burge, Stalnaker, van Gulick) about equivocation on "affects causal powers." I think that we can take Fodor's recent writings to provide the content of the notion of "affecting causal powers" by various tests. The cross-context test is discussed by Tyler Burge in "Individuation and Causation in Psychology," *Pacific Philosophical Quarterly* 70 (1989): 303–22, and by David Braun in "Content, Causation, and Cognitive Science," *Australian Journal of Philosophy* 69 (1991): 375–89, and by me in Chapter 2.
6 Jerry A. Fodor, *Psychosemantics: The Problem of Meaning in the Philosophy of Mind* (Cambridge MA: MIT/Bradford, 1987), 39.
7 Other forms of nonreductive materialism may also be committed to this thesis. In "The Metaphysics of Irreducibility," *Philosophical Studies* 63 (1991): 125–46, Derk Pereboom and Hilary Kornblith argue that explanatory properties are those in virtue of which their bearers have causal powers, and that all causal powers are

properties, whereas Fodor has been insistent that his view has room for relational explanations. Fodor insists that the property of being a planet is causally relevant to the planet's motion on grounds that objects have elliptical orbits in virtue of being planets.[8]

4. Finally, turn to a standard of adequacy on explanation elicited from Donald Davidson. Davidson speaks of events as spatiotemporal particulars, and of events as having various descriptions. Causation is a relation between events, no matter how they are described. Causal explanations are of events as described in one way or another. Put another way, a singular causal statement – 'a caused b' – is "transparent": Any co-referring term may be substituted for 'a' or 'b' without changing the truth value of the statement. Causal explanations are not likewise transparent. Under some descriptions, an event may causally explain another event; but under other descriptions, the same event may fail to be explanatory. For example, an event may causally explain the disarray if described as 'the break-in', but the same event (for Davidson, a spatiotemporal particular) may fail to explain the disarray if described as 'the event that led to a massive cover-up that finally brought down Nixon'.

Now on Davidson's view, every causal transaction is "covered" by a strict law, but there are no strict laws between mental events and physical events or between mental events and other mental events. Nonetheless, according to Davidson, belief explanations are causal explanations. Davidson reconciles these theses by taking mental events to be physical events described in a special mental vocabulary, and by allowing that the strict law that subsumes a causal transaction be in a vocabulary different from the vocabulary used in the explanation. Thus, your belief that it might rain casually explains your taking your umbrella, even though there are no strict laws between such beliefs and umbrella takings. But if your belief does explain your taking your umbrella, then your believing has a

constituted by (though not identical with) microphysical causal powers. Although they do not intend this as a constraint on causal explanation, it could easily be deployed for that purpose. If causal powers of x are constituted by microphysical causal powers of parts of x, then I think that the Pereboom-Kornblith view of explanatory properties would entail (F).

8 Discussion of Fodor's cross-context test in Chapter 2 gives reason to be dubious that (F) can admit relational properties as explanatory without also admitting broad contents. For further discussion, see my "Content and Context," in *Language and Logic* (Philosophical Perspectives 8), ed. James E. Tomberlin (Atascadero, CA: Ridgeview, 1994).

microphysical description, d_1, and your umbrella-taking has a microphysical description, d_2, such that it is a strict law that d_1 events cause d_2 events. Putting these aspects of Davidson's position into the language of properties that I have been using, we get another standard of adequacy on explanations:

> (D) A causal explanation is adequate only if the putatively explanatory properties and the explanandum property are coexemplified with properties projected by a strict law.[9]

Davidson's interest is purely metaphysical; he does not set out to give a condition that will allow us to determine which putative explanations are causal explanations. However, he does interpret causal explanations to entail singular statements of the form '*a* caused *b*', and he says that our only reason to believe such singular causal statements is that we have reason to believe that there are strict laws to the effect that 'all the objects similar to *a* are followed by objects similar to *b*'.[10] To that extent, at least, Davidson does expect his analysis to have epistemic import.

Now let us turn to some putative explanations, to which subsequently I shall apply these four standards.

NONPSYCHOLOGICAL CAUSAL EXPLANATIONS

With their almost exclusive focus on physical and psychological explanations, philosophers have given scant attention to an enormous class of explanations: nonpsychological intentional explanations. An explanation is intentional if it mentions an intentional property; and a property is intentional if it is a propositional-attitude property (e.g., the property of believing that health insurance is expensive) or if it presupposes that there are propositional-attitude properties (e.g., the property of passing a health-care reform bill). An explanation is nonpsychological if it does not cite any individual's propositional attitudes or other psychological states. Therefore, nonpsychological intentional explanations presuppose that there are propositional attitudes, without explicitly mentioning them.

Pretheoretically, I take a causal explanation to be an explanation

---

9 The explanandum property is the property to be explained, in contrast to the explanatory properties, which do the explaining.
10 Donald Davidson, "Causal Relations," in *Essays on Actions and Events* (Oxford: Clarendon Press, 1980), 160.

of why a particular phenomenon occurred in terms of the instantiation of some property that is not "definitionally" linked to the occurrence to be explained. By not being definitionally linked, I mean only this: For a competent speaker, knowledge of instantiation of the explanatory property would not suffice by itself for knowledge of the occurrence to be explained, nor would knowledge of the occurrence suffice for knowledge of instantiation of the explanatory property. For example, "The Greeks were outnumbered because the Persians had more men" would not count as a causal explanation.[11]

All explanations support counterfactuals. Causal explanations of individual occurrences support singular counterfactuals about those occurrences: If there had not been an F, then there would not have been a G. Although I am more precise in Chapter 5, here I want to rely only on pretheoretical intuitions about causal explanations. Thus, pretheoretically, I understand a causal explanation (1) to give information about why a particular phenomenon occurred, and (2) to mention explanatory properties that are instantiated before the occurrence of the phenomenon to be explained and that are not definitionally linked to the phenomenon to be explained, and (3) to support relevant counterfactuals about the phenomenon.

Since the class of explanations on which I want to focus has been ignored by philosophers, there are not standard philosophical examples to cite; and actual explanations from the social sciences are factually so complicated that they divert attention from the philosophical issues. For these reasons, I pare down explanations to the bare bones; but the explanations are in no way marginal or idiosyncratic. Nonpsychological intentional explanations are the primary means of explaining economic, social, legal, and political phenomena, and of explaining the behavior of individuals who participate in economic, social, legal, and political institutions – both in the social sciences and in everyday life. Not only do these sample explanations illustrate an enormous class of explanations, but also the intentional presuppositions of this class given them the same epistemic status (be it secure or precarious) as the class of belief explanations.

I shall sketch, briefly, four putative nonpsychological causal ex-

---

11 Richard Lederer, "The World according to Student Bloopers," *Funny Times* (1992): 7.

planations with intentional presuppositions, all of which draw on taxonomies that are actually found in the social sciences: economics, sociology, political science. The putatively explanatory properties were not discovered by the sciences, but were taken over (as is much of social-scientific taxonomy) from pretheoretical, commonsense classifications. After my brief sketches, I consider objections to regarding these as causal explanations. Then, in the next section I apply the proposed standards of adequacy to them.

1. The record drop in the New York Stock Exchange on October 19, 1987 ("black Tuesday"), is causally explained by program trading. The speed of program trading overwhelmed the mechanisms that were supposed to prevent a crash. By the time that trading was stopped on a particular stock, it was too late; program trading allows huge blocks of stock to be bought and sold in a few seconds.

2. Al's application for a gun permit was turned down. The causal explanation is that Al is a convicted felon. If he had not been a convicted felon, he would have received the gun permit.

3. Two people with the same incomes and assets in 1994 as in 1993, and with no change in the tax laws, owed more federal taxes in 1994. Why? They got married in 1994, and in the United States, for purposes of assessing one's income tax, there is something called the 'marriage penalty'.

4. In 1993, Janet Reno began to be accompanied by Secret Service agents. Why? She had been nominated to be attorney general, and her nomination triggered a sequence of events that led to her having Secret Service protection.

The examples, the likes of which could be multiplied indefinitely, seem to me clearly to be causal explanations. Before applying the proposed standards of adequacy to these explanations, let me entertain some important objections. The first two objections reject these examples as causal explanations: First, one may charge that they are not pretheoretically causal explanations; second, one may charge that the properties cited are not the relevant explanatory properties. The third rejects application of standards proposed for scientific explanation to such commonsense examples.

1. The first objection rests on the plausible notion that causes must be logically independent of effects; the link between explanatory properties and the phenomenon to be explained can not be definitional or analytic, but must be contingent, if the explanation

is to be a causal one. The charge is that my examples lack the requisite independence between explanatory properties and phenomenon to be explained.

Although I agree that explanans and explanandum must be logically independent, I think they are independent in the relevant sense in my examples. There is no "definitional" link between explanans and explanandum in any of the examples.[12] Here is an example at which the charge definitional dependence could justly be leveled: 'He was a lifelong bachelor because he never married'. This is not a causal explanation, because if one understands what a lifelong bachelor is, one already knows that he never married. The explanation is not causal because one knows the explanans simply by knowing the meanings of the words that express the explanandum and vice versa.

But this is not the case with my examples. One can know what program trading is without knowing anything about the connection between program trading and the crash on October 19, 1987; one can know what a convicted felon is without knowing anything about gun permits; one can know what marriage is without knowing anything about taxes; one can know what being nominated to be attorney general is without knowing anything about Secret Service protection. The explanans and explanandum of each of these examples (and myriads of others) are not connected by definition. Even a stout defender of the analytic–synthetic distinction would be hard pressed to claim that, in passing a law that denies gun permits to convicted felons, a legislature changes the definition of 'convicted felon'; rather, it changes the causal powers of convicted felons.

My guess is that underlying the objection is a kind of realism that sees intentional phenomena (like wars, presidential elections, and inflation) as "mind-dependent" or "subjective."[13] Perhaps the intuition is that since such intentional phenomena presuppose human institutions and statutory laws, they are under human control in a way that phenomena subject only to laws of nature are not. Al-

12 Although I do not want to presuppose the analytic/synthetic distinction, I want my arguments to apply to those who do endorse the distinction. Hence, in my reply to this objection, I assume (with the objector) that there is an analytic–synthetic distinction.
13 For a discussion of the idea of mind independence, and its lack of philosophical significance, see Chapter 8.

though it is true that "we" can change laws denying gun permits to convicted felons, whereas we cannot similarly change the law of gravitation, this fact seems irrelevant to causal explanation. Statutory laws themselves have consequences as serious as those of the law of gravitation. Making possession of a "controlled substance" a felony diverts resources into enforcement, new prisons and so on. Being arrested for possession of a controlled substance has a decided impact on one's causal powers. Hence, such properties as being arrested for possession should not be ruled out as causally explanatory.

Before moving to the second objection to my examples, let me mention a variant on the first objection. It is not intentional properties per se that fail to be causally explanatory; rather, it is only when the explanandum follows deductively from a description of the relevant institutions and statutory laws, together with the intentional properties, that the explanation fails to be causally explanatory. So, on this variant objection, Jack's calling a lawyer in the middle of the night because he had been arrested for possession is causally explanatory, but Jack's being taken to the police station because he had been arrested for possession is not a causal explanation. This is so, it may be claimed, because the law merely permits, but does not require, Jack's call to his lawyer; but it requires that anyone charged with possession be taken to the police station. Hence, one can "read off" the explanandum in the second case (Jack's being taken to the police station) from the relevant statute together with a description of the initial conditions (Jack's being arrested).

My reply, as earlier, is that this difference is irrelevant to causal explanation. There is no pretheoretical difference between explaining Jack's being taken to the police station and Jack's late-night call to a lawyer in terms of Jack's being arrested for possession. The explananda are on a par. The objector's worry that Jack's being taken to the police station can be "read off" a description of statute and initial conditions does not distinguish that explanation from venerable covering-law explanations. For one can equally "read off" a physical explanandum from descriptions of the physical law and the initial conditions; and many take such a covering-law explanation as a paradigm of causal explanation.

Finally, if the examples that I have given do not provide causal explanations, then it is unlikely that there are causal explanations for such intentional phenomenon as being denied a gun permit, or the crash of the New York Stock Exchange on October 19, 1987, or the owing of higher taxes, or the accompaniment by Secret Service agents. (See Chapter 5 for an argument that such intentional phenomena can not be explained by wholly nonintentional physical-counterpart explanations.) Surely, we would not want to give up on causal explanations of such phenomena. For these are exactly the kinds of phenomena for which we want to know causes.

Intuitively, causal powers often depend on social and linguistic environments. (Having a chauffeured limosine at one's disposal is a causal power.) Such causal powers, like others, are causally explanatory. In short, I see no use for the brand of realism that would demote phenomena with intentional presuppositions to a second-class status. Intentional phenomena have a kind of sturdiness and obduracy all their own. Pretheoretically, we count explanations in terms of intentional properties as explanatory, and the cost of ruling out such explanations on theoretical grounds just seems too high.

2. The second objection concerns the explanatory properties in my examples. Someone may object: The examples of the convicted felon and of getting married have the peculiar feature that the explanatory properties would not have the effects that they have if no one believed that they were exemplified. If no one had known that Al was a convicted felon, he would have received his gun permit. If no one had realized that you got married, then you would not have received a tax bill; though you still would have owed higher taxes, that effect is purely intentional. Moreover, if Al had not been a convicted felon but the clerk had mistakenly believed that he was, he still would not have received the gun permit; and if you had not really gotten married, but the Internal Revenue Service had mistakenly thought that you had, then you still would have received the tax notice. This suggests that the explanatory properties were not, say, being a convicted felon and getting married, but being thought to be a convicted felon and being thought to have gotten married.

My reply: First, note that the relevant contrast need not be between, say, being a convicted felon and *being thought to be* a convicted felon. The explanation of the denial of the gun permit would have been the same without anyone's actually thinking that Al is a convicted felon. For Al's application could have been processed entirely by a (dumb) algorithm with access to a huge data bank that included the information that Al was a convicted felon. So, the objection really has nothing to do with psychological states. In the slightly altered example, in which the application was mechanically processed by a computer, the objection should be this: It is not Al's being a convicted felon that explains his being denied a gun permit, but rather what explains the denial is that Al is listed as a convicted felon in the data bank.

So, let me formulate the objector's contrast in as neutral a way as possible: It is between a's being F and a's being represented as F.[14] The property of representing something as F is a property with intentional presuppositions, but one that can be instantiated by nonpsychological beings – by traffic signs and paintings, as well as by computers. Now the recast objection is this: The explanatory property is not being a convicted felon but being represented as a convicted felon.

My reply to the recast objection: Even if the objection were sustained in the case of the convicted felon, other examples – such as the explanation of the stock market crash – elude it, and such examples suffice to make my point. Moreover, even if one takes being represented as a convicted felon (rather than simply being a convicted felon) to be the relevant explanatory property, this property is still a relational property with intentional presuppositions, with all the attendant complications. When the property F (like the property of being a convicted felon) itself has intentional presuppositions, then the property of being represented as F is doubly intentional.[15] So, explanations in terms of *a's being represented as F* are as much a challenge to the proposed standards of adequacy as are explanations in terms of *a's being F,* where being F is a nonpsychological intentional property.

Nevertheless, I think that there are deep issues here. I want to press the point that being a convicted felon is itself an explanatory property – although many of the effects of having this property are mediated by the property of being represented as (being thought to be or being listed as) a convicted felon. As long as Al's being a convicted felon is in the causal background of the denial of the gun permit, being a convicted felon is a suitable explanatory property. On the other hand, I would agree with the objector that *sometimes*

14 I am using 'represented' here in a nontechnical sense. In particular, I am not implying that in order to represent that *p,* there must be an item in the head (a 'representation') that means that *p.*
15 For a discussion of the complications of double intentionality, see Chapter 7.

the relevant explanatory property is not a's being F, but a's being represented as being F. In what sorts of cases should a's being represented as F take precedence over a's being F as an explanatory property? I can think of two kinds of cases: (i) when a is not F; (ii) when a's being F is not in the causal history of the state of affairs to be explained. Let me illustrate:

i. Assuming that there are no witches, we explain the hysterics of certain children in seventeenth-century Salem not by the presence of a witch, but by the presence of someone the children took to be a witch. Hester has effects not by virtue of being a witch but by virtue of being represented as a witch. Or, to take another case: We explain the use of some apparatus of Priestley's by saying, "It was an oxygen detector," and we explain the use of some apparatus of Lavoisier's by saying, "It was thought to be a phlogiston detector." (It was only thought to be a phlogiston detector because there was no phlogiston to detect.) a's being thought to be F becomes explanatory when a is not F, or when the explainer doubts that a is F.

ii. Suppose that Sal, like Al, was a convicted felon who had his application for a gun permit rejected. But suppose that Sal's being a convicted felon had played no role in the rejection of the permit. For example, suppose that Sal's application had been processed by a computer that had listed Sal as a convicted felon but that Sal had gotten on the list by accident. Suppose that Sal was in the witness protection program and had not been supposed to be listed as a convicted felon; but the key-punch operator had been distracted by a ringing telephone and inadvertently had hit the key that entered Sal (under his new name) on the list of convicted felons. In this case, his being a convicted felon played no role in his being listed as a convicted felon. Hence, the correct explanation of the denial of Sal's application for a gun permit is not that he was a convicted felon (although he was) but that he is represented as a convicted felon. But Sal's is not the typical case; in the typical case (Al's), being a convicted felon is the explanatory property. In effect, the law says: No gun permits for convicted felons; it does not say: No gun permits for people represented as convicted felons. For if it said the latter, then someone who had never even been arrested but who was mistakenly represented in the data bank as a felon would *legitimately* be denied a gun permit. The innocent would have no recourse under such a law.

105

In cases in which a is F and in which a's being F are in the causal history of the state of affairs to be explained, then a's being F typically takes explanatory precedence over a's being represented as F. However, the objector may still persist in taking a's being represented as F as the explanatory property. The reason, the objector may say, that the real explanatory property is the representation of Al, rightly or wrongly, as a convicted felon is that this property "screens off" the property of Al's being a convicted felon. (Property A screens off property B from an outcome O iff the probability of O, given A and B, is no higher than the probability of O, given A alone.) Now, the objection is that the probability that Al is denied a gun permit, given that he is a convicted felon and is represented as a convicted felon, is no higher than the probability that Al is denied a gun permit, given only that he is represented as a convicted felon.

Without disputing the relative probabilities, I do not think that this is a good objection. For if it were, we would have no casual explanations of anything. If you assume that causes are events and that events are densely ordered (between any two there is a third), then any event cited as a cause is screened off from the putative effect by an event spatiotemporally between the putative cause and its effect. A foot injury would be screened off as a cause of your pain, since the probability of your being in pain, given your foot injury and the state of your nervous system, is no higher than the probability of your being in pain, given the state of your nervous system alone. But it would fly in the face of the purposes of causal explanation to deny that your foot injury causally explains your pain. Hence, the objection that being represented as a convicted felon screens off the property of being a convicted felon "proves too much." For that objection can be applied to (almost?) any putatively explanatory property. So, I set aside the objection that being represented as F screens off being F.

3. The third objection is a worry stemming from views on scientific explanation. Since some of the proposed standards are specifically aimed at scientific explanations, it may be objected that I am inappropriately applying standards for scientific explanations to commonsense explanations. My reply is that the proponents of the proposed standards typically assume that all genuine explanations are scientific explanations. For example, Stich proposes a standard of adequacy specifically for explanations of scientific psychology, but then takes the results to impugn the truth and explanatoriness

of ordinary attributions of attitudes. (Indeed, he goes out of his way to excoriate Dennett for trying to salvage any legitimate role, even a merely instrumentalistic role, for attributions of attitudes if they violate the standards that Stich accepts.)[16] Or to take an example removed from the issues of psychology, in the articles in an important recent collection entitled *Scientific Explanation,* the qualification 'scientific' is quietly dropped.[17] Thus, even if a standard of adequacy is proposed explicitly for scientific explanations, it is reasonable to consider it here since many philosophers assume that scientific explanation is the only kind of explanation worthy of the name. Later, I argue that explanations with intentional presuppositions are not merely second-class explanations, but here I want to consider how well such explanations fare under the constraints of the proposed standards.

My own view of the relation between theoretical explanations in physics, say, and the more commonsensical explanations I have set out is this: Garden-variety commonsense and scientific explanations are on a continuum, and what distinguishes one end of the continuum from the other concerns not the nature of the explanatory properties but the justification for taking the explanatory properties to be exemplified. The more that appeal to scientific theories is needed to justify attribution of a property, the more scientific are explanations that cite the property. For example, what justifies calling a blip on a screen an electron is scientific theory (understood only by initiates); but what justifies calling an icy slope slippery, or calling a person dependable, is ordinary experience (available to anybody without special training). Some properties, for example, geological properties, begin as common sense but then find their way into scientific research programs, in terms of which we may say that we now understand such properties better; but the ancients were as justified as we are in saying that, say, Pompeii was destroyed by a volcanic eruption.

If I am right, the sciences do not yield a privileged class of explanations isolated from everyday explanations. The main difference between so-called commonsense and scientific explanations resides in the source of putative epistemic legitimacy of the explanatory

16 Stich, *From Folk Psychology to Cognitive Science,* 243.
17 *Scientific Explanation* (Minnesota Studies in the Philosophy of Science, 12), ed. Philip Kitcher and Wesley C. Salmon (Minneapolis: University of Minnesota Press, 1989).

properties, not in their ontological status. My concern here, however, is not with the relations between scientific and commonsense explanations but, rather, with causal explanations, whether commonsense or scientific.

Let us now apply the proposed standards of adequacy to these examples. If a type of purported explanation violates a proposed standard, then either that standard is unacceptable or there are no adequate explanations of that type.

Begin with (K): Since the relations between being a convicted felon and being denied a gun permit, or between program trading and a stock market crash, can not be instantiated in worlds without intentional states, putative explanations that cite such properties violate (K). On (K), no explanation in terms of properties with intentional presuppositions is ever adequate. Hence, if (K) is accepted as a condition of adequacy on explanations, we can know a priori that explanations from the social sciences are generally inadequate. Moreover, many of the explanations offered and accepted as adequate in everyday life mention such properties: You were audited by the Internal Revenue Service because you deducted your home office in calculating your taxes. You paid a fine because your books were overdue at the library. You got a ticket because you were exceeding the speed limit. The properties of deducting your home office, of having overdue library books, of exceeding the speed limit – all of these and indefinitely many more – would fail to explain anything, if (K) were accepted as a standard of adequacy. So, allegiance to (K) would simply rule out, a priori, all putative explanations that mention nonpsychological properties with intentional presuppositions.[18]

Apply (S) to the examples. Call properties that supervene on the current, internal, physical states of their bearers "narrow properties." Is the causally efficacious property of being a convicted felon

---

18 Notice that modifying (K), in accordance with another of Kim's theses – namely, that macroproperties must be realized or grounded in microproperties – would not affect the point here. See Jaegwon Kim, "Epiphenomenal and Supervenient Causation," in *Theories of Causation* (Midwest Studies in Philosophy 9), ed. Peter A. French, Theodore E. Uehling, Jr., and Howard K. Wettstein (Minneapolis: University of Minnesota, 1984), 261.

a narrow property? Of course not. Al's physical constitution is independent of his property of being a convicted felon. Twin-Al, who is a physical duplicate of Al, may not be a convicted felon – although he may mistakenly think that he is. Twin-Al, who is not a convicted felon, may not even believe that he is a convicted felon; if Al was convicted in absentia (maybe as a war criminal), then he and his twin may have no beliefs at all about being convicted felons. So, no explanation that mentions the property of being convicted felon satisfies (S).

So, it seems that (S) would deem all the explanations to be inadequate. As with (K), if (S) is accepted, we would know a priori that all the social sciences, as well as much of common sense, fail to provide any adequate explanations of anything. Actually, (S) would rule out explanations that (K) may allow. For example, biological and other functionally defined properties, without intentional presuppositions, are (a priori) inadequate, according to (S). Not even is being a heart a narrow property, despite its taxonomic status in biology; for nothing is a heart unless it functions or was evolved to function in an organism in a certain way.[19] So, (S) would seem out of kilter with much of natural science too.

Now consider (F). In none of the examples are the putatively explanatory properties connected in any interesting way to the physical constitutions of their bearers. In the case of Al's being denied a gun permit, the property of being a convicted felon affects Al's causal powers – both positively and negatively. It not only resulted in his being refused a gun permit, but it also allowed him entry to a certain drug rehabilitation program. But however (or even whether) possession of the property of being a convicted felon affected Al's physical constitution is just irrelevant to the explanatory worth of explanations in terms of that property. In the case of the stock-market crash, it is not even clear what would count as the physical constitution of the New York Stock Exchange. Particular people, such as the president of the exchange, may act on its behalf, but their bodies are unlikely candidates to be the (scattered) physical constitution of the New York Stock Exchange. In the case of owing higher taxes, getting married had a clear effect, but not necessarily on either your or your spouse's physical constitution. Indeed,

---

19 For versions of this view, see Burge, "Individuation and Causation in Psychology," and Ruth Millikan, "Biosemantics," *Journal of Philosophy* 86 (1989): 281–98.

common-law marriages do not even require a ceremony, only the elapsing of time; yet, for all that, the causal and explanatory power of the property of your being married is unquestionable. You owe higher taxes because you got married. Indeed, owing higher taxes itself may be causally explanatory: if you owe but do not pay, you may end up in jail. So, the explanations fare no better on (F) than on the other putative standards of adequacy.

Now, turn to (D). It is difficult to see how we could ever know whether (D) was satisfied by any of our sample explanations. Although Davidson's views on the nomological nature of causation are purely metaphysical, he also says that "we have reason to believe the singular statement ['a caused b'] only in so far as we have reason to believe that there is such a law [to the effect that 'all the objects similar to a are followed by objects similar to b'].[20] But having reason to believe that there was such a strict law would not push us toward an explanation – for two reasons: First, since knowledge of strict laws is limited (to zero?), we would not know what the strict law was. Since we cannot now discern (and perhaps never will be able to) whether any particular explanations meet the condition given in (D), it would seem that we cannot enlist (D) as a usable standard of adequacy on causal explanation.

Second, knowledge of the identity of the strict law would not help us discover the appropriate descriptions for causal explanation. Suppose that a referee's call of a technical foul in the last second of a tied basketball game explains why the Panthers won. But the referee's call described as 'the seventeenth call of a technical foul in the season' does not explain the Panthers' victory. If there were descriptions of the referee's call in the last second in the tied game and the Panthers' victory, under which they were connected by strict law, then that same strict law would also connect the seventeenth call of a technical foul in the season and the Panthers' win. (This is so since, on Davidson's view of events, there is a single event, equally describable as 'the referee's call of a technical foul in the last second of the tied basketball game' or as 'the seventeenth call of a technical foul in the season'.) But in one case, we would have a causal explanation and in the other case, we would not. Since Davidson provides no way to determine under which descriptions

20 Donald Davidson, "Causal Relations," in *Essays on Actions and Events* (Oxford: Clarendon Press, 1980), 160.

events are causally explanatory and under which descriptions they are not, (D) is of little help in identifying adequate causal explanations.[21] In any case, it is unclear why a property is ever explanatory in virtue of being coexemplified with a different property that has a special feature. How does the special feature of being projected by a strict law rub off (as it were) on another property and make it explanatory? And why does the special feature rub off on some coexemplified properties and not others?

But there is a more serious problem with (D). Suppose that Reno's being nominated to be attorney general casually explains the onset of Reno's Secret Service protection. Then, on Davidson's view, the events described as 'Reno's being nominated to be attorney general' and 'the onset of Reno's Secret Service protection' have alternative descriptions in the vocabulary of microphysics, and these descriptions appear as antecedent and consequent of a strict law.[22] The problem is that there are not such redescriptions; therefore, by (D), Reno's being nominated cannot causally explain the onset of Reno's Secret Service protection. Even worse, the argument is generalizable to any putative explanation that mentions properties that are not projected by a strict law.

To see that there are no redescriptions of Reno's being nominated and of the onset of Reno's Secret Service protection that are antecedent and consequent, respectively, of a strict law, suppose that Reno had been struck by lightning between the time that she was nominated and the beginning of her Secret Service escort. In that case, the event of her being nominated would have occurred, but there would have been no event of her beginning to have a Secret Service escort. But if these events instantiate a strict law (under other descriptions), it is impossible for the first to occur without the second's also occurring. So, the events of Reno's being nominated and the onset of Reno's Secret Service protection cannot be connected by strict law under any descriptions. If there are any strict laws in the offing, they will have to rule out Reno's being hit by lightning in the interval between her nomination and the beginning of her escort. But the event of Reno's being nominated does not

---

21 For other criticisms of Davidson on causal explanation, see Louise Antony, "Anomalous Monism and the Problem of Explanatory Force," *Philosophical Review* 98 (1989): 153–87.
22 More accurately, there are a series of strict laws, $M \rightarrow M1$, $M1 \rightarrow M2$, . . . $Mn \rightarrow M'$.

rule out her being struck by lightning. So a redescription of the event of Reno's being nominated in the vocabulary of microphysics is not the antecedent of a strict law that has as consequent a redescription of the onset of Secret Service protection.

To put the point another way: Even though the event of Reno's being nominated did in fact cause the onset of Secret Service escort, the event of Reno's being nominated would not have caused the onset of Secret Service escort had she been hit by lightning. That is, it is *nomologically possible* that Reno had been nominated and yet that there was no Secret Service escort. But it is *nomologically impossible* for an event mentioned in the antecedent of a strict law to occur and yet for the event mentioned in its consequent to fail to occur. Therefore, there is no redescription of Reno's being nominated that is the antecedent of a strict law (or the first antecedent of a "linked" series of strict laws) whose consequent is a redescription of the onset of Secret Service protection.

Thus, on metaphysical grounds alone, the putative causal explanation of the onset of Reno's Secret Service protection in terms of her being nominated to be attorney general should be deemed inadequate by (D). Indeed, no explanation in terms of properties that are not themselves projected by a strict law can be adequate, according to (D). But since no known (or knowable?) explanations of macrolevel events mention properties projected by a strict law, no known explanations satisfy (D).[23]

On none of the proposals so far are explanations with intentional presuppositions explanatorily adequate. Perhaps the proposals can be modified in ways that would accord explanatory adequacy to explanations with intentional presuppositions. I consider two such modifications.

1. Fodor offers another way to formulate a standard of explanatory adequacy. Fodor holds that a covering law model of explanation allows properties projected by hedged or nonstrict laws – laws formulated with ceteris paribus clauses – to be explanatory.[24]

---

23 Geoffrey Goddu made this kind of argument against Jerry Fodor's views. See Fodor's "Special Sciences," in *Representations: Philosophical Essays in the Foundations of Cognitive Science* (Cambridge, MA: MIT/Bradford, 1980), 127–45, and his "Making Mind Matter More," *Philosophical Topics* 17 (1989): 59–79. I believe that Goddu's argument has wide application.
24 Fodor, "Making Mind Matter More," 59–79; "You Can Fool Some of the People All of the Time, Everything Else Being Equal; Hedged Laws and Psychological Explanations," *Mind* 100 (1991): 19–32.

"Strict laws and hedged laws with satisfied ceteris paribus conditions," he says, "operate alike in respect of their roles in covering causal relations and in respect of their roles in covering law explanations." So, "hedged laws can play the same role as strict ones in covering law explanations, so long as it's part of the explanation that the ceteris paribus conditions are satisfied."[25] This suggests the following:

(F*) A causal explanation is adequate only if the putative explanatory properties and the explanandum property are projected by a strict or nonstrict law.

All nonstrict laws, according to Fodor, must be "implemented" by physical (ultimately microphysical) mechanisms. He holds that ceteris paribus clauses existentially quantify over physical mechanisms. 'As cause Bs ceteris paribus', then, can "mean something like 'There exists an intervening mechanism such that As cause Bs when it's intact'." (Fodor's physicalism lies in the assumption that "all the mechanisms that mediate the operation of nonbasic laws are eventually physical," where a physical mechanism "is one whose means of operation is covered by a physical law (i.e., by a law articulated in the language of physics)."[26]

First, there are serious worries about Fodor's account of nomological sufficiency. Suppose that '$M{\rightarrow}B$ ceteris paribus' is a law. Then, according to Fodor's account, M is nomologically sufficient in worlds in which the ceteris paribus conditions are satisfied. As he puts it, "hedged (including intentional) laws necessitate their consequences when their ceteris paribus clauses are discharged."[27] Since nomological necessity is usually defined in terms of what would happen in any nomologically possible world, one may wonder about laws whose antecedents necessitate their consequents in some nomologically possible worlds but not in others. For example, is the antecedent of '$M{\rightarrow}B$ ceteris paribus' determinately satisfied in a world in which the ceteris paribus are *not* satisfied (i.e., in a world in which an M occurs but a B does not)? If so, then Ms are

---

25 "Making Mind Matter More," 75. According to Fodor, "Hedged laws necessitate their consequents in worlds where their ceteris paribus conditions are satisfied" (74). Some may find the notion of laws' necessitating their consequents in some worlds but not others baffling.
26 Ibid., 76, 79.
27 Ibid., 73.

not nomologically sufficient for Bs inasmuch as Ms occur without Bs. If not, then the law does not subsume an event in virtue of its being an M inasmuch as Ms occur without being subsumed by the law '$M{\to}B$'.

Putting aside qualms about the nomological character of non-strict laws, however, we still need an understanding of what is to count as a nonstrict law if (F*) is to be applicable. Here are three ways that (F*) may be interpreted.

i. If (F*) is interpreted in such a way that it is coextensional with (F) – as Fodor's remarks about intervening mechanisms strongly suggest – then (F*) too would disallow the examples as causal explanations.

ii. If (F*) is interpreted more broadly so that explanatory properties may supervene on physical properties that are not intrinsic to the individual, then (F*) would be as powerless to rule out any putative causal explanation as (D) is: Most explanations are such that it would be impossible to ascertain whether they conformed to (F*). A standard that can not be applied is no standard at all.

iii. Finally, if (F*) is interpreted so that any counterfactual-supporting claim can be turned into a nonstrict law, then I would have no objection to (F*). Suppose, for example, that (F*) were interpreted in such a way that all the following express nonstrict laws:

> Ceteris paribus, one can improve one's grade on an examination by preparing for it.
> Ceteris paribus, nominees to the Supreme Court show up for their confirmation hearings.
> Ceteris paribus, leaky pens stain the shirt pockets that contain them.

If such ceteris paribus sentences are construed as expressing non-strict laws, then I would consider (F*) harmless, because toothless. Now that I have suggested various ways that I would respond to a range of interpretations of (F*), I simply put (F*) aside as needing further specification.

2. Here is a second way to modify the proposed standards of adequacy. (S), as we have seen, was too restrictive; for it required explanatory properties to supervene on the intrinsic properties of their bearers. But suppose that we relaxed the requirement so that explanatory properties may supervene on the intrinsic properties of

their bearers and/or on the intrinsic properties of other things to which the bearers are related in some way; explanatory properties have to be *grounded* in intrinsic properties. For example, the property of believing that water is wet may supervene on the intrinsic properties of the believer and the intrinsic properties of water, where the believer is appropriately related to water. Informally, the idea of grounding is that for anybody (y) who believes that, say, water is wet, there are n objects ($x_1, \ldots x_n$) – including perhaps brain states and water samples – that have certain intrinsic properties ($A_1, \ldots A_n$), and, necessarily, if any n objects ($z_1, \ldots z_n$) have those properties, then somebody (w) believes that that water is wet, where there are particular physical or logical relations ($R_1, \ldots R_n$) between the believer and each of the n objects.[28] More formally, we can define grounding as a relation between properties:

Property B is *grounded in* intrinsic properties $A_1, \ldots A_n$ if and only if: For any y, if y has B, then

(i) there are $x_1, \ldots x_n$ such that x_1 has A_1, x_2 has $A_2, \ldots$, and x_n has A_n; and

(ii) there are physical or logical relations, $R_1, \ldots R_n$ [characterized in a certain way] such that y bears R_1 to x_1, y bears R_2 to $x_2, \ldots$ and y bears R_n to x_n; and

(ii) necessarily: For any $v_1, \ldots v_n$, such that v_1 has A_1, v_2 has $A_2, \ldots$ and v_n has A_n, and for any z, such that z bears R_1 to v_1, z bears R_2 to $v_2, \ldots$ and z bears R_n to v_n, z has B.

Now say that explanation E is grounded in explanation E^* iff the explanatory properties of E are grounded in the explanatory properties of E^*. For example, if one explanation cites a's being F as explanatory, where F is a relational property (like being a convicted felon), then the putative explanation may still be adequate if a's being F supervened on b's being G and c's being H, and so on (where G and H are intrinsic properties of b and c, respectively) and if a is suitably related to b and c, and so on. In that way, (S) could be revised to admit relational explanations that are grounded in explanations whose explanatory properties are intrinsic to their bearers. If relations were analyzed in a way that entailed that relational

---

28 Logical relations include the relation of identity.

properties supervened upon intrinsic properties, perhaps (S*) would be an acceptable standard of adequacy:[29]

> (S*) A causal explanation is adequate only if it is *grounded in* an explanation whose putatively explanatory properties supervene on the intrinsic properties of their bearers.

The big mystery is what relations are the grounding relations, $R_1, \ldots R_n$? What is grounding? As we have seen, the relation between the bearer of the grounded property and the bearers of the grounding properties is not just one of whole to part: There are no intrinsic properties of parts of a human being, such that, necessarily, if the parts have those intrinsic properties, then the human being is married. Nor is the grounding relation simply one of causality: Being a felon does not (or at least not obviously) entail that one is causally related to some set of objects with certain intrinsic properties. (The felon may be suitably related to a jury, but it is not in virtue of her intrinsic properties that someone is a juror.)

However, perhaps such relational properties as being a convicted felon could be explicated in terms of the intrinsic properties of their bearers *together with* the intrinsic properties of other things in the world. Call this a "Leibnizian" interpretation of relational properties.[30] Although I have no knockdown argument against a Leibnizian interpretation of relations, I want to show that the view is seriously incomplete. We can not specify the grounding relations R; we have no idea what kind of properties a relation must have to be a grounding relation. Moreover, I want to show, our ignorance of R makes absolutely no explanatory difference whatever. A Leibnizian interpretation of relations would be no help in our understanding of many relational properties inasmuch as the explanatory power of these properties does not seem to rest on the intrinsic properties of anything. Let me give a final example to this effect.

Consider a ring of counterfeiters who are so expert that they produce bills that are microphysical duplicates of genuine bills. Suppose that the police, in investigating the counterfeiting ring, have been tracking a number of hundred-dollar bills, some of which are know to be counterfeit and some of which are known to

---

29 (K), (D), and (F) could also be modified accordingly. For example, (K*): An explanation is adequate only if it is grounded in an explanation whose putatively explanatory properties can enter into an objective relation.

30 I am grateful to Derk Pereboom for discussing this possibility with me.

be genuine. The police question closely those with the counterfeit bills, but they detain those with the genuine bills (whom they think of as their control group) only long enough to identify them. Jane and Jill are microphysical duplicates, both of whom are handed hundred-dollar bills by twin shady-looking characters. Although the bills are themselves microphysical duplicates, Jane gets a counterfeit, and Jill a genuine bill, as the police are aware. The police stop Jane and Jill – Jane for close questioning, Jill for identification only. Jane's property of being in receipt of a counterfeit hundred-dollar bill causes the police to interrogate Jane at length; Jill's property of being in receipt of a genuine hundred-dollar bill causes the police simply to request identification. In consequence, Jane misses her flight to Paris; but Jill makes her flight. The difference between missing and not missing a plane is a clear causal, even a physical, difference.

Someone may note that if the police had had different beliefs, they would have behaved differently. I agree, but it does not follow that the bills' actually being counterfeit in the one case and genuine in the other made no difference in the case that I described. In my story, the bill's being counterfeit was partly responsible for the police's belief that the bill was counterfeit. If we trace the police's beliefs back to their causal origins, we find the belief of one bill that it was genuine originated (in part) in the fact that that bill was genuine; and the belief of the other bill that it was counterfeit originated (in part) in the fact that that bill was counterfeit. So, the actual properties of the bills of being, respectively, counterfeit and genuine play causal roles in the episodes that result in Jane's missing her plane and Jill's catching hers.[31]

If being counterfeit is a relational property that supervenes on the intrinsic properties of anything, whose intrinsic properties are those by virtue of which the bill is counterfeit? Since the counterfeit and genuine hundred-dollar bills are microphysical duplicates, the intrinsic properties of the engraved pieces of paper are irrelevant to

31 Notice that the "counterfeit" example shows that the purely intentional property of being counterfeit also would pass one of Fodor's necessary conditions on causal powers: It is no conceptual truth that causes that differ in that one has the property of being in receipt of a counterfeit bill and the other has the property of being in receipt of a genuine bill have effects that differ in that one is the beginning of a long interrogation and the other is a simple request for identification.

the difference between being counterfeit and being genuine. The physical manner of production of the bills is likewise irrelevant: The printing presses could also be microphysical duplicates, yet one bill but not the other may still be counterfeit. Maybe the property of being counterfeit supervenes on the intrinsic properties of the bills together with the intrinsic properties of certain individuals. But the intrinsic properties of which individuals? Perhaps unauthorized individuals. This would not help the Leibnizian, because a molecular duplicate of an unauthorized individual may be authorized to print genuine U.S. currency. (And a molecular duplicate of an authorizing individual may fail to be an authorizing individual, and so on indefinitely.) Hence, it is not the intrinsic properties of unauthorized individuals on which the property of being counterfeit supervenes.

This is not a refutation of a Leibnizian interpretation of relations. It is rather an argument that, even if the Leibnizian interpretation is correct, we have no idea on which intrinsic properties of which individuals the property of being counterfeit supervenes, and that furthermore – and here is the important point – our ignorance of such matters is no explanatory defect. It is not only that we do not know on which intrinsic properties of which individuals the property of being counterfeit supervenes, but rather that acquiring such knowledge would not further illuminate the original explanation.

In any case, we have no reason to think that (S*) would admit the sample putative explanations, except by default: Confidence in the explanatoriness of the sample explanations may simply lead one who is antecedently committed to (S*) to conclude that the explanations simply must satisfy (S*). The thought experiment about the counterfeit bill is intended, at a minimum, to show that (S*) does not provide a satisfactory constraint on explanation.

A VERDICT

We have considered six proposals for standards of explanatory adequacy. Each of the proposals for explanatory adequacy places a reductive, ontological requirement on properties that can be explanatory. Each would rule out, or else admit by default, not only the sample putative explanations that we began with, but a raft of commonsense and social-scientific explanations. So, either we give up the explanations or we give up the proposals as guides to explanatory adequacy.

Now, which should we give up – the proposed standards of adequacy or the examples? I think there is no contest. The proposed conditions of adequacy, at best, are irrelevant to actual evaluation of putative explanations and, at worst, would impugn, wholesale, successful nonpsychological causal explanations. In such a clash, in which successful, pervasive practice is pitted against a priori conditions of adequacy, it seems to me prudent to stick with what works – the successful explanatory practices – and to forsake the a priori conditions of adequacy.[32] The fact that our putative causal explanations do give us verifiable control over phenomena provides as much reason as we are going to get to think that we have discovered causally explanatory properties. A tip of the hat to G. E. Moore: We can be more certain that the causal explanations that afford control over phenomena are correct than of any metaphysical doctrine that would cast doubt on them.

Let me summarize some points from the examples. (1) The properties of being a convicted felon, of being married, of a stock market's crashing, of being nominated to be attorney general – properties that do not supervene on the intrinsic properties of their bearers – are taxonomic in economics, political science, and other social sciences. In addition, common sense regards them as causally efficacious: Indeed, what could be more fraught with causal consequences than being convicted of a felony, or being nominated to be attorney general? (2) Although these properties have intentional presuppositions for their exemplifications, they are cited as causes in unproblematic nonpsychological causal explanations, despite the fact that their causal efficacy derives from political, social and economic conventions. (3) The explanatory import of these properties does not depend on any information whatever about their physical realizations, if any. Yet, (4) these properties bear no taint of Cartesian immaterialism. The moral is that our preoccupation with the physical basis of all phenomena leads us astray in explanation.

32 The priority of explanatory practice over metaphysical speculation is a theme in the work of Tyler Burge. For example, see Burge's "Individuation and Causation in Psychology," 303–22, and "Mind-Body Causation and Explanatory Practice," in *Mental Causation,* ed. John Heil and Albert Mele (Oxford: Clarendon Press, 1993), 97–120.

In practice, there is no sharp line between nonpsychological explanations with intentional presuppositions, like those considered in this chapter, and psychological explanations. It would be arbitrary to hold belief explanations to special standards of adequacy to which other explanations are immune. So, if the proposed standards are unacceptable as general standards for nonpsychological explanations with intentional presuppositions, or are not clearly applicable to such explanations, then they are equally unacceptable as standards for belief explanations. There need be no general feature, which either can be known a priori or read off the results of past science, that causal explanatory properties must all share. So, belief explanations can not be deemed inadequate on the grounds that believing that p fails to live up to any such standard of explanatory adequacy.

I began with a widely accepted conditional: If beliefs causally explain behavior, then they must be (or be constituted by) brain states. That conditional is underwritten by a particular construal of causal explanation that I have tried to undermine. In the next chapter, I propose a general test of explanatory adequacy, which allows both psychological and nonpsychological intentional explanations to be adequate. On that account, the conditional is false: The explanatoriness of belief does not require that beliefs be brain states.

5

How beliefs explain

We have seen that metaphysical constraints on properties that can be causally explanatory lead to grief for many kinds of non-psychological explanations that are routinely and successfully accepted as causal explanations. This result suggests – rightly, in my opinion – that the Standard View conception of causal explanation is too restrictive. In response, I propose a test for a certain common and important kind of causal explanation. After defending the test against objections, I argue for the autonomy of intentional explanations, and then use the resulting thesis – that intentional explanations are not replaceable by physical explanations of the constituents of the intentional phenomena – to undermine the motivation for the Standard View of causal explanation. I argue that it is not in virtue of being brain states that beliefs are causally explanatory – even if they were brain states. Finally, I argue that the Standard View does not show how beliefs can be causally explanatory in any case. In the next chapter, I propose an alternative to the Standard View.

A TEST FOR EXPLANATORY ADEQUACY

A great deal rides on our finding causal explanations of such intentional phenomena as the defection of the working class from the Democratic party, Ross Perot's appeal, child abuse, the growth of the deficit. Hence it seems methodologically misguided to begin with a Standard View metaphysics that precludes the causal explanations we want, need, and are willing to pay millions to find. It is better to start with explanations that work.

What I offer is only a test for determining that one has a causal explanation. It is not an analysis or a theoretical account of causation or of causal explanation. Indeed, the test purports to provide only a sufficient condition for a causal explanation; many causal explanations will elude the test. The basic idea is that we know that

121

we have an adequate causal explanation when it affords control over phenomena of the type explained. When we can produce or prevent a phenomenon at will, we know that we have found a cause.[1] So, if control of some property yields control of some phenomenon, we have a causal explanation of the phenomenon. Here, then, is what I call the 'Control Test': Let C be circumstances in which someone can produce or prevent an occurrence of a certain type of phenomenon, G, by producing or preventing an occurrence of another type of phenomenon, F, where an occurrence of F is temporally distinct from an occurrence of G and an occurrence of F does not itself entail an occurrence of G.[2] Then:

> (CT) An occurrence of F in C causally explains an occurrence of G in C if: (i) If an F had not occurred in C, then a G would not have occurred in C; and (ii) given that an F did occur in C, an occurrence of G was inevitable.

I make no great claims for (CT); indeed, I do not find it very illuminating. But as unrobust as (CT) is, it is useful for its generality: There is no special pleading for intentional explanations, psychological or nonpsychological. The vagueness of the expressions 'someone' and 'can produce or prevent' does not matter here; for in the examples at issue, it is not only empirically possible but even feasible to bring about the phenomena in question.

(CT) does not require causal explanations to be claims about the internal states of anything.[3] Although some philosophers hold that

---

1 Richard Miller has pointed out, "all means of control are causes, even if the converse is not true." Richard Miller, *Fact and Method: Explanation, Confirmation and Reality in the Natural and Social Sciences* (Princeton: Princeton University Press, 1987), 104.

2 The requirement of temporal distinctness is intended to rule out constitutional explanations as causal explanations. (An arrangement of molecules in marble does not causally explain a statue.) The requirement that an occurrence of F not entail an occurrence of G is intended to rule out cases in which explanans and explananda would be "definitionally" linked. (One's sister's having a baby does not causally explain one's becoming an aunt.) Recall that the term 'phenomenon' is a general term that covers properties, conditions, and states of affairs.

3 (CT) differs from other counterfactual approaches to mental causation in its indifference to internal states. Contrast (otherwise congenial) views of causal explanatoriness of properties in Terence Horgan, "Mental Quasation," in *Philosophy of Mind and Action Theory, 1989* (Philosophical Perspectives 3), ed. James E. Tomberlin (Atascadero, CA: Ridgeview, 1989), 47–76; and Ernest LePore and Barry Loewer, "More on Making Mind Matter," *Philosophical Topics* 17 (1989): 175–91. Also see John Haugeland, "Phenomenal Causes," in *Spindel Conference 1983: Su-*

causal explanations explain by citing underlying physical mechanisms,[4] we have seen that intentional explanations generally do no such thing; explanations that do cite underlying physical mechanisms are a special case, useful in some of the physical sciences, but by no means exhaustive of causal explanations. Indeed, many kinds of causation, intentional and nonintentional, are right out in the open: Julia Child sees the knife *slice* the bread; the eyewitness saw the defendant *push* the victim; I smelled the gas *filling* the room: she heard someone *light* a match; he felt a bee *sting* his arm; he heard the high note *shatter* the glass; she saw the building *crush* the automobile; I saw her *copying* the list of phone numbers; she saw the burglar *pick* the lock.[5] These straightforward causal judgments are not hypotheses about internal states of anything: The causation is right on the surface for anyone to see. In some of these examples, the causation is intentional: The defendant pushed the victim; the burglar picked the lock; the assistant copied the list. But with respect to causal explanatoriness of properties, the intentional-nonintentional distinction just fades in importance.

Let me entertain some objections to (CT):

1. (CT) is obviously circular: The idea of producing and preventing phenomena is itself clearly a causal notion. It's no good to use causal notions to understand causation. *Reply:* (CT) is not an analysis or a theory of causation; it is a test to determine whether we are in possession of a certain kind of causal explanation. We discover causes (and we philosophize about them) *in media res,* so to speak, not in a Cartesian vacuum.

2. (CT) is intentional and hence its use as a test for causal explanations begs the question in favor of intentionality. *Reply:* (CT) no more presupposes intentionality than does scientific experimentation. If someone gives a good account of scientific practice that has no presuppositions about intentionality, then that account can be used to explain away the appearance of intentionality in (CT).

pervenience, ed. Terence Horgan (*Southern Journal of Philosophy* 22, suppl. [1984]), 63–70.

4 See, for example, Wesley C. Salmon, *Scientific Explanation and the Causal Structure of the World* (Princeton: Princeton University Press, 1984).

5 G. E. M. Anscombe makes a similar point in "Causality and Determination," in *Metaphysics and Philosophy of Mind, Collected Papers* vol. 2 (Minneapolis: University of Minnesota Press, 1981), 133–47. Also see Frederick Stoutland, "On Not Being a Behaviorist," in *Perspectives on Human Conduct,* ed. L. Hertzberg and J. Pietarinen (Leiden: E. J. Brill, 1988), 48–60.

3. (CT) is subject to counterexamples. *Reply:* (CT) correctly withholds its imprimatur from standard counterexamples to accounts of causal explanation:

a. Counterexamples based on "preemption": For example, it would seem that we could causally explain Henry's weight gain one morning by his having eaten chocolate cake the night before. But Henry's having eaten chocolate cake may not pass (CT). For suppose that Henry liked pie almost as much as he liked cake, and if in the circumstances he had not eaten the cake, he would have had pie (and gained weight overnight). So, even with total control over Henry's cake consumption, we may have no control over his weight gain. *Reply:* I am not claiming that passing (CT) is a necessary condition of the causal explanatoriness of a property, only that it is a sufficient condition. My aim is to come up with a general test the passing of which assures us that we have a causal explanation; so if (CT) misses some causal explanations, that is all right so long as there are no "false positives." No doubt there are many causal properties beyond our ability to control, even in principle, but intentional properties are not – or not always – among them.

b. Counterexamples based on "common cause": Suppose that Jack and Jill went on a picnic and both ate poisonous mushrooms and became ill.[6] If Jack had not got sick, Jill would not have got sick; yet, we do not want to say that Jack's getting sick causally explains Jill's getting sick: Each got sick because he or she had eaten poisonous mushrooms. *Reply:* Fortunately, Jack's getting sick does not pass (CT) as a causal explanation of Jill's getting sick. For if an experimenter had prevented Jack's getting sick by not allowing him to eat the poisonous mushrooms, and not interfering in any other way, Jill (who ate the mushrooms) would still have gotten sick. Preventing or producing Jack's getting sick in the circumstances does not prevent or produce Jill's getting sick.

c. Counterexamples based on explanatory irrelevance:[7] Suppose that Al takes his wife's birth-control pills right on schedule and

---

6 This is a simplified example along lines of one offered by Salmon in *Scientific Explanation and the Causal Structure of the World*, 158.

7 For detailed discussion of famous counterexamples to the deductive-nomological model of explanation, see Wesley C. Salmon, "Four Decades of Scientific Explanation," in *Scientific Explanation,* ed. Philip Kitcher and Wesley C. Salmon (Minneapolis: University of Minnesota, 1989), 3–219.

does not get pregnant. As constant as the conjunction of his taking the pills and not getting pregnant is, we do not want to explain his not getting pregnant by his taking the pills. *Reply:* Fortunately, again, (CT) gives the right result. If we had prevented Al from taking the pills, he still would not have become pregnant. So, the property cited in the bogus explanation of Al's not getting pregnant does not pass (CT).

Now let me turn to the virtues of (CT):

1. (CT) accords with the fundamental idea of causes as "making a difference" to their effects. It may be used in conjunction with Mill's methods; yet, it is neutral with respect to accounts of the nature of causation (e.g., Humean regularity accounts vs. Lewisian counterfactual dependence accounts).

2. (CT) is perfectly general: It is not tailored to accommodate psychological (or any other special kind of) explanations. Although (CT) only reaches a certain kind of causal explanation – explanations of phenomena within our control – it has the advantage of being a single test for all explanations of such phenomena. With respect to causal explanatoriness, (CT) makes no distinction between intentional and nonintentional explanations; it draws no a priori line that relegates some class of explanations to second-class status; it neither mandates nor precludes reductions. (Methodologically, this is as it should be: Reductions are where you find them; they are not the deliverances of metaphysical speculation – even of speculation on the future of science.)

3. (CT) is compatible with materialism without entailing it. Methodologically, (CT) gets things right. Rather than deriving standards of adequacy on explanations from a metaphysical picture (and ruling out most otherwise successful explanations), (CT) allows us to reverse the order. The explanations that pass (CT) are reliable, and, for my money, reliability is a better mark of truth than is conformity to metaphysical strictures.

Although my concern here is with causal explanation, not with the metaphysics of causation per se, it is noteworthy that (CT) seems compatible with various metaphysical theories of causation. One such theory that seems at least in part congenial is Richard Miller's. According to Miller, 'cause' is *a core concept:*

The concept of a cause, like the concept of a number or of a work of art, centers on a diverse but stable core of cases: impact's causing motion, pain's causing crying, and so on through the paradigmatically banal examples (compare counting and measuring numbers, or representational easel paintings and statues, as part of the core for 'work of art').[8]

Miller goes on to say, "Further development from the core outward is governed by science, not by a general analysis." Although I heartily agree that further development is not governed by a general analysis, I would not envisage science (at least in any disciplinary sense) as the only source of development from the core: changes in our practices and institutions generate new causal patterns. In any case, the idea of a core-plus-development allows that certain "specific, elementary interpretations of events as involving genuine causation, not just correlation, have no justification and need none."[9] Indeed, reasons belong to the core, and thus need no special justification as causes. It is no more surprising that we should have a capacity to identify motives than that we have a capacity to identify physical shapes.[10]

Here are some important features of Miller's view for my purposes: (1) It is antipositivistic: Causal explanations are not understood in terms of deduction from covering laws. (2) It is nonreductive: There are no microphysical constraints on explanatory properties. (3) It allows that standards of explanatory adequacy be field-specific and pragmatic: Practical concerns may dictate choice of a standard causal pattern – as when we seek the causes of racial prejudice in order to reduce it.[11]

Many philosophers may accept (CT) as a test for causal explanatoriness, but go on to insist that while (CT) may yield a kind of low-grade or second-rate causal explanation, genuinely adequate explanations explain wholly in terms of physical properties of internal states. It is to this view – which is based on an illusion of "depth" – that I now want to turn.

THE AUTONOMY OF INTENTIONAL EXPLANATIONS

Some philosophers take intentional explanations as a kind of resting place on the way to deeper, physical explanations that will ulti-

---

8 Miller, *Fact and Method*, 6.
9 Ibid., 82.
10 Ibid., 128, 129.
11 Ibid., 94.

mately replace them.[12] I think that such a view is profoundly mistaken: Intentional explanations are autonomous and irreplaceable by physical explanations. In this section, I argue for the autonomy of intentional explanations, and in the next section, I use this thesis to help undermine a major motivation for the Standard View.

The relevant contrast is between intentional explanations (that ignore physical constituents of intentional phenomena) and physical explanations of the constituents of those phenomena. For example, an intentional explanation of why Bush pardoned Weinberger may advert to Bush's assessment of the political situation, to his own long-standing beliefs and desires, to the influence of advisers, and so on. A physical explanation with which this may be contrasted – call it a 'physical counterpart' of the intentional explanation – may advert to all manner of bodily motions, to marks on paper, to audible emissions, and so on. The physical-counterpart explanation gives causal information about the physical events that constituted the pardon of Weinberger. Ultimately, physical-counterpart explanations cite fundamental properties of microphysics. For whatever would impel one to take intentional phenomena (e.g., pardoning, believing) to be constituted by nonintentional phenomena (e.g., audible emissions, brain states) in the first place would also impel one to take brain states to be constituted by molecular states and so on "down" until one reaches entities that have only such properties as expressed by predicates like 'is a neutrino'.

If a physical-counterpart explanation of, say, the pardoning of Weinberger is to replace the intentional explanation, then either the physical-counterpart explanation is a "deeper" explanation of the pardon than the intentional explanation, or the physical-counterpart explanation simply supersedes the intentional explanation, as Copernican astronomy supersedes Ptolemaic astronomy.[13] First, I ar-

12 For example, Daniel C. Dennett said, "Of course, if some version of mechanistic physicalism is true (as I believe), we will never *need* absolutely to ascribe any intentions to anything." "Conditions of Personhood," in *Brainstorms: Philosophical Essays on Mind and Psychology* (Montgomery, VT: Bradford Books, 1978), 273.

13 It may be supposed that one explanation may replace another if they are merely equivalent, with neither being superior to the other. The argument in the text against a physical-counterpart explanation's being deeper than an intentional explanation may also be deployed against a physical-counterpart explanation's being equivalent to an intentional explanation.

gue that a physical–counterpart explanation is not a "deeper" explanation of the intentional phenomenon; and then I argue that the physical–counterpart explanation can not simply supersede the intentional explanation. Therefore, I conclude, intentional explanations are irreplaceable by physical–counterpart explanations.

Consider a particular savings and loan institution (S&L) that failed. An explanation of its bankruptcy in terms of its investments is an intentional explanation. Nothing is a bankruptcy or an investment in a world without complex economic practices, practices that could not exist in a world without attitudes. So, to say that 'being an investment' is an intentional property in the relevant sense is not just to say that nothing is an investment unless it is done for a reason. (Being done for a reason is much more psychological than what is intended here.) A particular electronic transfer may be an investment even if it was made accidentally; what makes it an investment is not that it was done for a reason, but that it occurred in the context of certain financial practices. So, suppose that a single disastrous investment in condominiums and office buildings causally explains the S&L's bankruptcy. This explanation is a non-psychological intentional explanation.

Consider a physical counterpart of such an explanation. The physical counterpart would be an explanation of the microphysical state that constituted the collapse of the S&L in terms of the microphysical state that constituted the making of the investment.[14] Suppose that the fatal investment had been made by electronic transfer from point A to point B. Call the microphysical state that constituted (i.e., materially composed) the making of the investment a 'U-state', where U-states are defined by the local physical properties of a certain kind of stream of electrons. Also suppose that the moment of insolvency is identified with another electronic event that requested transfer of funds that the S&L did not have.[15] Call the microphysical state that constituted this electronic request an 'F-

14 The physical explanations must bottom out in explanations in terms of fundamental physics. The relations between macrophysical explanations (e.g., lightning caused the tree to fall) and microphysical explanations (e.g., electrons, perhaps quarks, instantiated certain laws) are as murky as any; but for some reason, physicalists do not seem to find these puzzling.
15 As a simplification, I am identifying the onset of bankruptcy with the moment of insolvency. Actually, since bankruptcy is a legal state, the onset of bankruptcy should be identified with microphysical events underlying a certain judge's bodily motions. This point makes no difference to the example.

state', where F-states are also defined by the physical properties of a kind of stream of electrons. Now suppose that, by an extremely complex physical process, U caused F. (If this seems unlikely to you, then you are already skeptical that a physical–counterpart explanation is a deeper explanation of the bankruptcy than is the intentional explanation.)

For the purposes of this argument, I am stipulating the following: (1) An explanation of this particular S&L's bankruptcy in terms of its investment is an acceptable explanation of the bankruptcy (as acceptable as intentional explanations get); and (2) the investment is constituted by a complex physical state that I am calling a 'U-state', and the event of bankruptcy is constituted by a complex physical state that I am calling an 'F-state'; and (3) there are complex physical laws in virtue of which U-states cause F-states. According to the view that I want to refute, an explanation in terms of U-states is a deeper explanation of the failure of the S&L than is the explanation in terms of investments. On the contrary, I try to show that, even with the given stipulations, the microphysical states are explanatorily irrelevant to the failure of the S&L.[16]

There are both epistemological and metaphysical points to be made here. First, an epistemological point: The justification for claiming that the investments caused the failure of the S&L needs no recourse to anything specifiable in terms of microphysical states. Justification of the intentional explanation would invoke intentional phenomena; for example, if the S&L had not made the fatal investment but had invested in another venture that had been considered, it could have covered its small other losses and remained solvent. If justification of the intentional explanation depended on knowing anything about such underlying physical states, we would never be justified in claiming that the bad investments, or any other investments, ever caused anything. Indeed, we do not even know any nonintentional *macrophysical* explanations for bankruptcies. (Explanations in terms of contracts, cash flow, or even data entries all have intentional presuppositions.)

Furthermore, although a main purpose of looking for causes of

16 David Owens takes a similar position. He holds that "the primacy of physics does not entail the hegemony of physical explanation." See his "Levels of Explanation," *Mind* 95 (1989): 59–79. My objective is somewhat different from his, however. My argument against explanatory reduction is intended to open up space, as it were, for an alternative to the Standard View.

the failure of an S&L is to prevent such costly debacles in the future, knowing the underlying physical states U and F would not help prevent future S&L failures. Since any single investment may be constituted by indefinitely many different combinations of microphysical states – quadrillions, perhaps – a physical explanation in terms of the U-state's causing the F-state would not be "projectable" to future S&L failures: Two similar S&L failures would almost surely be constituted by wholly dissimilar microphysical phenomena, and hence almost surely have wholly different physical-counterpart explanations. Thus, to count the physical explanation an explanation of the S&L's collapse would simply defeat the point of explanation.

The reason that a physical-counterpart explanation would give no predictive grip on future failures of S&L's leads to the metaphysical point. Under what conditions would a physical-counterpart explanation of an intentional phenomenon be a deeper explanation than the intentional explanation? The answer concerns supervenience. The root idea of supervenience is that some properties (the supervening properties) depend on underlying properties (the subvening, or base, properties). Two things that are just alike in their base properties are just alike in the properties that supervene on the base properties. For example, if being a good person supervenes on being a kind, honest, and generous person, then two people who are just alike in terms of kindness, honesty, and generosity are just alike in terms of goodness. One of them is good if and only if the other is good. So: A property P supervenes on a property P^* only if, necessarily, for any instantiation of P^* there is an instantiation of P.[17] Say that an explanation E supervenes on an explanation E^* only if for any property mentioned in E, there are properties mentioned in E^* on which the E-property supervenes. Now: Explana-

17 As I am characterizing it, supervenience is a reflexive, nonsymmetrical, and transitive relation that allows for multiple realizability of supervening properties. Jaegwon Kim, whose articles have generated the current discussion of supervenience, defines 'supervenience' as a relation between *families* of properties. Assuming, as do many proponents of the Standard View, that any Boolean combination of properties is a property, reference to families is dispensable. But even if we retain the terminology of 'families', supervenience requires that each member of the supervening family depends on some set of properties in the base family in this sense: Necessarily, if the relevant properties in the base family are instantiated, then the supervening property is instantiated. For a more precise discussion of supervenience (and varieties of supervenience), see Chapter 7.

tion E^* is a deeper explanation of the phenomenon explained by E only if E supervenes on E^*.

Is the explanation in terms of U-states a deeper explanation of the S&L's collapse than the explanation in terms of investments? The answer is yes if and only if the worlds in which both the U-state and the F-state obtain are worlds in which the S&L made certain investments and went bankrupt. But the supervenience relations do not hold.

To see that the relevant supervenience relations do *not* hold, notice that U-states and F-states could occur spontaneously in outer space, or in a world just like ours after nuclear war. (A few years ago, our politicians were warning us that a world like ours that had been obliterated by nuclear war was a very nearby world.) But in the absence of an economic system, such states would constitute neither the making of bad investments nor financial failure. A U-state constitutes an investment in the actual world, and an F-state constitutes a bankruptcy in the actual world; but *in the world without an economic system,* the macrostates constituted by the U-state and the F-state would not have the properties of being an investment and being a bankruptcy, respectively. Hence, being an investment does not supervene on the property of being a U-state, and being a bankruptcy does not supervene on the property of being an F-state. Since the property of being an investment does not supervene on the property of being a U-state, and the property of the S&L's collapse does not supervene on the property of being an F-state, the explanation of the F-state in terms of the U-state is not a deeper explanation of the S&L's collapse. To summarize:

1. Explanation E^* is a deeper explanation of the phenomenon explained by E only if E supervenes on E^*.
2. The explanation of the S&L's bankruptcy in terms of investments does not supervene on the explanation in terms of U-states.

Therefore,

3. The explanation in terms of U-states is not a deeper explanation of the S&L's bankruptcy than is the explanation in terms of investments.

Intuitively, this conclusion seems to me unsurprising. Explanations always support counterfactuals. The antecedents and consequents of counterfactuals supported by the purely physical explanation do not "track" the antecedents and consequents of counterfactuals supported by the intentional explanation. The counterfactuals supported by an explanation of the S&L's failure should include this one: If the S&L had not made the investments, it would not have failed. However, the physical explanation would only support a counterfactual like this: 'If the U-state had not occurred, the F-state would not have occurred'. But to say that the U-state did not occur (in some other world) says nothing about whether an S&L failed in that world. For, as we have seen, the occurrence of these microphysical states is neither necessary nor sufficient for the S&L's failure: The occurrence of the U-state is not necessary for the S&L's failure since the failure could have been constituted by quadrillions of other microphysical states, had they occurred instead of the F-state;[18] the occurrence of the U-state is not sufficient for the S&L's failure since in worlds without the embedding economic systems, the U-state (and F-state) obtain without being S&L failures.

Let me venture a diagnosis of the situation. Philosophers have conflated supervenience (a relation among properties) with constitution (a relation among things). Let me explain. A statue is constituted by (or, some may hold, is identical to) some bunch of molecules, but its property of being a statue does not supervene on the properties of the molecules. The thing is a statue in virtue of its place in the art world, or the intention of its designer, or its aesthetic qualities (such as expressiveness), or maybe something else. But none of these potential art-making properties supervenes on the properties of the molecules that constitute the statue. The properties of constituent molecules are not what makes something a statue. The fact that the statue is constituted by molecules does not imply that its property of being a statue supervenes on the properties of its constituent molecules.

What is true of the property of being a statue is true of (wide) intentional properties generally: *supervenience* relations (among properties) diverge from *constitution* relations (among things). This point has gone unnoticed, I think, because of excessive concern for

18 Someone may object that had some non-F states constituted the failure of the S&L, there would have been a different failure. But we do not individuate economic (or other social phenomena) this way. If there had been a different guest list, there may have been a different dinner party; but there would not have been a different dinner party if one of the guests had had her hair cut a millimeter shorter. There would be no explanatory value in individuating macroevents so finely, even if we could do it.

nonrelational properties of the physically described world.[19] For nonintentional macrophysical properties, supervenience and constitution go together: A sample of water is constituted by a group of H_2O molecules, and the (macrophysical) properties of the water sample, like wetness, supervene on the properties of the molecules. But in the case of intentional properties, supervenience and constitution come apart. Even though a counterfeit bill is constituted by a certain group of molecules, the bill's property of being counterfeit does not supervene on any properties of those molecules: Of two molecularly identical pieces of paper, one may be counterfeit and the other genuine. What makes a bill a counterfeit is not its physical structure. A physical duplicate of a genuine bill may be counterfeit if printed by an unauthorized person.

Apply this point to the case of the S&L. If we assume that the U-state is the microphysical state constituting the bad investment, and that the F-state is the microphysical state constituting the S&L's failure, what would make a physical explanation of the F-state in terms of the U-state an explanation of the S&L's failure? One may be tempted to say: The S&L's investments supervene on the U-state, and the S&L's failure supervenes on the F-state. But this answer harbors the fatal equivocation: The S&L's investments *are constituted by* the U-state, but the property of being an investment does *not supervene on* the property of being a U-state. This is the reason that a physical explanation of the F-state would not be an explanation of the S&L's failure, even though (by hypothesis) the S&L's failure is constituted by the F-state.

The fact that the F-state constitutes the S&L failure in the actual world depends on the social and economic institutions of the actual world. It is not in virtue of supervenience that the F-state constitutes the S&L failure; for there is no such supervenience relation between the property of being F and the property of being an S&L failure. This result is not at odds with a suitably relaxed materialism. Although the property of being an S&L failure does not supervene on the property of being an F-state, it may well supervene on widely distributed physical properties; if so, the relevant physical properties would be those that determine a certain kind of econom-

19 As I elaborate in Chapter 6, the conflation is abetted by equivocal use of the term 'physically realized by' sometimes to refer to a relation among things and sometimes to refer to a relation among properties.

ic system – a whole complex set of practices – not just the local properties that determine F-states. A supervenience base for the property of being a bank failure or for the property of being an investment would include properties instantiated over vast reaches of space and time, extended far enough to include all the physical property instantiations on which economic practices depend – perhaps back to Adam Smith's day, or even to the Big Bang.[20] Therefore, the fact that the S&L collapse does not supervene on the property of being an F-state leaves open the possibility that it does supervene on properties of (widely scattered) physical states.

Even if a physical explanation of the microstate that constituted the S&L's failure is not a deeper explanation of that failure, one may be thinking along eliminativist lines, like this: "Nevertheless, the physical explanation could totally supersede the intentional explanation. The relation between the physical and intentional explanations may not be one of deep to shallow, but rather one of true to false. The explanation of combustion in terms of oxygen is not deeper than an explanation in terms of phlogiston, but it supersedes the phlogiston explanation nonetheless. Why shouldn't the relation between intentional and physical explanations be like the relation of explanations in terms of phlogiston to those in terms of oxygen?"

My reply: The situations are disanalogous. First, there are reliable (though hedged) generalizations about investments that are part of a network of economic generalizations, but not about phlogiston that are part of a network of chemical generalizations. Second, phlogiston explanations and oxygen explanations were competitors within a single science; they could not both be correct. Investment explanations and U-state explanations are not even obvious competitors. They find their places in very different sciences (economics and fundamental physics), and there is no prima facie reason that they cannot both be correct in their respective domains.

The third reason the investment versus U-state explanations are not analogous to the phlogiston versus oxygen explanations is that the phlogiston and oxygen explanations share a single explanandum, for example, the calx's getting heavier. But there is a sense in which the U-state explanation and the investment explanation ex-

---

20 Since I take explanations to have epistemic import, I would not call anything requiring reference to such a vast array of unspecifiable properties an 'explanation'.

plain different things: The U-state explanation explains a physical phenomenon (the occurrence of the F-state) that also happened to constitute a bank failure; the investment explanation explains the bank failure *as* a bank failure. (To put this in the perhaps unfortunate language of essence and accident: The U-state explanation explains a phenomenon that is accidentally a bank failure; the investment explanation explains a phenomenon that is essentially a bank failure.)

Fourth, there is a single explanatory interest that either the phlogiston explanation or the oxygen explanation would have been equally able to satisfy. The U-state explanation and the investment explanation, however, answer to quite different explanatory interests. The U-state explanation would be useless to anyone interested in bank failures per se; it would support no predictions about future bank failures. Since we obviously have explanatory interests in bank failures, and intentional explanations can serve such interests while physical explanations cannot, intentional explanations cannot be replaced by or made redundant by physical–counterpart explanations. I take the S&L case to be exemplary; similar arguments apply to other cases of nonpsychological intentional phenomena.

To sum up the argument for the autonomy of intentional explanations: Physical–counterpart explanations can replace intentional explanations only if either the physical–counterpart explanations are deeper explanations of the intentional phenomena or they drive out the intentional explanations as true theories drive out false ones. Since intentional explanations do not supervene on physical–counterpart explanations, physical–counterpart explanations are not deeper explanations of intentional phenomena; and since physical–counterpart explanations cannot serve the predictive and explanatory purposes that are well served by intentional explanations, physical–counterpart explanations do not drive out intentional explanations. Therefore, physical–counterpart explanations cannot replace intentional explanations.

Many philosophers believe that the only genuine explanatory properties are physical properties, but that explanations that cite nonphysical properties still may have a lower-grade explanatory value.[21] Thus, on this view, although we use intentional explana-

21 Variations on this theme of reductive materialism may be found in Wesley C. Salmon, Jaegwon Kim, and W. V. O. Quine.

tions for practical affairs, their causal-explanatory value depends upon their relation to explanations in terms of wholly physical properties. Far from providing deeper explanations, however, I have tried to show that physical-counterpart explanations cannot replace intentional explanations.

In general, we should distinguish between having an adequate causal explanation and knowing the physical conditions that in fact obtain when the explanatory properties are instantiated.[22] Knowing physical conditions for the instantiation of explanatory properties may be irrelevant to assessing the putative explanation. Similarly, knowing the physics of television broadcast transmission may be irrelevant to understanding the influence of television on children who watch it; knowing the chemistry of paint may be irrelevant to assessing Raphael's place in the history of painting. On the other hand, knowing the physics of television broadcast transmission may be just what you need if you want to sabotage Saturday morning cartoons; and knowing the chemistry of paint may be just what you need if you want to restore *The School of Athens*. But we should not conclude that the adequacy of an intentional explanation depends on any particular relation between the intentional properties and physical properties.

From the S&L case, I want to draw two morals: (1) Appeal to constitution is generally irrelevant to explaining intentional phenomena; for facts about constitution do not support the counterfactuals needed for explanation of intentional phenomena. (2) Intentional causal explanations need not (indeed, generally do not) cite "inner causes" of physical objects. Both morals apply to belief explanations – as we shall see when we turn to the Practical Realist alternative to the Standard View.

MOTIVATION FOR THE STANDARD VIEW UNDERMINED

The major motivation for the Standard View is that the Standard View seems required in order to understand how beliefs can be causally explanatory. In this section, I want to meet the challenge of the Standard View by arguing that, even if beliefs were constituted by brain states, it would not be by dint of their being so constituted

22 Tyler Burge has made this point. See his "Individualism and Psychology," *Philosophical Review* 95 (1986): 3–45.

136

that they are causally explanatory. I shall put this point variously by saying that beliefs need not be (or be constituted by) brain states in order to be causally explanatory, or that the causal explanatoriness of beliefs does not require them to be brain states. My aim here is to undermine a central motivation for the Standard View, the first premise of the Argument from Causal Explanation in Chapter 1:

> (IIIa) Unless beliefs were brain states, they could not causally explain behavior,

and thereby to clear the way for supplanting the Standard View with a Practical Realist view of belief.

Call (IIIa) – the thesis that, unless beliefs were (either identical to or constituted by) brain states, they could not causally explain behavior – the "brain explain" thesis.[23] In this section, I argue that the "brain explain" thesis is false.[24] To avoid begging the question against the Standard View when I undermine its motivation, at this stage I must not take the Standard View to be false. So the argument against the "brain explain" thesis in this section is that the "brain explain" thesis is false, whether the Standard View is true or false. The argument against the "brain explain" thesis has as an outermost shell a simple dilemma:

> If the Standard View is true, then the "brain explain" thesis is false; if the Standard View is false, then the "brain explain" thesis is false. Therefore, the "brain explain" thesis is false.

Most of my effort in this section is directed toward establishing the first premise of the shell argument: If the Standard View is true, then the "brain-explain" thesis is false. To this end, I shall present a conditional proof, with the weakest version of the Standard View as conditional premise.

The weakest version of the Standard View, entailed by all other versions, is that beliefs are constituted by brain states, where consti-

---

23 Robert van Gulick suggested the label in his comment on my "Attitudes as Nonentities" at the Oberlin Colloquium on April 17, 1993, to be published in *Philosophical Studies*. His acute comments prompted many improvements in my arguments.
24 I want to be clear about the dialectic here. The argument against the "brain explain" thesis is not itself intended to refute the Standard View. My direct arguments against the Standard View are directed at specific versions of it in Chapters 2 and 3.

tution is understood as material composition. Just as for each statue, there is a chunk of marble, wood, or something else that constitutes (i.e., materially composes) that statue, so – according to the
Standard View – for each occurrence of a belief, there is a particular
brain state that constitutes that occurrence of that belief. The general metaphysical picture is that things have constituents, and that
those constituents have further constituents, and so on. The ultimate constituents are those with fundamental physical properties.
Constitution is supposed to be a very general phenomenon: Rain is
constituted by drops of water, which are constituted by molecules;
wars (e.g., the U.S. Civil War) are constituted by battles (e.g., the
Battle of Gettysburg), which are constituted by troop movements
(e.g., Pickett's Charge), which are constituted by the advancing of
individual soldiers, which are constituted by bodily motions, and
so on. Since constitution is a transitive relation, once we get started
on this road to the physical, there is no stopping at the level of
macrophenomena.

Here is the argument – a conditional proof with the weakest
version of the Standard View as conditional premise (CP) – that if
the Standard View is true, then the "brain explain" thesis is false:[25]

(CP) Beliefs have brain states as constituents.

(P1) No intentional explanation is replaceable by physical explanations of the constituents of the intentional phenomena.

(P2) Belief explanations are intentional explanations.

From (P1), (P2), and (CP), we have

(C1) No belief explanation is replaceable by brain-state explanations.

(P3) If the "brain explain" thesis is true, then belief explanations
are replaceable by brain-state explanations of the same phenomena.

From (P3) and (C1), we have

(C2) The "brain explain" thesis is false.

Discharging the assumption (CP) of the conditional proof, we have

25 Goeffrey Goddu helped improve this argument.

138

(C3) If beliefs have brain states as constituents, the "brain explain" thesis is false.

That is, even if the Standard View is true, beliefs need not be (identical to or constituted by) brain states in order to be causally explanatory. The argument for (C3) is valid, but are its premises true?[26]

(P1)

The preceding section was an extended argument for (P1). In a nutshell, intentional explanations are irreplaceable by physical explanations of the constituents of intentional phenomena, because the identity of an intentional phenomenon is independent of the identity of its physical constituents.

(P2)

Turn now to (P2). Belief explanations are intentional explanations by definition. Nevertheless, there may be a worry here about "direction of fit": In effect, I am treating belief explanations as simply one kind of intentional explanation. To some philosophers – "methodological individualists" – this line will seem wrongheaded. Methodological individualism, as it was debated a couple of decades ago, is the view that facts about social groups (e.g., nations) were to be understood as facts about individuals (e.g., presidents, legislators, generals). From the point of view of the methodological individualist, it may seem that I am going in the wrong direction: In their view, social-scientific explanations should be reduced to belief explanations.

The worries of this kind of methodological individualist do not concern me. First, my position bypasses the old debate in the philosophy of the social sciences. My position concerns the explanatory status of relational properties with intentional presuppositions (like being counterfeit, being married), not with whether group behavior can be analyzed in terms of individual behavior. Even if a Supreme Court decision may be understood as the product of indi-

---

26 Reductive materialists are likely to resist (P1) and endorse (P3); nonreductive materialists are likely to endorse (P1) and resist (P3). Both reductive and nonreductive materialists take issue with (C3).

vidual decisions of the justices, the contents of those individual decisions almost surely have intentional presuppositions. My claim is that properties cited in belief explanations have the same explanatory status (they explain in the same way, and just as well) as other properties with intentional presuppositions, not that psychological properties are analyzable in terms of social properties. (I am making no claims about any kind of analysis.) The doctrine of methodological individualism concerns the conditions under which social properties are exemplified. But the explanatoriness of a property is guaranteed by (CT), regardless of the conditions under which the property is exemplified. Hence, I am not begging questions against any theories of what conditions must be satisfied for a given property to be exemplified. When a property is explanatory, when it plays a systematic role in explanations that are reliable, then we have good reason to think that the conditions for its exemplification, whatever they are, are fulfilled.

Second, if beliefs are individuated relationally – and there is an emerging consensus that they are – then one already holds that belief properties do not supervene on the intrinsic properties of believers. If belief properties supervene on physical properties at all, they supervene on the believer's intrinsic properties together with other properties in the environment. In this respect, belief properties are no different from other (more obviously social) properties with intentional presuppositions. Relational individuation of belief, by itself, rules out reduction of social properties to individuals' intrinsic properties. For even if one reduced social properties to psychological properties of individuals, those psychological properties would themselves be relational. And this is so, whether methodological individualism, as it has been debated in the social sciences, is correct or not. Thus, I see no objection to (P2).

(P3)

Finally consider (P3): If the "brain explain" thesis is true, then belief explanations are replaceable by brain-state explanations of the same phenomena. (P3) follows from a very general principle. Let E be a causal explanation that cites property P to explain some phenomenon F. Then, the causal explanatoriness of P depends on the relation of P to some lower-level property P^* only if E is replaceable by an explanation E^*, where E^* cites P^*. Since E is replaceable by E^* just in case either E is a deeper explanation of the same phenomenon than E^*, or E supersedes E^*, (P3) follows as an instance of the general principle. However, I really have no argument for the general principle other than intuition. So, let me try to defend (P3) in another way.

Some may object that (P3) is too strong. They may urge that the "brain explain" thesis is true *even if* belief explanations are not replaceable by brain-state explanations.[27] Such an objector may claim that if beliefs are actually constituted by brain states, then the "brain explain" thesis is true, regardless of whether or not belief explanations are replaceable by brain-state explanations.

I want to show that even if beliefs were constituted by brain states, it is not in virtue of their being so constituted that they are causally explanatory. I can agree that having certain kinds of brain states is a *necessary condition* for humans to have beliefs (and, of course, having beliefs at all is a necessary condition for having beliefs that are causally explanatory). But even if having certain kinds of brain states is a necessary condition for having beliefs, the "brain explain" thesis may still be false. Any time that a belief explains behavior, then all the necessary conditions for the having of the belief ipso facto are satisfied – whether the necessary conditions are that the believer have certain kinds of brain states, or that the believer be in a world with H_2O, or that the believer have been born more than five seconds ago. But, if we assume the "constitution" version of the Standard View to be contingent, the causal explanatoriness of belief does not require that beliefs be constituted by brain states (even if in fact they were so constituted). Suppose that the universe had turned out to have been Aristotelian. How would that have affected assumptions about the attitudes' being brain states? A lot: An Aristotelian (according to some interpretations) would not construe beliefs as brain states.[28] How would a supposed Aristotelian universe have affected our explanations of intentional phenomena? Not one whit: If the sensible and social world were the same as our world, we would have had the same range of explanations, deployed in the same ways and with the same degree of success, that we actually have. In an Aristotelian

---

27 I take this to be the view of nonreductive materialists like van Gulick.
28 For a discussion of various interpretations, see Michael V. Wedin, *Mind and Imagination in Aristotle* (New Haven: Yale University Press, 1988).

universe, we would still have explanations in terms of beliefs, as well as explanations in terms of making bad investments. Thus, since the explanatoriness of belief is compatible with the world's being Aristotelian, but beliefs' being brain states is not compatible with the world's being Aristotelian, it follows that the explanatoriness of the attitudes does not require that attitudes be identical to or constituted by brain states.

Some philosophers may be unconvinced by a thought experiment about an Aristotelian universe. One may suppose that nothing follows about our world, which is not Aristotelian. From the fact that we can imagine a world in which genes did not turn out to be sequences of DNA, it would not follow that the causal explanatoriness of genes in our world does not depend on their being sequences of DNA.[29] However, I believe that this analogy misfires.

First, we expect the difference between having blue eyes and having brown eyes to show up in DNA sequences in some way that is detectable by looking at DNA. But we (or I) do not expect the difference between believing that shooting an intruder is often excusable and believing that shooting an intruder is seldom excusable will ever be apparent from a purely neurophysiological point of view. Yet, the difference in the latter beliefs is important: If I were a defense attorney for the person accused of shooting an intruder, I would be quite interested in whether jurors had one belief rather than the other (or neither). Second, I believe that the gene-DNA analogy (like the water-H_2O analogy) is generally misleading as a guide to belief. There is a genetic *code* to break; the relationship between genes and DNA sequences is a kind of relativized type identity. Inquiry into DNA will trump any other consideration about which features are genetic features; but inquiry into brain states will not trump other considerations about whether a person has a certain belief, as I argue in Chapter 6.

Finally, and most important, we should distinguish between the issue of which properties are causally explanatory and the issue of what is required for a property to be causally explanatory. Although *which* properties are causally explanatory changes from world to world, the relation of causal explanatoriness itself does not. What makes it the case both in our world and in the Aristotelian world that beliefs are causally explanatory is that certain

29 I owe the objection to Robert van Gulick.

counterfactuals hold.[30] ("If she had not believed that the door would be unlocked, she would have taken the key.") Indeed, the same high-level counterfactuals about social and sensible phenomena hold in both worlds, and it is these counterfactuals that secure the causal explanatoriness of belief in both the actual world and the Aristotelian world, regardless of the issue of the constitution of belief. Thus, the fact that the actual world is not Aristotelian does not impugn the thought experiment.

In defense of (P3), I proposed (but did not argue for) an intuitive general principle of which (P3) is an instance; then I rebutted a nonreductive Standard View claim that if beliefs are actually constituted by brain states, then the causal explanatoriness of beliefs depends on beliefs' being brain states – even if belief explanations are not replaceable by brain-state explanations. On the contrary, I argued that even if beliefs in the actual world were constituted by brain states, the causal explanatoriness of beliefs would not depend on their being so constituted. Therefore, I see no good reason to reject (P3).

If (P1)–(P3) are true, then so is the first premise of the dilemma: If the Standard View is true, then the "brain explain" thesis is false. If the Standard View is false, then beliefs do not have brain states as constituents; so if the Standard View is false and if beliefs are causally explanatory, then the "brain explain" thesis is false. In either case, the "brain explain" thesis is false: Beliefs need not be identical with, or constituted by, brain states to be causally explanatory. Therefore, the argument from causal explanation for the Standard View (in Chapter 1) – the first premise of which is the "brain explain" thesis – is unsound.

To say that the *explanatoriness* of beliefs (or investments) is independent of their being brain states (or computer states) is not to say that beliefs or investments are in some sense "immaterial." They could not be immaterial – any more than our practices could be. Our practices are embodied: The macrophysical world provides brute constraints on what we do and how we do it – for example, we build sofas in the shapes that we do because our bodies bend the way they do and are comfortable in some positions and not in

---

30 Later in this chapter, I present an argument counter to the view that the term 'belief' rigidly designates whatever brain states cause intentional behavior. Such a view is not at issue in this section, however; here, I am considering 'beliefs are constituted by brain states' as a contingent thesis.

others – and we mold our practices around the relevant macro-physical facts.

HOW BELIEFS DO NOT EXPLAIN: THE STANDARD VIEW

So, even if beliefs were constituted by brain states, their causal explanatoriness would not derive from their being so constituted. Moreover, I do not think that the Standard View has any account of how beliefs construed as brain states can be causally explanatory anyway. On the Standard View, beliefs (if there are any) are explanatory because they are brain-state (tokens) that interact with other brain-state tokens to produce the behavior to be explained. This picture cannot account of the causal explanatoriness of belief.

Suppose I showed up at a lecture hall at four o'clock because I thought a lecture I wanted to hear would be delivered there then. Proponents of the Standard View would say that there was a brain-state token that was my belief that a certain lecture would be delivered in that place at that time, and that that token interacted with another brain-state token that was my desire to attend the lecture; and that this interaction produced further brain states that eventuated in the bodily motions that took me to the lecture hall. But on this view, the causal explanatoriness of the token neural state derives from its *intrinsic* physical properties; if we assume externalism (i.e., the view that beliefs are individuated in part by extrinsic properties, by reference to the individual's environment), what makes the brain state a belief that *p* are *extrinsic* properties. So, the fact that the brain state was a belief about a certain lecture was irrelevant to its interactions with other neural states. On this token-identity account, the property of believing that *p* just drops out of the causal-explanatory picture.[31] Hence, even if beliefs were token-identical to brain states, that fact would not show how believing that *p* could be causally explanatory.

One impressive attempt to reconcile an externalist version of the

---

31 Whence 'the problem of mental causation'. There is a huge literature on this problem. For example, see Stephen Yablo, "Mental Causation," *Philosophical Review* 101 (1992): 245–80; Robert van Gulick, "Who's in Charge Here? And Who's Doing All the Work?" in *Mental Causation*, ed. John Heil and Alfred Mele (Oxford: Clarendon Press, 1993), 233–56; Tyler Burge, "Mind-Body Causation and Explanatory Practice," ibid., 97–120. For my own direct response to the problem, see my "Metaphysics and Mental Causation," ibid., 75–95.

Standard View with the causal explanatoriness of beliefs has been presented by Frank Jackson and Philip Pettit. Construing beliefs as brain states, they agree that the property of believing that p is not a causally efficacious property. Nevertheless, Jackson and Pettit urge, the property of believing that p may still be causally explanatory.[32] In their view, belief explanations explain by quantifying over a range of efficacious properties (such as physical properties of brain states). Let's look at this account of how beliefs explain.

Jackson and Pettit try to show how beliefs (individuated by broad content) can be explanatory by showing how they may "programme" the phenomena that they explain without actually producing those phenomena. Program explanations "tell us about the range of states that do or would produce the result without telling us which state in fact did the job."[33] An attribution of belief in a program explanation picks out a range of internal states, "each member of which would have produced the result and one of which did in fact produce the result."[34]

If I am right, then this is *not* the way that belief explanations explain. To see that belief explanations could not explain by picking out a range of internal states, consider three questions: (1) What is the extent of the range? (2) How can individual brain states in the range be identified by investigators? (3) How do explanatory locutions ever acquire such a range as their extension? I believe none of these questions has a satisfactory answer. Suppose the explanation of Fox's vote against the school budget is that he believed it would raise taxes too much, and suppose the attribution – 'Fox believed that the proposed school budget would raise taxes too much' – picks out a range of internal states as Jackson and Pettit claim.

First, what is the extent of the range of brain states? All the states that would have caused Fox to vote against the school budget are in the range. What states are those? If the vote had been by secret ballot, the brain states would have included all those brain states that would have caused his hand to move in any of the ways that would have produced on paper what would count as a "no" vote; if the vote had been by right-hand raising, the states would have

---

32 Frank Jackson and Philip Pettit, "Functionalism and Broad Content," *Mind* 97 (1988): 381–400.
33 Ibid., 396.
34 Ibid., 393.

included all those brain states that would have caused his right hand to go up at a time that would count as a "no" vote; and so on for all the other ways the vote could have been taken. When we attribute the belief that the proposed budget would raise taxes too much, are we quantifying over all the brain states that would have produced any movement that would have counted as a "no" vote, no matter how the vote was taken, or are we only quantifying over those brain states that would have produced a movement that counted as a "no" vote, given the manner in which the vote was actually taken? The very meaning of the explanation rides on how this question is answered, but it is difficult to see what answer could be given. It is not even obvious that there is a fact of the matter about how many ways the vote could have been taken.

Second, how could the range – if there is a fact of the matter about what range it is – be identified by investigators? We must have some way of identifying the range other than as 'any of the brain states that would have caused a motion that would be a "no" vote'. Otherwise, recourse to program explanations is vacuous. To see this, suppose that we disagree about why Fox voted against the school budget. I attribute to him the belief that it would raise taxes too much; you attribute the belief that the school board takes kickbacks. If the only way to identify the relevant ranges of brain states is 'any of the brain states that would have caused a motion that was a "no" vote', there is no way to distinguish between your explanation and mine; the attributions would purport to pick out the same range, namely, the range that includes any of the brain states that would have caused a "no" vote. We have no nonintentional way to identify any particular brain state (much less a range of possible brain states) as being a belief that the school budget would raise taxes too much as opposed to a belief that the school board takes kickbacks. Nothing weaker than a type-identity theory – the prospects for which are dim – would yield a way to identify the range other than vacuously as the range any of whose states would have produced a motion that would have counted as a "no" vote.

Finally, how could the English ascription – 'believed that the proposed school budget would raise taxes too much' – ever have come to refer to such a motley of existing and nonexisting states? We attribute beliefs and successfully explain behavior in total ignorance of brain states. Our ability to use belief ascriptions in the way

146

that we do would be wholly mysterious if they explained by denoting brain states or by quantifying over brain states.

Proponents of the Standard View may reply like this: Just as people could use 'water' to pick out H_2O before anyone knew the chemical composition of water, so too we use 'belief' to pick out an internal state (or a range of internal states) before we know what neurophysiological states we are referring to. Such physicalists, I believe, err in assimilating 'belief' to physical natural kinds of terms like 'water'. For there are lots of nontrivial ways to pick out what 'water' refers to: 'That stuff [demonstrating a body of water]', 'the liquid with the same chemical composition as the stuff in mountain streams', and so on. Then, later it is discovered that that stuff is H_2O. But, in the absence of type identity, there is no similar way to identify a physical entity as a belief, and then later discover that it was a particular brain state. (Indeed, if connectionism is true, it would seem hopeless to suppose that particular brain-state tokens – global and distributed, as well as local and discrete – could be singled out as being particular beliefs. This result, I hasten to add, would cast no doubt on belief, but on the Standard View that takes beliefs to be identical to or constituted by brain states.)

So, if we need some account of how beliefs explain, Jackson and Pettit's view does not fill the bill. Indeed, I do not think that any account that bases the explanatoriness of belief on the putative connections between beliefs and brain states will succeed. As I have argued, the explanatoriness of belief – like the explanatoriness of the S&L's investments – depends in part on our practices and institutions, not wholly on physical states that constitute beliefs (still assuming that beliefs are constituted by anything at all). So, if we need a philosophical account of how beliefs explain, the thesis that beliefs are brain states will not supply it. Therefore, consideration of the causal explanatoriness of beliefs provides no ground for the Standard View of beliefs as brain states.

Philosophy of mind has gone astray in construing psychological properties like belief on the analogy of physical natural kinds like water.[35] To find the nature of water, identify the stuff that constitutes it: H_2O. But the analogy with belief does not hold: It no more

---

35 Even functionalists, who define beliefs in terms of causal role, typically identify a belief with the physical state that has the role in question.

follows that to find the nature of belief, identify the stuff that constitutes it than it would follow that to find the nature of money, find the stuff that constitutes it. There may or may not be something economically interesting about the physical constitution (or the physical realization) of, say, a bank's asset-to-debt ratio, but economists (and philosophers of economics) need take no special interest in physical realizations per se. So, too, there may or may not be something psychologically interesting about the physical realization of, say, a person's belief that she is being followed, but psychologists (and philosophers of psychology) need take no special interest in physical realizations per se. The legitimacy of psychology no more depends on particular physical realizations of explanatory states like belief than does the legitimacy of economics depend on particular physical realizations of explanatory states like the national debt. It should be obvious that it does not follow from any of this that beliefs (or the national debt) are realized in, or constituted by, some nonphysical stuff. The point that I am urging is that physical realization or constitution is simply irrelevant to the justificatory, explanatory, and predictive uses to which we put beliefs (or the national debt).

As a final example of the irrelevance of physical constitution to explanation of behavior, consider again the example of Fox's voting against the school budget because he thought that it would raise taxes too much. Suppose that the vote had been taken at a meeting with the following instructions in order to save time: "Raise your right hand if you are in favor of the budget, and your left hand if opposed." Finally, suppose that Fox had raised his left hand, thereby voting against the budget as he had intended.

According to the Standard View – and its ally, the so-called causal theory of action – Fox's "no" vote is to be understood as follows: Fox had a particular brain state that constituted his belief that the budget would raise taxes too much, and that brain state (partly) caused Fox's left arm to rise; and in the context, the left hand's rising constituted a "no" vote. There are three reasons why this Standard View picture seems not to illuminate either belief or action:

1. Amid all the electrical and chemical activity in the brain, there may not be any particular brain state identifiable as a belief that the budget would raise taxes too much among the myriad of brain states that contributed to Fox's left hand's going up.

148

2. The physical constitution of the action to be explained (e.g., the left hand's rising) is irrelevant to the identity of the action. Had the voting instructions been slightly different – "Raise your left hand if you are in favor of the budget, and your right hand if opposed" – the "no" vote (the *very same* "no" vote) would have been constituted by Fox's right hand's going up.

3. Anyone concerned with school budgets wants to predict and explain Fox's vote, not his left hand's rising – even if one agrees that there is a mechanistic, neurophysiological explanation of Fox's left hand's rising. Even if we take actions to be events, and even if we take the "no" vote actually to be constituted by the left hand's rising (in a certain context), the essential property of the event to be explained is that it is a "no" vote; its being a left hand's rising is the sheerest of accidents. Attention to the physical constitution of actions just diverts attention from what we want to explain. But if the physical constitution (the left hand's rising) of an action (the "no" vote) is not what needs explaining, then the motivation to advert to putative physical constitution (a brain state) of the causally explanatory property (the belief that the budget would raise taxes too much) is undercut.

In short, taking beliefs to be constituted by brain states does not shed light on the explanatoriness of the attitudes. Only in cases in which there is some malfunction (e.g., a brain tumor) or some interference (e.g., an implanted electrode) do particular brain states become relevant to explaining action – and even in those cases, there may be no "isomorphism" between particular brain states taxonomic in neurophysiology and particular attitudes.[36] When the brain is functioning normally, it is explanatorily irrelevant whether or not there are particular brain states that constitute each explanatory attitude.

CONCLUSION

The explanatoriness of belief explanations does not depend on relations that attitudes may bear to certifiably physical properties. In this respect, belief explanations are a species of explanations with

---

36 For a discussion of the role of the brain in mentality that is congenial to the views I am advocating, see Oliver Sacks, *The Man Who Mistook His Wife for a Hat* (New York: Summit, 1985).

intentional presuppositions. Belief explanations, I have argued, are not just stand-ins for deeper explanations. In normal cases, where there is no neurological or gross anatomical breakdown, belief explanations are as deep as we can get – without changing the subject – when we explain intentional action.[37] We do not use belief attributions to pick out brain states. The undeniable fact that brain damage interferes with mental functioning no more shows that belief attributions pick out a range of brain states than does the fact that damage to the wood interferes with the musical functioning of a violin show that aesthetic terms pick out a range of states of the wood.

Belief explanations, and intentional explanations generally, form patterns of explanation that require no vindication in terms of underlying mechanisms. Their justification resides in the reliability and indispensability of belief explanations – just as the justification of explanations of the behavior of gross material objects resides in their reliability and indispensability. There may well be scientifically fruitful investigation of the mechanisms that underlie, say, change of belief, but understanding such mechanisms should not be confused with understanding belief and its causal role in behavior – any more than understanding the mechanisms of broadcast transmission should be confused with understanding television and its causal role in contemporary society.

Philosophers of mind typically begin with a metaphysical conception of the nature of explanatory properties and then ask whether putative causal explanations (such as explanations in terms of attitudes) fit into the preset framework. I am urging a methodological about-face. Instead of beginning with metaphysical intuitions about science or reality, we should take our metaphysical cues – more empirically – from a consideration of successful explanatory practice. A defeasible test like (CT), I have argued, is well suited to actual everyday and scientific practice, as well as to the aims of explanation. Moreover, belief explanations, and intentional explanations generally, are certifiably causal explanations on (CT). Intentional explanations are neither replaceable by nonintentional explanations nor "merely heuristic." Without retreating to dualism, intentional explanations uniquely illuminate parts of reality that matter to everybody.

37 On this point, I agree with Davidson.

PART III

Practical Realism and its prospects

6

Belief without reification

The Standard View of the attitudes – shared by reductive, non-reductive, and eliminative materialists – takes beliefs, if there are any, to be constituted by brain states. In Part I, I criticized the Standard View directly, in both its eliminativist and noneliminativist versions. In Part II, I examined a central motivation for the Standard View – namely, the view that the causal explanatoriness of belief requires the Standard View – and found that the conception of causal explanation on which that motivation rests is too restrictive. To accommodate causal explanations that are successfully deployed in science and in everyday life, I proposed a general test for causal explanatoriness, which, I argued, belief explanations easily pass.[1] In this chapter, I ask, How should the attitudes be understood if they are to play their explanatory roles? If beliefs are not brain states, what are they? I offer what I am calling 'Practical Realism' as an alternative to the Standard View.

WHAT ARE BELIEFS?

According to Practical Realism, believing that *p* is an irreducible fact about a person. Although it may be extended to things other than organisms, Practical Realism (like the Standard View) in the first instance applies to paradigmatic believers: human beings.[2] The first claim of Practical Realism is that a belief is a global state of a whole person, not of any proper part of the person, such as the brain.[3] Persons have beliefs; brains have neural states. Having cer-

---

1 As we saw in Chapter 2, some may suspect that the defeat of belief explanations is imminent at the hands of connectionism. But such a suspicion simply presupposes the Standard View; on Practical Realism, connectionism offers no threat to belief.
2 I am not here attempting to give conditions for something to be subject to intentional states like belief. Rather, I am specifying conditions under which *S* believes that *p,* where *S* is a human being. Human beings have beliefs if anything does.
3 I agree with Daniel C. Dennett when he says: "The subject of all the intentional attributions is the whole system (the person, the animal, or even the corporation

tain neural states is, presumably, necessary for people to have beliefs; but it does not follow that for a person to have a particular belief, there is a neural state that constitutes that belief. Compare: Horses win races; legs have states. Having certain leg states is, presumably, necessary for horses to win races; but it does not follow that for a horse to win a particular race, there is a leg state that constitutes the winning of the race.

An attitude is a state in the attenuated sense in which a state of financial health or a state of emergency or a state of physical fitness is a state. Consider financial health. First, there are genuine facts about financial health even though 'state of financial health' does not refer to anything inside a person or to anything inside an institution like a Savings and Loan (S&L) – if it makes sense to say of an S&L that it has an inside. S&Ls are not just arrangements of matter, with clearly defined "insides." The state of an S&L's financial health cannot be identified with any particular internal state; financial health is a relational state of the S&L as a whole. Although there are borderline cases of financial health, there are many clear cases in which one S&L is financially healthy and another is not; and it is of great moment to discern which is which. Finally, a state of financial health (or the property of being physically fit) is causally explanatory in a straightforward sense; for example, the Lincoln Savings and Loan filed for Chapter 11 bankruptcy because of the state of its financial health, not because, say, its officers were seeking publicity. (If anyone doubts that this is a good causal explanation, then she should find a better one or hold that there are no causal explanations of such things as filing for bankruptcy.) So, if a state of belief is like a state of financial health, then we should not expect to identify it with any particular internal state of the believer.

The thesis of Practical Realism is this: Whether a person S has a particular belief (individuated by a 'that' clause in its attribution) is determined by what S does, says, and thinks, and what S *would* do, say, and think in various circumstances, where "what S would do"

or nation) rather than any of its parts, and individual beliefs and desires are not attributable in isolation, independently of other belief and desire attributions." "Three Kinds of Intentional Psychology," in *The Intentional Stance* (Cambridge MA: MIT/Bradford, 1987), 58. As I argue later, I disagree that this prevents realism about belief.

may itself be specified intentionally.[4] So, whether 'S believes that p' is true depends on there being relevant counterfactuals true of S. The antecedent of a relevant counterfactual may mention other of S's attitudes, but not, of course, the belief in question. If S is a speaker of a language, then the relevant counterfactuals concern her linguistic as well as her nonlinguistic behavior. These counterfactuals bear the weight of revealing the "nature" of having beliefs and the other attitudes – regardless of what is going on in the brain.[5] (Similarly, an S&L is in a certain state of financial health if and only if certain counterfactuals are true – e.g., if one of its investments went bad, it would cover the loss.)

Practical Realism allows that one may have a belief even if one never manifests it in overt behavior. Perhaps more significantly, Practical Realism allows that one may have a belief even if there are no relevant nonactual circumstances in which one would manifest it in overt behavior. For according to Practical Realism, S may believe that p even if there are no nearby possible worlds in which S would manifest the belief in any observable way. Suppose that Sims has a secret belief that Stalinism is the best form of government, but that she is always careful not to betray her belief in anything that she says or does. Also suppose that, as it happens, throughout Sims's life there is never a nearby possible world in which the belief would affect what she said or did in a relevant way. (Following Gordon Liddy, she has trained herself to withstand pain, and so would not divulge her belief even under torture.) Still, having that belief must make some difference, in this case a difference in her thoughts. For example, if Sims were to read of the demise of Stalinism, she would regret its passing. Depending on Sims's circumstances, the regret may or may not affect Sims's overt behavior. But even if it does (perhaps the regret leads Sims to decline an invitation to celebrate the downfall of Stalinism with her acquaintances), the behavioral effect may not allow detection of the regret by an observer (perhaps Sims begs off the celebration by pleading a headache). So Practical

---

4 I am proposing a kind of "holism" about belief. In *Holism* (Oxford: Blackwell, 1992), Jerry Fodor and Ernest LePore criticize what they call "meaning holism."
5 Although it is beyond the scope of this work to give an account of counterfactuals, I would begin with the Lewis-Stalnaker truth conditions, with a suitably chosen "similarity metric." 'If a had not been F, then b would not have been G' is true if and only if in the nearest world in which a was not F, b was not G.

Realism should be considered not a form of behaviorism but a form of radical relationism.

The relation between the meaning of the 'that' clause of a true attribution of belief and the relevant counterfactuals is rather like the relation between the meaning 'is in excellent financial health' (said of a prudent and fortunate S&L) and a set of statements about its debt, assets, investments, cash flow, management, and so on. Even if the statements about assets are not themselves counterfactual, their significance for the financial health of the S&L depends on counterfactuals that they support. For example, the relevance of some asset to the financial health of the institution may lie in its liquidity, and the notion of liquidity is overtly counterfactual: An asset is liquid if you can get rid of it in a hurry at full value. Now consider the parallels with belief. Believing that p is a state of a person that depends on the truth of counterfactuals. We know what counterfactuals are relevant in part by understanding the 'that' clause of the attribution, in part by knowing generalizations about how people behave, and in part by knowing the circumstances and other attitudes of the believer. And just as there are many different ways in which an S&L can be financially healthy, so too there are many different conjunctions of relevant counterfactuals that are sufficient for believing that p.

In general, the fact that a person believes that p is not the same fact as the fact that certain counterfactuals about the person are true.[6] This is so because 'x believes that p' may be true of S and S' even if the relevant counterfactuals for S and S' have few, if any, members in common. Suppose that in 1992 Dan Quayle and Al Gore had very different attitudes regarding the environment, but suppose that they both believed that the Competitiveness Council inhibited environmental regulation. 'If x had the opportunity, x would disband the Competitiveness Council' may have been one of the relevant counterfactuals for Gore's belief, but not for Quayle's. 'If x had the opportunity, x would increase the powers of the Competitiveness Council' may have been one of the relevant counterfactuals for Quayle's belief, but not for Gore's. Yet, they still *shared* the belief that the Competitiveness Council inhibits environmental reg-

---

6 Thus, I am not providing an analysis of 'believes that p'.

ulation.[7] (In my view, correct attribution of this shared belief does not require postulating "a similarly structured object in each head.")[8]

In short, S's believing that p is an irreducible fact about S, and is no more mysterious than S's owing a hundred dollars in income tax, or an S&L's being in good financial health. Just as two persons could not differ in their beliefs unless there were other differences between them (perhaps differences in counterfactuals true of each), so too two S&Ls could not differ in their state of financial health unless there were other differences between them (perhaps differences in counterfactuals true of each). But it does not follow in either case that there is any reduction of the highly complex state of affairs, easily designated by, for example, 'The S&L's being in good financial health' or 'S's believing that p' to any nonintentional state of affairs – certainly not to a nonintentional state of affairs knowable by a finite mind. The examples have illustrated the stubbornly nonreductive character of belief, on the Practical Realist's view.

Many proponents of the Standard View assume that anything less than a reductive account of the attitudes is "circular": Their methodological worry is how to break into the sphere of intentionality from a wholly nonintentional perspective. I have several responses to such a worry: First, I think that the worry is ill-motivated.[9] Different sciences study phenomena in different domains. Surely, the credibility of, say, economics does not rest on giving even a noneconomic account (much less a nonintentional account) of goods and services. Second, all inquiry takes place from within the sphere of intentionality. Scientific activity (formulating and testing hypotheses, e.g.,), as well as practical reasoning, would be unintelligible without intentional assumptions, at least at the present. And I do not foresee any science that is free of intentional presuppositions that treats the mind in a reasonably comprehensive

7 An observer must know a great deal about someone to know what the relevant counterfactuals for a given belief are; but my concern here is with the conditions under which someone has a certain belief, not with how we ascertain that she has it. Even so, we ascertain people's beliefs by seeing what they do and say.
8 For different purposes, Dennett makes this point about belief in "Three Kinds of Intentional Psychology," 55.
9 See Chapter 7, where I argue that the so-called naturalization project – which aims to supply nonintentional and nonsemantic conditions for intentional states – is ill-motivated.

way.[10] Trying to break into the intentional realm from the "outside" is like trying to break into the room where you are sitting. Third, intentional concepts are not circular in any ordinary sense. Definitions are the sorts of things that are circular, but I doubt that intentional concepts are susceptible to explicit definition, circular or not. Finally, if intentional concepts do form a circle (in some sense), the "circle" is all-encompassing. Beliefs and the other attitudes are part and parcel of a comprehensive, and thoroughly intentional, conception of reality – a conception whose legitimacy rests on its reliability in practice in science and everyday life.[11]

CAN COUNTERFACTUALS UNDERWRITE BELIEF?

The Practical Realist holds this: S believes that p if and only if, in S's context, there are relevant counterfactuals nonvacuously true of S.[12] The qualification 'in S's context' is to signal two kinds of context dependence: (1) The fact that which counterfactuals are relevant to a particular person's believing that p – and how their truth should be determined – depends on features on the particular person, her history, and her physical, social, and linguistic environment,[13] and (2) the fact that it is only relative to a context that the counterfactuals are sufficient for S's believing that p: There are no noncircular context-independent sufficient conditions for S's believing that p, where 'S' ranges over human beings and 'p' over propositions.

For simplicity, I am using the term 'counterfactual' in what is perhaps an extended sense, so that a subjunctive conditional with an antecedent that is true in the actual world counts as a counterfactual.[14] Thus, the counterfactual account of belief is to cover what

10 See Lynne Rudder Baker, "Content Meets Consciousness," *Philosophical Topics,* forthcoming.
11 See Chapters 3 and 8.
12 To require nonvacuous truth is to rule out counterfactuals that are true in virtue of there being no possible world in which the antecedent is true. Such a counterfactual, as Mark Lukas pointed out, should not be relevant to anyone's believing anything. Hereafter, I omit the qualification 'nonvacuous'.
13 Recall Quayle's and Gore's shared belief about the Competitiveness Council; the relevant counterfactuals may be quite different for two people who believe the same thing.
14 If one does not like this usage, then one may replace the term 'counterfactual' in such cases with the term 'indicative counterpart of a counterfactual', and adjust the Practical Realist account accordingly: "S believes that p if and only if, in X's

the believer actually does, says, and thinks, as well as what the believer would do, say, and think in nonactual circumstances. Sometimes beliefs, like causes, are right out in the open. Just as we see Julia Child *slice* the bread (cause the bread to break), so too we see beliefs exhibited in an action. When we see the flames shooting up from the house, and an ill-clad person running into the frigid night shrieking "Fire!", we see a belief made manifest in actual (not merely counterfactual) behavior. So, some of the counterfactuals relevant to believing that *p* have antecedents and consequents that are true in the actual world.

Pretty clearly, to have relevant counterfactuals true of *S* is a *necessary condition* for *S* to believe that *p*. If there are no possible circumstances in which *S*'s putative belief that *p* would make some difference in what *S* does, says, or thinks, then *S* has no such belief. Again, this is not to say that all beliefs must actually be manifested in behavior or thought, but only that there must be (possible) circumstances in which any belief would be so manifested.[15] The difficulties arise with considering the truth of counterfactuals to be sufficient: Do relevant counterfactuals provide even a relativized *sufficient condition* for *S* to believe that *p?* Unfortunately, there are complications.

Although this example is vastly oversimplified, suppose that the following is a relevant counterfactual allegedly sufficient for *S*'s belief that Clinton is president: If *S* were asked who was president, and *S* understood the question, and *S* wanted to be cooperative, *S* would respond by saying that Clinton is president. How do we determine whether such a counterfactual is true or false? To evaluate a counterfactual, we look to the nearest possible world in which the antecedent is true and see whether the consequent is true in that world. If so, the counterfactual is true; if not, it is false. To determine which possible world is nearest, we must hold some facts about the actual world constant and let others vary. Holding constant the physical laws of nature, we tell a story about the actual world in enough detail to determine the minimal change that would make the antecedent of the counterfactual true. Then, the nearest possible world is one in which that minimal change has been made.

context, there are relevant counterfactuals and indicative counterparts of counterfactuals nonvacuously true of *S*."

15 This point seems to me phenomenologically correct. Sometimes I do not know what I believe until I see what I do.

We cannot, however, evaluate the counterfactuals simply by see-ing whether, in the nearest possible world in which the antecedent is true, the consequent is also true. For if there are no restrictions on worlds relevant to a person's believing that p, this account would allow anybody (or anything!) to believe almost anything. For ex-ample, suppose that Joey is a precocious newborn baby, and we want to evaluate the counterfactual "If Joey were asked who is president, and Joey understood the question and Joey wanted to cooperate, then Joey would say that Clinton is president." If we do not restrict possible worlds for evaluating the counterfactuals, we just look to the nearest world in which the antecedent is true, that is, the nearest world in which Joey is asked who is president, Joey understands the question, and Joey wants to cooperate: In *that* world, Joey would be much older (in order to understand the ques-tion) and would answer that Clinton is president. In that case, the counterfactual would be true in the actual world, by the procedure just outlined for evaluating counterfactuals. But such a result should not be relevant to attributing to infant Joey (in the actual world) the belief that Clinton is president. For infant Joey has no such belief.[16]

So, we must restrict the possible worlds in which we evaluate relevant counterfactuals for belief. Call the possible worlds in which relevant counterfactuals for belief may be evaluated 'belief-relevant' worlds. For example, almost always belief-relevant worlds should be those in which S's physiology is not radically different from what it is in the actual world. This restriction on belief-relevant worlds rules out evaluating relevant counterfactuals in worlds in which S has changed from being dead to being alive, or from being an infant to being an adult, or from being comatose to being healthy.[17] Thus, with this restriction, the account of belief does not accord infant Joey beliefs that he does not have, but that he would have if he were older.

Although we can say that belief-relevant worlds are those in

16 Mark Lukas pointed out this kind of problem. Geoffrey Goddu, Mary Litch, and Neil Feit also helped sort out the issues.
17 If Practical Realism is extended to things other than organisms, then the require-ment should be that in belief-relevant worlds, S is not radically different physi-cally from the actual world. For example, if S is a computer, a counterfactual relevant to S's belief should not be evaluated in a world in which S has been smashed with a sledgehammer.

which S's physiology is unaltered, we cannot fully specify noncircular context-independent constraints on belief-relevant worlds. For belief-relevant worlds are worlds in which certain features of the actual world are held constant and other features are varied; but which features should be held constant and which features varied depends on facts about the particular person, her history, and her physical, social, and linguistic environment.[18] The range of beliefs is so vast and dependent on so many different kinds of relations, that it is impossible to specify sufficient conditions for anyone's believing that p, for all p. Even though there are no general specifiable conditions for belief-relevant worlds, however, it is worthwhile to try to show in piecemeal fashion how counterfactuals provide noncircular sufficient conditions, in given contexts, for S's believing that p. I shall show how to respond, in what seem to me natural and non–ad hoc ways, to various counterexamples to the claim that counterfactuals true of S are sufficient, in noncircularly specified contexts, for S's believing that p.

Consider first a simple example. Suppose that Peter asks Paul for Mary's telephone number, and that Paul looks it up in the local directory. Indeed, whenever Paul is asked about Mary's telephone number, he always consults the directory and produces the correct number, 765-4321. Since Paul is a reliable informant about Mary's telephone number, he seems to satisfy at least one counterfactual relevant to believing that the number is 765-4321: If he were asked what the number is, he would produce it. Intuitively, however, Paul does not have the belief that Mary's number is 765-4321, but only a belief about how to find the number.[19] Does Practical Realism have the unhappy consequence that Paul believes that Mary's telephone number is 765-4321 when he has to look it up each time? No. We can easily constrain the counterfactuals that suffice for believing that p in a way that accords with what we ordinarily take belief to be. The counterfactuals should not allow the ability to acquire the information that p from an outside source to suffice for believing that p. Information that p from an outside source should

18 If we could fully specify noncircular context-independent conditions for belief-relevant worlds, we would have a context-independent account of context (and a solution to the frame problem). I am informed by a physicist, Annette Prieur, that results in quantum mechanics depend on selection of a context, for which there are no generally specifiable conditions.

19 Jay Garfield and Joe O'Rourke offered this example.

include any information obtained via the senses. For example, if Paul painted Mary's number on his hand, which he consulted each time he was asked for the number, he still would not believe that Mary's number was 765-4321. So, the counterfactual "If Paul were asked for Mary's telephone number, and Paul understood the question and he wanted to be helpful, he would report that the number is 765-4321" does not suffice for Paul's believing that Mary's number is 765-4321. The counterfactual relevant to this particular case would be the following: "If Paul were asked for Mary's telephone number, and Paul understood the question and he wanted to be helpful, he would report that the number is 765-4321 without obtaining additional information through his senses."

Still, another problem looms. If Smith believes that it may rain in Seattle, then there must be some counterfactual true of Smith such as this: "If y had borrowed x's only umbrella and x believed that she was about to go to Seattle and x always wants to keep dry, then x would ask y to return the umbrella." Is some such counterfactual sufficient for S to believe that p? Clearly not. For the counterfactual may be true of Smith when (intuitively) she does not believe that it may rain in Seattle. Suppose that Jones had borrowed Smith's only umbrella, and Smith believed that she was about to go to Seattle and Smith always wants to keep dry, and Smith asked Jones to return the umbrella. Now also suppose that the reason that Smith asked Jones to return the umbrella was that Smith wanted to lend it to Abel. Thus, the counterfactual is not sufficient for Smith's believing that it may rain in Seattle. The problem here is general: The counterfactual may be true of S for the wrong reason – a reason having nothing to do with S's having the belief in question.[20]

This difficulty can be repaired, however. The single counterfactual by itself is not sufficient for Smith to believe that it may rain in Seattle. In addition to it, we need a "negative" counterfactual. Perhaps together, these counterfactuals comprise a sufficient condition for Smith's believing that it may rain in Seattle: "If y had borrowed x's only umbrella and x believed that she was about to go to Seattle and x always wants to deep dry, then x would ask y to return the umbrella; and if it is not the case that (y had borrowed x's only umbrella and x believed that she was about to go to Seattle and x

20 Don Gustafson pressed on me the need to discuss this issue.

always wants to keep dry), then it would not be the case that x asked y to return the umbrella." Now the claim is that this pair of counterfactuals is sufficient for Smith's belief that it may rain in Seattle.

Does the counterexample show also that the pair of counterfactuals is insufficient for Smith to believe that it may rain in Seattle? It does so only if both counterfactuals are true when Smith lacks the belief in question. So the issue now is to determine whether at least one of the counterfactuals is false when Smith does not believe that it may rain in Seattle. The addition of the negative counterfactual seems to rule out the counterexample based on Smith's wanting to lend the umbrella to Abel. For suppose that we fill in the story so that intuitively the nearest belief-relevant world in which the negative antecedent is true is one in which Smith has no plans to travel and hence does not believe that she was about to go to Seattle; then, the negative consequent is false: Smith would still have asked Jones to return the umbrella anyway since she wanted to lend it to Abel. Thus, the putative sufficient condition for Smith's believing that it might rain in Seattle is not satisfied in the case in which intuitively Smith lacks the belief in question.

Inclusion of negative counterfactuals as parts of sufficient conditions for belief also wards off another kind of potential counterexample to the account. Suppose that Jones has borrowed Smith's umbrella and that Smith is about to go to Seattle, where she wants to keep dry, and that Smith asks Jones to return the umbrella. But this time, let us suppose, a brain tumor causes Smith to ask Jones to return the umbrella. Again, Smith intuitively does not believe that it might rain in Seattle, but the affirmative counterfactual is true. So, the affirmative counterfactual alone cannot be claimed to be sufficient for Smith's belief that it might rain in Seattle. Again, the negative counterfactual blocks the counterexample. The negative consequent is false in nearby belief-relevant worlds in which the negative antecedent is true: The brain tumor would have caused Smith to have asked Jones to return the umbrella in nearby belief-relevant worlds in which Smith did not believe that she was about to go to Seattle. Good news!

Now for the bad news. What otherwise seem to be sufficient conditions for S to believe that p turn out to be insufficient when the nearest belief-relevant world is one in which the believer's belief itself is altered. To simplify the example still further, suppose that we offer the following as sufficient for Smith's believing that she is holding an umbrella.[21]

    (i) If Smith wanted to keep dry and Smith believed that it was raining, then Smith would raise her arm; and

    (ii) If it is not the case that (Smith wanted to keep dry and Smith believed that it was raining), then Smith would not raise her arm.

Now suppose that at the moment, Smith does not believe that she is holding an umbrella. (It's a sunny day, and she does not have her umbrella.) Now are the counterfactuals (i) and (ii) true? Unfortunately, they may be. Since it is not raining and Smith does not raise her arm, the negative counterfactual (ii) is true. Sad to say, the affirmative counterfactual (i) may also be true. For suppose that Smith carries an umbrella always and only when it rains;[22] so, in the nearest belief-relevant world in which it is raining, Smith is holding an umbrella, and, wanting to stay dry and believing that it is raining, in that world she does raise her arm. That is, in the nearest belief-relevant world in which the antecedent of the counterfactual is true, the consequent is also true; so, if Smith wanted to keep dry and Smith believed that it was raining, Smith would raise her arm – because in that world she would also believe that she is carrying an umbrella. But if the counterfactuals are true in a case in which Smith does not believe that she is holding an umbrella, then they cannot be sufficient for Smith's believing that she is holding an umbrella.[23]

The obvious way to try to avoid the counterexample would be to hold constant Smith's belief about whether she has an umbrella from world to world for purposes of evaluating the counterfactual. We could rule out the counterexample if we constrained nearness of

---

21 Notice that the conjunction of counterfactuals cannot be transformed into a single counterfactual with a hugely complicated conjunctive antecedent. For there is no possible world in which the antecedents of both (i) and (ii) are true. Yet both (i) and (ii) may both be nonvacuously true.

22 We also must require that in the nearest belief-relevant worlds Smith carries an umbrella always and only when it is raining. Although such a stipulation is empirically implausible, I accept it to keep the example simple. The point of the example is to illustrate a difficulty in principle.

23 I am indebted to Mark Crimmins for the counterexample.

possible world like this: "If S believes that p in the actual world, then S believes that p in the nearest belief-relevant world; and if S does not believe that p in the actual world, then S does not believe that p in the nearest belief-relevant world." But such a constraint would render the account of sufficient conditions for S's believing that p circular. Since we are looking for a sufficient condition for Smith's belief, we cannot determine which is the nearest belief-relevant world on the basis of information about whether she does or does not believe that she has an umbrella. The problem with taking counterfactuals to be sufficient for S's believing that p, then, is this: In order to evaluate the truth of the counterfactuals, we must look to other belief-relevant worlds similar to the actual world. But similar in what respects? Even if we rely on our intuitions to determine a suitable "similarity metric," those intuitions cannot include information about the very facts for which we are proposing a sufficient condition.[24]

So, we seem to have a dilemma. The proposed counterfactuals seem to be either insufficient or question begging in this sense: In order to rule out as nearest a belief-relevant world that makes the counterfactuals true even though Smith (in the actual world) lacks the belief in question, we must disallow worlds in which Smith's belief is different from her actual belief (e.g., disallow the belief-relevant world in which Smith carries an umbrella always and only when it is raining). That is, we must assume that Smith's belief state does not change from what it is in the actual world; but in the context of supplying sufficient conditions for Smith's having the belief, such an assumption is question begging. Call this difficulty 'the sufficiency problem.'

The Practical Realist solution to the sufficiency problem is to concede that the pair of counterfactuals, (i) and (ii), are indeed insufficient for Smith's believing that she is holding an umbrella. But it does not follow that there are *no* counterfactuals true of Smith that are (non–question beggingly) sufficient for Smith to believe that she is holding an umbrella. What follows is only that we may be mistaken that we are in possession of sufficient conditions for Smith's belief. We may even be justified (though wrong) to think

---

24 Note that this problem afflicts any counterfactual account of sufficient conditions. It is not peculiar to Practical Realism. See C. B. Martin, "Dispositions and Conditionals," *Philosophical Quarterly* 44 (1994):1–8.

that (i) and (ii) are sufficient for Smith to believe that she is holding an umbrella. What we are missing is not information about Smith's beliefs or change of belief, but rather other relevant information: An Omniscient Being would know that Smith carries an umbrella always and only when it is raining; such an Omniscient Being would then know that (i) and (ii) are not sufficient for Smith's believing that she is holding an umbrella, and would know this without relying on any knowledge about whether Smith believes that she is carrying an umbrella. And if we were to discover that Smith carries an umbrella always and only when it is raining, then we would withdraw our claim that (i) and (ii) are sufficient for Smith to have the belief – again, without discovering (or stipulating) anything about Smith's beliefs or change of belief.

To evaluate counterfactuals proposed as sufficient for Smith's believing that she is carrying an umbrella, we select the nearest possible world in the usual (intuitive, context-dependent, but non–question begging) way on the basis of the information that we have, excluding information about the subject's belief in question. If we had had further information about Smith's umbrella-carrying habits, we would not have supposed that the truth of (i) and (ii) guarantee that she believes that she is carrying an umbrella. As long as there are some such counterfactuals, perhaps knowable only by an Omniscient Being, and their evaluation does not require knowledge of Smith's beliefs, then Practical Realism is safe from the counterexample and the charge of circularity.

The Practical Realist claim is that if there is no conjunction of true counterfactuals that is non–question beggingly sufficient for Smith's believing that she is carrying an umbrella, then she does not have that belief. But it is consistent with this claim that we may be mistaken about the sufficiency of any particular conjunction of counterfactuals because we lack relevant information – information that makes no assumptions about whether Smith has the belief. Since we are fallible and our knowledge is limited, and the appropriate counterfactuals whose truth would guarantee that Smith believes that she is carrying an umbrella are highly context-dependent, it is unsurprising that we cannot be certain of the sufficiency of any conjunction of counterfactuals for Smith to have the belief in question. The problem with specifying sufficient conditions for believing that p, then, is that for any proposed conjunction of counterfactuals, there may be further relevant (and non–question begging) information that is not available to us, which, if we had it, would induce us to withdraw the claim that the proposed counterfactuals were sufficient for the belief in question. But this is a problem about the limitations of our knowledge, not about the account of belief in terms of counterfactuals. As in any other domain about which one is a realist, one may be justified but mistaken in one's judgments.

In sum, my solution to the sufficiency problem is this: I grant that, in the case described, (i) and (ii) are not sufficient conditions for Smith's believing that she is carrying an umbrella – although we may have mistakenly thought them sufficient until we found out that Smith carries an umbrella always and only when it rains. But there are counterfactuals that are sufficient for her believing that she is carrying an umbrella, and the evaluation of which does not require any question-begging selection of the nearest possible world. Those counterfactuals that really are sufficient take into account all the relevant information about Smith – information to which we may not be privy – but they can be evaluated without knowing whether Smith has the belief in question in the actual or any nonactual possible world. Therefore, there is no circularity. Since it is not my intention to give a reductive account of belief in terms of counterfactuals (or of anything else), I need not *specify* counterfactuals that would guarantee that S believes that p. I can rest here with exposing and exploring the substantive metaphysical fact that the existence of relevant counterfactuals true of S is both necessary and (non–question beggingly) sufficient, given a context, for S's believing that p. The claim of Practical Realism is that counterfactuals, and counterfactuals alone, reveal the nature of belief.

To sum up: S believes that p just in case there are relevant counterfactuals nonvacuously true of S, where relevant counterfactuals concern what S would do, say, or think in various circumstances. The counterfactuals are to be evaluated in worlds in which S's physiology is not radically different from what it is in the actual world. Just as there is no context-free way to specify a context of ordinary life, there is no general method for determining which are the belief-relevant worlds for the counterfactuals sufficient for belief. In many cases, the belief-relevant worlds will have the same physical laws as the actual world; but also in many cases, what matters for belief-relevant worlds is similarity of macrophysical behavior intentionally specified – whatever the underlying physical

167

laws. So, often what is more important than keeping constant the basic laws across worlds is keeping constant macrophysical phenomena and the conventions of S's society.

Before contrasting Practical Realism with the Standard View, let me allay two potential worries. The first is that appeal to relevant counterfactuals may seem to impugn the causal explanatoriness of beliefs. The second is that reliance on counterfactuals undercuts the realism of Practical Realism.

Can beliefs be causally explanatory if the truth of relevant counterfactuals is necessary and sufficient, in the context, for having a belief? The discussion of the collapse of the S&L in Chapter 5 heads off the charge, I hope, that beliefs must be internal states to be causally explanatory. But there may remain another worry: Since the relevant counterfactuals concern what the believer would do, say, or think in various circumstances, it may be charged that beliefs are "conceptually" related to behavior – in the way that being a bachelor is related to being unmarried – and hence not available for causal explanation. This worry may be particularly acute in the case of explaining linguistic behavior; for a single pair of counterfactuals may be sufficient for S's believing that p: If x believed that she were asked seriously whether p is true, and x understood the question and x wanted to cooperate and x was a competent speaker, then x would assert that p; and if it is not the case that (x believed that she were asked seriously whether p is true, and x understood the question and x wanted to cooperate and x was a competent speaker), then x would not assert that p. But if the truth of these counterfactuals is sufficient in the context for believing that p, then S's saying that p can not be causally explained by S's believing that p. But surely, one may object, we want to explain what one says in terms of what one believes.

So we do – and so we can. For I am not giving an analysis of 'S believes that p', nor making any claims about semantics. I am rather giving necessary and sufficient conditions for someone's having a belief. As long as there is at least one conjunction of counterfactuals sufficient for S's believing that p that does not contain reference to saying that p, then S's believing that p is logically independent of the assertion in this sense: S would still have had the belief even if S had not said that p. In general, if S's believing that p is to explain causally S's doing A, then there must be at least one conjunction of

168

counterfactuals sufficient for S's believing that p that contains no mention of S's doing A. In effect, this restriction insures that S has the belief that p independently of her doing A. The restriction guarantees that the inference from behavior to belief is contingent.[25]

The second worry to allay here is that no kind of realism can rest on counterfactuals. As we have seen, counterfactuals are notoriously context-dependent. But to say that counterfactuals are context-dependent is not to say that they always lack truth value. It is context-dependent that it is now four o'clock, but there is a fact of the matter about the time for all that. Counterfactuals such as 'If you had not taken your umbrella, you would have gotten wet' seem to be straightforwardly true or false. However, counterfactuals about a person may leave it indeterminate whether a person has a particular belief: Even an Omniscient Being would be unable to decide. But this feature, I think, accords with the facts of believing. In such cases, which are not typical, there is a fact of the matter about the indeterminacy – whether we actual observers are in a position to ascertain the fact or not.

Counterfactuals are ubiquitous in cognitive practices. The assumption that counterfactuals may be ascertainably true is embedded in the conception of a ceteris paribus clause, and in the conception of a law of nature. The hypothetical reasoning that drives scientific research would be unthinkable unless counterfactuals were assumed to be true. The assumption that counterfactuals are true is enshrined in law and custom, and is required for our practices of praise and blame. A recent Supreme Court decision in an antidiscrimination case held that even when an employer is found to have sexually discriminated against a fired employee, the firing is permissible provided that the employee would have been fired in

---

25 Note that a critic can not induce circularity by conjoining the antecedents and consequents of all the relevant counterfactuals sufficient for S to believe that p to form one very large counterfactual. For the nearest possible world in which the antecedent of one of the individual counterfactuals is true may be different from the nearest possible world in which the antecedent of another of the individual counterfactuals is true; the nearest possible world in which all the antecedents of all the counterfactuals are true is (most likely) different still. Indeed, there may be no possible world in which the antecedent of counterfactual formed by conjoining the antecedents of the individual counterfactuals is true. Compare: "If it doesn't rain, I'll have a picnic; and if it rains, I won't." If we conjoined the antecedents of these counterfactuals, we would have an antecedent ("If it rains and if it does not rain") that is true in no possible world.

the absence of the discrimination. To make such a decision is to assume that there is a fact of the matter about the truth of counterfactuals, and that the truth of relevant counterfactuals may be ascertained.

In practice – scientific, legal, and moral – a lot rides on assumptions about counterfactuals. In the Cartesian tradition, it is the task of philosophy to evaluate such assumptions and to discard those that fail to pass metaphysical muster. Although I agree that philosophy has an important critical task, I see no privileged standpoint from which to discard the assumptions without which there would be no recognizably human life. In any case, we rely on counterfactuals in many contexts that have nothing to do with attitudes. Although I discuss counterfactuals in terms of possible worlds, Practical Realism is compatible with any account of counterfactuals according to which some counterfactuals are determinately true. If Practical Realism is correct, belief-supporting counterfactuals are among those that can be determinately true.

In short, there is often a fact of the matter about whether there are relevant counterfactuals true of an individual; and when there is not a fact of the matter about whether there are such true relevant counterfactuals, there is a fact of the matter about the indeterminacy of the individual's having the belief.[26] So, appeal to counterfactuals is no source of antirealism about belief.[27]

Even if counterfactuals can be determinately true or false, there may be a residual worry that mere counterfactuals are too puny to settle whether someone really believes that p.[28] Although I think this is a deep concern to which I cannot do justice here, let me try to alleviate this worry by interpreting it in various ways:

1. If the worry is that belief is an actual state of a person, and actual states cannot be understood wholly in terms of counterfactuals, then I would ask for clarification of 'actual state'. I have argued at length against the various versions of Standard View, according to which belief is an actual internal state (a brain state). There is a sense of 'state' in which I agree that belief is an actual state

---

26 I think that indeterminacy is morally important in, for example, assessing one's culpability for what one does.
27 At the end of Chapter 7, I discuss the issue of realism about belief in greater detail. Here I simply want to counter a charge of antirealism based on the fact that Practical Realism rests on counterfactuals.
28 The discussion that follows was prompted by comments from Mark Crimmins.

– as in my state of readiness to help you move your books; but counterfactuals seem the right approach to understand actual states in that sense. I agree with Peirce: "Belief does not make us act at once, but puts us into such a condition that we shall behave in a certain way, when the occasion arises."[29] The relevant "condition" should not be identified with any particular molecular configuration in the person.[30] (See the disanalogy with fragility in the next section.)

2. If the worry is that all the Practical Realist offers for understanding beliefs is a net of counterfactuals, into which we have no entrance from the actual world, then I would recall that the relevant counterfactuals include conditionals with antecedents and consequents that are true in the actual world – and that these antecedents and consequents mention behaviors and perceptual states as well as other attitudes. Whether a person actually behaves in a certain way is a determinate fact about the person in this world, independently of what is the case in other possible worlds. So, even on the counterfactual approach, the property of believing that p is not solely a matter of what happens in nonactual worlds.

3. If the worry is that an account of belief ought to specify necessary and sufficient conditions for believing that p in terms of properties such that whether they apply is metaphysically prior to whether 'believes that p' applies, then I do not think that we will ever have any adequate account of belief that satisfies that condition. The nature of belief is not to be found in "deeper facts" about the person than the counterfactuals provide. Even though there are many necessary conditions for believing that p (e.g., having a functioning brain), believing that p does not supervene on them, and the nature of belief is not disclosed in them.

CONTRASTS WITH THE STANDARD VIEW

According to the Standard View, a belief attribution is true only if there is a brain-state token that constitutes the belief. According to Practical Realism, the story is different. Suppose that, by ordinary

29 Charles S. Peirce, "The Fixation of Belief," in *Selected Writings*, ed. and introd. Philip P. Wiener (New York: Dover Publications, 1966), 99.
30 This point should not tempt one to mind-body dualism. It would be fallacious to argue that if the condition in question is not identical with a particular material state, it must be identical with a particular immaterial state.

171

standards of evidence, Bob appears to believe that grass is green. When asked what color grass is, he replies that it is green; when asked to describe Kelly green, he says that it is the color of grass; when queried about chlorophyll, he says that it makes grass green, and so on. In this case, according to Practical Realism, Bob can not be shown to lack the belief that grass is green simply by citing neurological evidence.[31] On the other hand, according to the Standard View, if, say, the most theoretically refined description of brain states never turned up brain-state tokens that plausibly could be said to constitute his belief tokens, then we should withdraw attribution of the belief.[32] The Practical Realist, who does not construe beliefs as brain states in the first place, would remain unfazed: Failure to find a plausible brain-state token to constitute a belief token would not impugn attribution of the belief.

On some versions of the Standard View, counterfactual-supporting generalizations connecting beliefs to actions are deemed false unless there are computational mechanisms that "implement" the generalization.[33] To say that a computational mechanism implements a psychological generalization is to say at least that for every person whose behavior is subsumed by the generalization, there are

31 Here is a dissimilarity between beliefs and the S&L case discussed in Chapter 5: If, in the S&L case, it is discovered that there had been no electronic transfer (there was just a malfunction on the other end), no investment would have been made. But discovery that there had been no brain state that could be identified as a particular belief would not impugn the attribution of belief, provided that there were relevant counterfactuals true of the person. On the other hand, discovery that none of the money in the S&L is my money does not impugn the claim that the S&L has my money; similarly, discovery that none of S's brain states can be identified as S's belief that p does not impugn the attribution of belief that p to S.

32 If the token-identity (or token-constitution) claim is to be nonvacuous, then the brain-state tokens that are candidates to be Bob's belief that grass is green would have to have in common some property taxonomic in neurophysiology. Since token-identity theorists are not committed to type identity, they need not suppose that there is a single type of brain state shared by everyone who has a single type of belief; but in order to *establish* token identity, they will have to find – at least within a given individual's brain – enough neurophysiological similarity among brain-state tokens to warrant calling them all tokens of the belief that grass is green. It is an empirical question whether neurophysiology will develop in a way that would permit token identification; I am dubious, and even more so as I consider social and political beliefs, rather than beliefs about one's perceptual environment. But if there is no neurophysiological basis for saying of particular brain-state tokens that they are tokens of S's belief that p, the claim of token identity (or token constitution) seems empty.

33 For example, see Jerry A. Fodor, "The Elm and the Expert: Mentalese and Its Semantics" (1993 Jean Nicod Lectures).

particular computational states that are reliably coinstantiated with the mental states mentioned in the antecedent of the generalization. Since such computational states are defined by properties wholly intrinsic to the brain, there must be neural states that are sufficient for the relevant computational states. Now if we understand the computational mechanisms to be mechanistic processes of particular brain states, and we understand brain states to be states taxonomic in neurophysiology, then, according to the Standard View, a generalization like 'People who believe that p and desire that q (ceteris paribus) do A' is false unless there are particular brain states reliably coinstantiated with the properties of believing that p and desiring that q.

The Practical Realist would disagree. For most propositions, the property of believing that p is a relational property. With respect to generalizations mentioning *nonintentional* relational properties, an individual is subsumed by the generalization in virtue of its relational properties, not its internal states. For example, to explain why planets travel in elliptical orbits, an astronomer would be on the wrong track if he focused on the material constitution of planets. The only relevant properties are the mass of the planet, the mass of the star around which it is revolving, and the distance between the two. Hold these properties constant, and replace the material constitution of the planet by anything you like, and you have not affected the orbit. The planet's trajectory is fully explained by the inverse square law. We need look no further for internal mechanisms that implement the law.[34] This general point about relational properties and generalizations mentioning such properties has obvious application to intentional psychological properties.

Consider this counterfactual-supporting generalization:

(G) If a member of the school board believed that the school budget would raise taxes too much, and he wanted to keep

---

34 Someone may object that the inverse square law is a basic law, and hence needs no implementing mechanism, but that psychological laws are nonbasic and so require mechanisms for their implementation. Such an objection would be beside the point. For I am denying not that psychological laws have implementing mechanisms but, rather, that such mechanisms must be neural mechanisms (where neural properties are intrinsic properties). If the inverse square law is a basic law, then some basic laws mention relational properties (e.g., distance between two bodies).

his pledge to stop tax increases, then (ceteris paribus) he would vote against the school budget.

(G) is the kind of counterfactual-supporting generalization that is typically used in everyday explanations of behavior. Either scientific psychology will be concerned with such generalizations or not. If not, then there will be important and extensive ranges of behavior outside the purview of scientific psychology. So, suppose, as psychologists typically do, that scientific psychology aims at encompassing all human behavior and hence will be concerned with generalizations like (G).

Now suppose that neurophysiologists undertook to discover a relevant neural mechanism – one on which the computational mechanism that implements (G) is to supervene – in a particular member of the school board, Fox. Suppose that the neurophysiologists had a (fantastic) total brain monitor that recorded all the chemical and electrical activity in the brain. Suppose that Fox were monitored as he attended board meetings, where, meeting after meeting, he voted against the school budget – always giving as his reason that he thought that the budget would raise taxes too much. Judging by the behavioral evidence, including frequent interviews with Fox and his own confidential diary entries, Fox's voting behavior is subsumed by (G).

Now suppose that the monitoring of Fox's brain took place during a period when the school budget was first voted down and then re-presented (in the same form) to the board for another vote. (Suppose that the superintendent thought that, second time around, he had swayed enough board members to pass the same budget that previously had been turned down.) Also suppose that to save time (as in Chapter 5), pro and con votes were always cast for and against the school budget simultaneously: At the first meeting, the board members raised their left hands to vote "no" and their right hands to vote "yes" (all at once); at the second meeting, the board members raised their right hands to vote "no" and their left hands to vote "yes" (all at once). So the same type of motion that was a vote *against* the school budget in the first meeting was a vote *for* the school budget at the second meeting.

Finally, suppose that the neurophysiological data revealed mechanisms that controlled Fox's arm motions, but that these mechanisms did not contain any particular brain state (or nonheterogeneous disjunction of brain states) taxonomic in neurophysiology that was reliably coinstantiated with Fox's belief that the school budget would raise taxes too much. For example, suppose that there was no brain state taxonomic in neurophysiology that was an element both in each of the mechanisms that produced Fox's various arm motions at the board meetings and in each of the mechanisms that produced Fox's sounds when interviewed about his reason for voting against the school budget.[35] Moreover, the same neural mechanisms that produced Fox's arm motions in the board meeting also produced arm motions that, in other circumstances, were variously tests of the windy conditions, requests to address meetings, exercises in a physical fitness program. In the case that I am imagining, all the behavioral evidence indicates that Fox's voting behavior is subsumed by (G); but since there is no particular brain state (or nonheterogeneous disjunction of brain states) that plausibly may be said to constitute the belief mentioned in the antecedent of (G), there is no evidence for a computational (ultimately neural) mechanism in Fox that plausibly may be said to implement (G).

The proponent of the Standard View who holds that psychological laws must be implemented in the brain should conclude in such a case that, all nonneurophysiological, behavioral evidence to the contrary, (G) is *false*.[36] For one who holds that psychological laws must be implemented by neural mechanisms, the only alternatives to taking (G) to be false seem to be these: (i) Although (G) is a true, counterfactual-supporting generalization that explains Fox's voting behavior, (G) is not a genuine law; or (ii) although (G) is a true, counterfactual-supporting generalization, it does not explain Fox's voting behavior. Since what matters in psychology are true, counterfactual-supporting generalizations that explain behavior, endorsement of (i) would just raise the question of the relevance of

35 In *From Folk Psychology to Cognitive Science: The Case against Belief* (Cambridge, MA: MIT/Bradford, 1983), chap. 11, Stephen P. Stich cited an empirically real case in which the subsystems that are responsible for verbal reporting are different from (and may be isolated from) the subsystems that are responsible for nonverbal behavior. Whereas Stich took such a case to be evidence that there are no beliefs, I take it to be evidence that beliefs need not be (or be constituted by) particular brain states. Once again, one philosopher's *modus ponens* is another philosopher's *modus tollens*.
36 See Fodor, "The Elm and the Expert." In discussion, Fodor made a similar point on August 18, 1993, at the NEH Institute on Meaning at Rutgers University, where I presented a version of this argument.

"genuine laws" (construed so that (G) is not a genuine law) to psychology. On the other hand, endorsement of (ii) seems unprincipled: Since changing Fox's beliefs about the effects of the school budget would change Fox's voting behavior, it seems ad hoc to deny that (G) explains Fox's "no" votes while conceding that (G) is a true, counterfactual-supporting generalization. So, neither of these latter Standard View alternatives seems any more acceptable than taking (G) to be false – in the face of overwhelming behavioral evidence to the contrary.

By contrast, the Practical Realist, who never identifies beliefs with brain states in the first place, holds that it is misguided to accord decisive weight to neurophysiological evidence for this kind of generalization; the evidence for the generalization is not to be found "in the head" but in ordinary actions. As long as people continue to behave as they now do, (G) needs no further vindication from the discovery of any special kind of neural mechanisms. Moreover, even if there are mechanisms that implement generalizations like (G), they need not be *neural* mechanisms. Perhaps psychological generalizations depend only on a normally functioning brain and particular relations to various features of the environment – as the inverse square law depends only on each body's total mass and the distance between them – without regard for any particular neural states. So, the Practical Realist makes two points: If (G) is implemented by some mechanistic process, the mechanism need not be a neural mechanism; and in any case, the adequacy of (G) does not depend on the discovery of any mechanisms, neural or not.

Let me try to sharpen the contrast between the Standard View and Practical Realism by considering three responses to Practical Realism that are inspired by the Standard View.

1. The first Standard View response is an objection that the distinction between believing as a property of whole persons and of brains is ill-founded. The objection may be pressed by an unfortunately gruesome thought experiment (suggested by Fred Feldman). Call this "the Monty Python" objection: Suppose that persons are identical with their bodies, and that Brown is a person who believes that *p*. Now suppose that experimenters start chopping away at parts of Brown – first a finger here and there, then more centrally (being careful to hook the remaining parts of Brown's body to life-support systems), until finally all that is left of Brown's

body is his brain – call the brain 'b'. Now if the brain continues to function normally, Brown could still believe that p, even in the absence of the rest of the body. (For the sake of argument, I am assuming with my critics that a person is identical to her body, and that the remaining brain, b, suffices for the person still to exist. If this seems outlandish to you, stop the thought experiment at the "amputation" right before the point at which you would say that the person no longer exists.) Thus, since Brown still has the belief that p and the person Brown is here identical with the brain b, the belief that p is a property of S's brain. So goes the objection.

The thought experiment "proves too much." For suppose that Brown is the owner of the National Football League (NFL) champions. Still assuming that a person is identical with her body, and that Brown is now identical to brain b, we should conclude – by the same reasoning as the objector's – that brain b now has the property of being the owner of the NFL champions. The bizarre conclusion that brain b has the property of being the owner of the NFL champions is simply a deduction from premises that being the owner of the NFL champions is a property of Brown, and that (what is left of) Brown is identical to brain b. Even if – by default, so to speak, on the assumption that a person is identical to her body – in this extreme case, being the owner of the NFL champions is a property of brain b, it does not follow that the property of being the owner of the NFL champions is, in the first instance, a property of brains; still less does it follow that having a certain brain state constitutes being the owner of the NFL champions. Exactly the same reasoning applies to the objector's example about belief: We should not conclude that believing that p really is a property of the brain any more than being the owner of the NFL champions really is a property of the brain. Although having certain brain states is a necessary condition, on the one hand, for believing that p and, on the other hand, for being the individual who owns the NFL champions, in neither case is the property constituted by a particular brain state.

Even if one takes a person to be identical to her body, it is not in virtue of that identity that one has beliefs. Compare: Being sentimental is a property of some songs; a song is just certain kinds of physical vibrations; but it is not in virtue of being vibrations that the song is sentimental. Again, what makes it the case that S believes that p is that relevant counterfactuals are true of S. Brown still believes that p, according to Practical Realism, in virtue of there remaining relevant counterfactuals true of Brown. (Again: one may need a brain in order for the counterfactuals to be true of one.)

In Brown's diminished condition, one may well wonder, what are the relevant counterfactuals? Presumably, the counterfactuals will concern only her thoughts. For example, suppose that the belief in question is that Brown's lover is in New York.[37] Then the following may be a relevant counterfactual: If Brown were to think of her lover, then she would wish that she were in New York. Now I can agree that Brown could have neither the thought of the lover nor the wish that she were in New York without having certain kinds of brain states. But it is in virtue of the true counterfactuals about the thought and the wish that Brown believes that her lover is in New York. If Brown had had the same brain states, but in a world in which those brain states were not the relevant thoughts, then, on my view, she would not have had the belief that her lover was in New York. Thus, a Practical Realist can handle this extreme case: We need not suppose that a belief is constituted by a brain state even when a brain is all that remains of a person who, we agree, has a certain belief.

2. The second Standard View objection is that the Standard View is needed for certain kinds of explanation. For example, Robert van Gulick tells his class something they did not know: that his grandmother was named 'Agnes' and lived to be 101 years old. When queried soon after about the name and age of van Gulick's grandmother, the students give the right answer. According to the Standard View, the brain of each person in the class changed on hearing what van Gulick said about his grandmother; and those changes causally explain the students' ability to give the grandmother's name and age when she died. How should a Practical Realist respond?

A Practical Realist should agree with van Gulick that the students acquired the beliefs in question when he told them about his grandmother, that at that time each of their brains changed in whatever ways were necessary for the acquisition of the beliefs, and that the newly acquired beliefs explain their behavior. Now all of our brains

37 The issue here only concerns Brown's *retaining* beliefs when the "whole person" Brown is now identical to brain *b*. I am not conceding, even for the sake of argument, that brain *b,* unattached, so to speak, to a human body with appropriate causal connections to the environment, could acquire the belief that her lover is in New York.

are changing in all manner of ways all the time. The question for the Standard View, however, is whether for *each* belief acquired, there is a *particular* brain change that can be coherently identified as constituting the acquisition of just that belief. Although this is an empirical question, my strong hunch (which I share with the eliminativists) is that neuroscientists will not come up with a theory that identifies brain states in such a way that, for every belief acquired, there is a particular (token) brain state – either local and discrete, or global and distributed – that constitutes the acquisition of that belief.

To see the difficulty, suppose that, as you are listening to the weather report, you hear a car drive up; and you thereby simultaneously acquire both the belief that it will snow tomorrow and the belief that the guests have arrived. If any version of the Standard View is correct – even the weakest "constitution" version – then there is one brain state (token) that constitutes your coming to believe that it will snow tomorrow and a second brain state (token) that constitutes your coming to believe that the guests have arrived. Now maybe neurophysiologists will countenance states in such a way that they can distinguish tokens that constitute coming to believe that p from simultaneous tokens that constitute coming to believe that q – as I mentioned, this is an empirical question – and maybe not. (If neuroscientists do not find such states, then proponents of the Standard View should either become eliminative materialists or give up the Standard View altogether; if they opt for the latter, Practical Realism waits in the wings.)

In any case, according to Practical Realism, the fate of the attitudes does not hinge on speculation about the future of neuroscience. For even if neuroscientists did consider a particular brain change to be Sam's acquisition of a belief that van Gulick's grandmother was named "Agnes," what makes it the case that Sam has acquired the belief is that there is now a relevant set of counterfactuals true of Sam – no matter what happened in his brain. So, the Practical Realist can agree that there is a moment of acquisition of a belief, that there were (a myriad of) changes in the brain at the moment of acquisition without which the belief would not have been acquired, and that the belief so acquired causally explains the students' subsequent verbal behavior. But none of this requires the Standard View.

3. The third Standard View objection is that Practical Realism is

not really an alternative to the Standard View, but rather can be conjoined to it. Even if the property of believing that p is best understood in terms of relevant counterfactuals, the objector may urge, beliefs could still be constituted by brain states. A proponent of the Standard View may agree that people, not brains, have beliefs; after all, people, not lungs, have emphysema – notwithstanding the fact that to have emphysema is to have one's lungs in a certain state.[38] Likewise, the proponent of the Standard View may insist that to have a belief is to have one's brain in a certain state. The Practical Realist sees a disanalogy between having beliefs and having emphysema. Investigators can look inside at a person's lungs and see whether she has emphysema. But lacking brain writing, investigators cannot look inside a person's brain and see whether she believes that winters are long in Vermont, still less whether she believes that if she had left an hour earlier, she would have avoided the storm.

Nonetheless, a proponent of the Standard View may insist, appeal to relevant counterfactuals may be just a step on the way to an account of belief as brain states – in the way that appeal to counterfactuals about the conditions under which an object would break is just a step on the way to an account of fragility as a physical state of an object. But, again, there is an important disanalogy between the property of believing that p and the property of being fragile. Suppose that we understand fragility in terms of the state of breaking when struck with impact i or greater (where the value of i varies with the type of object under consideration). Now if object O is fragile, there are microphysical properties $P_1, \ldots, P_m$ such that O instantiates one of them, and O's instantiating that microphysical property is sufficient for it to be true that if struck with impact i or greater, O would break. To see the disanalogy between fragility and belief, suppose that an untenured faculty member, Jones, believes that publications are required for being granted tenure. Among the counterfactuals relevant to Jones's belief is this one: "If child care were available to x, x would work on a journal article." Now if Jones's believing that publications are required for tenure were parallel to O's being fragile, then the following would be the case: There are neural properties $N_1, \ldots N_n$ such that Jones instantiates one of them, and Jones's instantiating that neural property is

<hr>

38 This analogy comes from Robert van Gulick.

sufficient for the relevant counterfactual to be true of Jones. But it is *not* the case that Jones's neural properties suffice for it to be true of Jones that if child care were available, she would work on a journal article. No matter how we augmented the antecedent of the counterfactual, in order for Jones's behavior to count as working on a journal article, Jones must be embedded in a complex social and professional environment.

The property mentioned in the consequent of the counterfactual associated with fragility – O's breaking – supervenes on O's microphysical properties; but it is not the case that the property mentioned in the consequent of the counterfactual associated with the belief – the property of working on a journal article – supervenes on Jones's neural properties or on any other of her intrinsic properties. If the property of working on a journal article supervenes on anything, it supervenes on the properties of Jones's physical, social, and linguistic environment together with her intrinsic properties. In cases of belief generally, the relevant counterfactuals individuate behavior by means of ordinary action descriptions – for example, work on a journal article, cook dinner, mail the check, ask for the umbrella back. Behavior so individuated does not supervene on any intrinsic properties of the believer.

So, while ordinary dispositional properties like fragility may be understood in terms of the intrinsic physical properties of their bearers, the properties mentioned in the counterfactuals relevant to belief may not be so understood. For their instantiation depends not only on the intrinsic properties of their bearers, but also on environmental conditions too complicated to begin to specify physically. Thus, accounts of ordinary dispositional properties like fragility provide no reason to think that appeal to relevant counterfactuals is just an intermediate step on the way to understanding beliefs as brain states.

Nevertheless, since much of what I have argued here is congenial to the view that beliefs are constituted by brain states, some may retain allegiance to the Standard View. After all, the "depth" metaphor runs deep, and reality, many are persuaded, must be unified. I would reply that unity is where you find it, and in the unity that we find the intentional and the nonintentional are thoroughly interwoven in ways that we cannot begin to disentangle. (Better, perhaps: There is a unified reality from which we abstract the intentional and the nonintentional.) So, I would urge abandoning the

Standard View. In addition to the difficulties with varieties of the Standard View that I have already discussed, I have two further reasons for rejecting the Standard View: (1) The most plausible version of the Standard View is, at best, a bare metaphysical thesis with no explanatory or epistemological import. (2) The Standard View rests on (what used to be called) a category mistake.

1. On the Standard View, belief states are said to be physically realized in the brain. But the term 'physical realization' oscillates between two distinct relations – supervenience and constitution.[39] As we saw in Chapter 5, supervenience is a relation between properties; constitution is, in the first instance, a relation between an object and the (material) elements that compose it.[40] As I pointed out, the distinction between supervenience and constitution is important. A contract may be constituted by a group of molecules that make up a certain piece of paper, but its property of being a contract does not supervene on the properties of the molecules. With the distinction between supervenience and constitution in mind, my initial reason for rejecting reconciliation with the Standard View is twofold: First, supervenience versions of the Standard View are false; second, even if a constitution version (or a token-identity version) of the Standard View were true, the fact – if it were a fact – that beliefs are constituted by brain states would not be explanatorily significant.[41]

Consider first supervenience versions of the Standard View. Af-

39 In *Physicialism: The Philosophical Foundations* (Oxford: Oxford University Press, 1994), Jeffrey Poland argues that materialism needs a realization theory that explains how base properties determine higher-level properties. Such a theory requires a relation stronger than strong supervenience, and stronger than strong-supervenience-cum-constitution.

40 Some may extend the notion of constitution to properties, but when they do, the "constitution" relation seems to turn out to be supervenience with a huge number of distinct supervenience bases. For example, in "The Metaphysics of Irreducibility," *Philosophical Studies* 63 (1991): 125–45, Derek Pereboom and Hilary Kornblith formulate a thesis of the "token-constitution of causal powers" as follows: "The causal powers of a token of kind F are constituted of the causal powers of a token of kind G just in case the token of kind F has the causal powers it does in virtue of its being constituted of a token of kind G" (131). As I understand it, token constitution of causal powers of the token of kind F by those of the token of kind G implies that (1) the causal powers of tokens of kind F are multiply realizable; (2) the causal powers of tokens of kind F are not identical to the causal powers of tokens of kind G; and (3) the causal powers of the token of kind F supervene on the causal powers of the token of kind G.

41 Of course, as I argue in Part I, I think that there are direct arguments against the currently available versions of the Standard View.

ter a decade and a half of argument, most philosophers agree that the property of believing that p (at least for most replacements of 'p') does not supervene on intrinsic properties of the believer.[42] In retrospect, it is difficult to see how anybody ever seriously thought that one's believing that, say, *Roe v. Wade* was an important Supreme Court decision supervened on the believer's intrinsic properties. Since brain states are determined wholly by the intrinsic properties of persons with brains, beliefs do not supervene on brain states. And this would be so even if beliefs were constituted by brain states. So, whether beliefs are constituted by brain states or not, the thesis that beliefs supervene on brain states is false.

Now turn to the other possible version of the Standard View – the thesis that, although beliefs do not supervene on brain states, they are nonetheless constituted by brain states.[43] This thesis fails to have epistemological or explanatory import. Unlike supervenience – which, although theoretically interesting, does not hold between beliefs and brain states – constitution is simply not a theoretically interesting relation for most intentional phenomena. The fact that a contract is constituted by a piece of paper reveals nothing about the nature of contracts. This point holds for intentional phenomena in general: Even when there is an undisputed relation of constitution between an intentionally identified object and material elements that constitute it, the constituting elements shed no explanatory light on the constituted object as intentionally identified.

For example, all college professors are constituted by human bodies. But to understand what college professors are, no one would study anatomy. Indeed, being constituted by a human body does not distinguish college professors from felons, judges, kings, soldiers, husbands, and wives. So, it is hardly surprising that human bodies are not the focus of inquiry into higher education, crime, justice, monarchy, war, or marriage. As already noted, there may be two people with no bodily difference whatsoever, one of

42 I am not supposing that the Standard View is individualistic. (What I am calling 'constitution versions' of the Standard View plainly are not individualistic.) As long as brain states are individuated in terms of a person's intrinsic properties, however, the mind–brain supervenience thesis is individualistic.

43 Richard Boyd pointed out to me in conversation that materialists still need to appeal to constitution as well as to supervenience. For supervenience alone would not rule out vitalism, or other claims about nonphysical "emergent" properties, that may be thought always to appear whenever the physical world is in such and such a state.

whom is a husband and the other of whom is not. In understanding intentional phenomena, material constitution is simply not the important relation, even when there is no uncertainty about what constitutes what.

Here we have a marked contrast between the physical and social sciences. In the physical sciences, where the phenomena under investigation are nonintentional, constitution is a crucially important relation: To understand lightning, find what constitutes it. Indeed, in the physical sciences, we take discovery of something's constitution to be discovery of its nature: It is the nature of water to be H_2O. In the social sciences, where the phenomena under investigation are intentional, material constitution is largely irrelevant. (Biology seems to be on the fence.) Even though personal-income-tax payers are constituted by human bodies, knowledge of that fact does not enhance understanding of anything about the tax system. What it means to be a person-income-tax payer or a schoolteacher or a husband is not determined by what constitutes (in the sense of materially composes) the taxpayer for felon or husband. Even if all money were constituted by pieces of paper, knowing that fact would bring us no closer to understanding the nature of money. Similarly, even if beliefs were constituted by brain states, that fact would no more illuminate the nature of belief than does the fact that the U.S. Declaration of Independence is constituted by a piece of parchment illuminate the nature of the early U.S. Republic. So, the constitution version of the Standard View is epistemologically idle.

Therefore, the Standard View does not reveal the nature of belief. The thesis that beliefs supervene on brain states is false, and the thesis that beliefs are constituted by brain states, if true, would not illuminate the nature of belief.

2. The second, and more important, reason not to try to reconcile Practical Realism with the Standard View is that the Standard View rests on a category mistake. The Standard View mistakes a necessary condition for belief for a relation of material constitution. Having certain kinds of brain states may be necessary for having beliefs; but it does not follow that particular brain states constitute particular beliefs. Brain states are ordinary spatiotemporal entities. Spatiotemporal entities are not widely scattered objects, but are compact objects that have more or less definite boundaries in space in time. A belief is no more constituted by an ordinary spatiotem-

poral entity than is the British Constitution.[44] To look for a spatiotemporal entity that constitutes either a belief or the British Constitution would be to make a mistake about the sort of thing under investigation.

The term 'belief' is a nominalization of 'believes that'.[45] I doubt that any particular spatiotemporal object has the property of *being a belief that* Clinton is president, but I do not doubt that people have the property of *having a belief that* Clinton is president (or, equivalently, the property of *believing that* Clinton is president). Since 'belief' is a noun, philosophers have been misled into thinking either that there are spatiotemporal entities that constitute beliefs or else that it is not literally true that we have beliefs. But if, as the Practical Realist urges, we understand the object of investigation not to be an ordinary entity at all, we see that the Standard View alternatives are not exhaustive. It is importantly *false* that S has a belief if and only if S has a particular brain state that satisfies the open sentence '*x* is a belief that *p*.' (Arguments for eliminative materialism depend crucially on not recognizing this fact.)[46]

On the Standard View, belief attributions are ultimately hypotheses about brains. By contrast, according to Practical Realism, as long as there are relevant counterfactuals, S believes that *p* – however the brain is organized. The overwhelming evidence that there are beliefs stems from our success in explaining behavior on the basis of attitudes, and from the fact that attitudes are constitutive of successful cognitive and social practices. Our confidence in the truth of sentences of the form '*S* believes that *p*' rests upon this sort of evidence, which has been available for millennia, and which is independent of any hypotheses about the brain. Presumably, one cannot believe that *p* without having certain brain states; but believ-

---

44 Note that denial that the British Constitution (as well as belief) is constituted by a spatiotemporal entity is compatible with materialism, understood as global supervenience or as the old-fashioned view that nothing exists but atoms and the void. Thus, no one needs the Standard View as a hedge against mind-body dualism. I discuss this further in Chapter 7.

45 Many have noted that 'belief' is ambiguous. Sometimes it refers to the proposition believed, and sometimes it refers to the state of believing. Although my interest is in the latter, I do not think that it is coherent to try to distinguish a state of believing from a state of believing that *p* (as Fodor did at one time). There is no state of believing without something believed.

46 For example, see Stich, *From Folk Psychology to Cognitive Science.*

ing that p is no more a property of a brain than writing bad checks is a property of a hand.

One does not understand the state of believing that a good publication record is required for getting tenure unless one understands the proposition that a good publication record is necessary for tenure; to understand that proposition, a theorist must understand not brains but employment practices (intentional!) and professional standards (also intentional!) of the modern academy (also intentional!). Neural processes no doubt "subserve" some of the indicative counterparts of the antecedents and consequents of the counterfactuals in humans, but the relation between beliefs and brain states bears scant resemblance to the relation between genes and DNA. For a more apt comparison to the relation between beliefs and brain states, we should look to the relation between winning a horse race and the physiology of horses' legs. To understand properties such as believing that a good publication record is required for getting tenure and what it is to have such properties, one need not look inside people's heads. Even if it were the case that there are belief tokens such that for every belief token, there is a brain-state token, that fact would be inessential to a belief's being a belief. What makes it the case that a person has a belief is that there be a set of counterfactuals true of the person. No account in terms of brain states could capture the class of beliefs except *per accidens*.[47]

Therefore, I urge resistance to combining Practical Realism with the Standard View: First, the supervenience version of the Standard View is false, and the constitution version is unilluminating. Second, the Standard View rests on a category mistake. Let me emphasize that rejection of the Standard View is not rejection of the relevance of neurophysiology to the mind (nor is it rejection of materialism; see Chapter 7). It is, rather, rejection of the claim that each instance of each belief is identical with, or is constituted by, some particular state of the brain.

Here is a catalog of the differences between the Standard View and the Practical Realist View. According to the Standard View at its most robust:

1. One has a belief that p by virtue of being in a particular brain state that *is* a belief that p or that *constitutes* a belief that p.

47 This sentence is a paraphrase of Daniel Dennett's comment on Ryle's account of intelligent action in "Three Kinds of Intentional Psychology," 45.

2. Beliefs are subpersonal; the bearer of a belief in the first instance is a brain.
3. The explanatory power of beliefs requires that beliefs be "isomorphic" to (perhaps distributed) brain states.
4. We must await the outcome of science to tell us what beliefs are (and whether there are any at all).

According to the Practical Realist View:

1. One has a belief that *p* by virtue of there being a conjunction of relevant true counterfactuals that mention a range of circumstances in which the believer would perform a range of intentional actions – thinkings, doings, and sayings.
2. Beliefs are not subpersonal: They are global states of whole persons, in the same sense that actions are.
3. The explanatory power of beliefs derives from the fact that their role in our practices makes it possible to manipulate behavior by manipulating attitudes – without regard for hypotheses about brain states.
4. We need not await the outcome of science for a verdict on belief. Understanding our cognitive practices tells us what beliefs are, and the reliability of those practices in the sciences and in everyday affairs assures us that there are beliefs.

LANGUAGE AND THE INNER LIFE

A prominent feature of our existence – of mine, at least – is what I shall call an 'inner life'. Not only do we have beliefs, but we also consciously entertain our beliefs and other attitudes. I can call to mind my college graduation; I can "replay" the events of the day; I can recite poetry without moving my lips; I can silently rehearse my lines in a skit; I can set about examining my conscience. All of these are episodes of first-personal awareness.[48] (Let 'thoughts' refer to the objects of any such episodes.) My inner life consists of first-personal episodes that are private, in the sense that I may choose not to divulge it to anyone else.[49] To investigate the epistemic status and ontology of first-personal episodes is far beyond the scope of my project.[50] Here I only want to see whether the

---

48 John R. Searle has proposed that there is no mental state that is inaccessible to consciousness. See *The Rediscovery of the Mind* (Cambridge, MA:MIT/Bradford, 1992). We need not go that far to concede that many mental states are accessible to consciousness.
49 They are not private in the sense in which Wittgenstein denied that there could be a private language.
50 One important study is Gareth B. Matthews's *Thought's Ego in Augustine and Descartes* (Ithaca, NY: Cornell University Press, 1992).

(admitted) existence of first-personal episodes constitutes a threat to Practical Realism.

Considerations like the following may lead one to think that first-personal episodes present a difficulty for Practical Realism: "When I entertain the thought that *p*, something is going on inside me. If what is going on inside me is not constituted by brain states, by what is it constituted? The only possible answer seems to be: soul states. But appeal to soul states is untenable. So, first-personal episodes (e.g., consciously entertaining a belief that *p*) must be constituted by brain states even if believing that *p* is not."

This line is precisely the Cartesian reasoning against which I have been arguing (and about which I have more to say in Chapter 7). The mistake is to think that constitution is a universal relation – so that it makes sense to ask of *everything*, By what is it constituted? – and then to suppose that there are only two possible answers, material things or immaterial things. But if I have been right, the question – By what is such and such constituted? – cannot meaningfully be asked of just anything. The question may be asked meaningfully of material objects (buildings, diamonds); but it does not follow from this that the question may be asked meaningfully of intentional phenomena, first-personal or not.

First-personal episodes are obviously intentional: Entertaining the belief that *p* presupposes that there be beliefs that *p* (where there is a belief that *p* just in case someone believes that *p* and someone believes that *p* just in case there are relevant counterfactuals true of the believer). From the Practical Realist point of view, first-personal episodes are in many ways like other intentional episodes.[51] Although some intentional episodes may be constituted by physical episodes (e.g., the S&L's investment was constituted by an electronic impulse), we can deny that other intentional episodes (e.g., the founding of the U.S. Republic) are constituted in the relevant sense by molecules. And this denial does not force us to suppose that the founding of the U.S. Republic is constituted by

---

51 I take there to be an irreducible distinction between a first-personal perspective and a third-personal perspective, and first-personal episodes are available only from a first-personal perspective. For a provocative discussion of "the incompleteness of objective reality," see Thomas Nagel, *The View from Nowhere* (New York: Oxford University Press, 1986). Also, see my "Why Computers Can't Act," *American Philosophical Quarterly* 18 (1981): 157–63. Although important, this issue is not directly relevant to the current discussion.

immaterial objects. I think that the worry about first-personal episodes is as misplaced as a similar worry about the founding of the U.S. Republic would be. Even if molecular motion is a necessary condition for the founding of the U.S. Republic, we need not conclude that the founding is constituted by such molecular motion. Similarly (again!), even if having certain brain states is a necessary condition for entertaining the thought that p, it does not follow that those brain states constitute the episode.

So, I do not think that the existence of first-personal episodes poses a threat to Practical Realism.[52] If *having a belief that p* is a relational property of a whole person, then so is *entertaining a belief that p*. Furthermore, there are relevant counterfactuals for entertaining thoughts. Here is a candidate to be a relevant counterfactual for entertaining thoughts about one's trip to Alaska: If x were asked what she was thinking about, and x were a competent speaker, and x understood the question, was not laboring under self-deception, and wanted to cooperate, then x would say that she was thinking about her trip to Alaska.

This candidate for a counterfactual relevant to one's thinking about one's trip to Alaska also illustrates a special feature of first-personal episodes: They are linguistic episodes. Unlike Davidson, I hold that nonlinguistic beings have beliefs, for example, the belief that there is food over there, or even the first-personal belief that could be expressed by the English sentence, 'I am in danger'. But the range of their beliefs is severely limited. Perhaps it extends little farther than to beliefs about the present environment. By learning a language, we are able to have thoughts (and hence beliefs) about anything – about events in the past and future; about theoretical entities; about abstractions like beauty, truth, and goodness; about divine beings; about irrational numbers – about anything for which we have a concept or word in our language. (I think that recent philosophers of mind have underestimated the role of public language in making possible people's beliefs.) The vast majority of our beliefs are thus "language-dependent": We could not have them if we lacked the requisite public-language apparatus. First-personal episodes having language-dependent beliefs as objects are themselves linguistic episodes.

52 Practical Realism can treat the problem of qualia in the same way that it treats first-personal episodes. Qualia should no more be reified than beliefs.

I would like to go farther, however, to suggest that all first-personal episodes are linguistic in the sense that only creatures with a public language can have them. Although I cannot defend this view here, I can illustrate it. (1) On the one hand, it may seem that we have first-personal episodes that are independent of language: Suppose that you have some ineffable experience that seems beyond the powers of language to describe (other than to say that it is ineffable). I would concede that this is possible, but suggest that the ability to have such an experience derives from your being a language user. I do not think that dogs and cats have such ineffable experiences. (2) On the other hand, dogs and cats may have some beliefs. Suppose, as seems likely, that a nonlinguistic creature can have a belief expressible in English by 'I am in danger.' I can agree that it can have this belief without agreeing that it can entertain a first-personal episode with the content that it (itself) is in danger. Speaking metaphorically, to entertain such a thought is to hold it before one's mind – whether it is believed or not, whether it is true or not, whether it is prompted by some present environmental stimulus or not. This suggests – rightly, I think – that first-personal episodes should be thought of as inner speech, as utterances of unvocalized sentences in a public language.[53]

Again, my view contrasts with the Standard View on the relation between thought and spoken language. There are several versions of the Standard View, all attempting either to reduce language to thought or to reduce thought to language: Suppose that (a) there is a language of thought ("Mentalese"); then on the Standard View, either (i) spoken language is reducible to the language of thought, and we need a theory of the language of thought that does not presuppose the existence of a public language, or (ii) the language of thought is itself a public language, and we need a theory of public language that does not presuppose the existence of the representational character of mental states. On the other hand, suppose that (b) there is no language of thought; then, on the Standard View, spoken language is reducible to (nonlinguistic) representational mental states, and we need a theory of the mental states that

53 In this respect, I agree with Wilfrid Sellars. See Jay L. Garfield, "The Myth of Jones and the Mirror of Nature: Reflections on Introspection," *Philosophy and Phenomenological Research* 50 (1989): 1–26.

makes no reference to their representational character.[54] However, if I have been right, then none of the proposed reductions will be satisfactory: The fact that nonlinguistic animals can have rudimentary beliefs notwithstanding, for linguistic beings thought and spoken language develop together.

CONCLUSION

According to Practical Realism, beliefs are states of persons – like states of matrimony, states of bankruptcy, and states of disgrace. Practical Realism accords with common practice – practice that extends to every part of human life. By appealing to counterfactuals to account for belief, Practical Realism shows why our ability to make correct attributions of belief is independent of knowledge of brains: We know a great deal about what a person would do in various circumstances, even though we have no access to the person's internal states. In some domains, the metaphor of "depth" pays off: Isolation of HIV viruses provided a much deeper understanding of the disease known as AIDS. But the attitudes are not like AIDS: There are no comparable "deeper" facts to be discovered.

Practical Realism explains what Jerry Fodor has called "the persistence of the attitudes,"[55] but without Fodor's commitment to the existence of mental representations constituted by brain states. By not requiring beliefs to be brain states, Practical Realism explicitly abandons mentalism. By not giving conditions for believing that *p* solely in terms of behavior, it implicitly abandons behaviorism. (I take it to be a signal virtue that this approach shows that mentalism and behaviorism are not exhaustive alternatives.)

Practical Realism has two advantages over the Standard View: First, it avoids problems of prominent versions of the Standard View discussed in Chapters 2–4. Second, regardless of the future of neurophysiology, true counterfactuals relevant to *S*'s believing that *p* will almost surely be available; hence, attitudes are not held hos-

54 For example, see, respectively, Jerry A. Fodor, *Psychosemantics: The Problem of Meaning in the Philosophy of Mind* (Cambridge MA: MIT/Bradford, 1987); Gilbert Harman, *Thought* (Princeton: Princeton University Press, 1973); and Robert Stalnaker, *Inquiry* (Cambridge MA: MIT/Bradford, 1984).
55 Fodor, *Psychosemantics,* chap. 1.

tage to developments in neuroscience. Thus, we have good reason to avail ourselves of this alternative to the Standard View. Otherwise, in light of the vulnerability of the claim that there are beliefs-construed-as-brain-states to disconfirmation by neuroscience, we may find ourselves at the mercy of a nonintentional version of Descartes's Evil Genius.

7

Mind and metaphysics

Just as the Standard View finds its home in a particular metaphysical picture, so does Practical Realism. In Chapter 8, I sketch the larger metaphysical picture from which my account of belief is an abstraction. In this chapter, however, I want to defend Practical Realism from objections based on the metaphysics of the Standard View. The first objection is that the account of the attitudes is not "naturalistic": It does not provide (nor does it aim to provide) nonintentional and nonsemantic conditions for having an attitude. The second objection concerns scientific psychology: It may be charged, on the one hand, that Practical Realism renders attitudes unsuitable for any theoretical role in science and, on the other hand, that, anyway, psychological research relies on (and hence indirectly confirms) the conception of beliefs as brain states. The third objection is that Practical Realism may be incompatible with materialism. The last objection is that Practical Realism is no realism at all.

NEED INTENTIONALITY BE "NATURALIZED"?

Many philosophers suppose that there is an important pretheoretical distinction between intentional and nonintentional properties. Say that a property is intentional if and only if either it is a propositional-attitude property – for example, the property of believing that such and such – or its instantiation presupposes instantiation of propositional-attitude properties.[1] Whereas nonintentional properties, such as the property of being constituted by H_2O,

---

1 A simpler, but faulty, way to characterize intentional properties is as properties that cannot be instantiated in a world without attitudes. This characterization is unsatisfactory since it would rule out reduction of intentional to nonintentional properties a priori: Any physical properties nomologically sufficient for instantiation of any intentional property would be counted as intentional on the simpler definition. I am grateful to Jeffrey Poland, Robert Pennock, Mark Webb, and Michael Patton for discussion of this point.

seem to reside safely in molecular reality, intentional properties seem to be uncertainly rooted in the physical world. In response to such worries, philosophers have undertaken to "naturalize" intentionality by showing how intentional properties depend on nonintentional properties. As Jerry Fodor vividly put it in a now famous passage:

I suppose that sooner or later the physicists will complete the catalogue they've been compiling of the ultimate and irreducible properties of things. When they do, the likes of *spin, charm,* and *charge* will perhaps appear upon their list. But *aboutness* surely won't; intentionality simply doesn't go that deep. It's hard to see, in face of this consideration, how one can be a Realist about intentionality without also being, to some extent or other, a Reductionist.

Fodor concludes: "If the semantic and the intentional are real properties of things, it must be in virtue of their identity with (or maybe of their supervenience on?) properties that are themselves *neither* intentional *nor* semantic. If aboutness is real, it must be really something else."[2]

Such considerations give rise to a stringent methodological demand: For any putative reality, either "naturalize" it or give it up as illusory. Naturalization of intentionality is just one step on the way to satisfying this general demand. Say that an intentional property is naturalized if and only if we can specify nonintentional and nonsemantic conditions for its instantiation. The naturalization project is thus a *project* – something that either is or is not successfully carried out. It is not a bare metaphysical thesis.

My aim in discussing the naturalization project is partly negative and partly positive. On the negative side, I hope to show that the project of naturalizing intentionality need not be undertaken at all, and is unlikely to be completed if undertaken. The distinction between intentional and nonintentional properties marks no gap that requires theoretical closure. On the positive side, I hope to demonstrate the pervasiveness of intentionality and its resistance to any formulable reduction to the nonintentional.

Many of the properties that interest us are intentional: Intentional properties, of course, comprise not only properties like regretting

---

2 Jerry A. Fodor, *Psychosemantics: The Problem of Meaning in the Philosophy of Mind* (Cambridge MA: MIT/Bradford, 1987), 97.

that such and such, or of missing someone who has left town; but also nonpsychological properties of legal, social, aesthetic, religious, economic, and political institutions are intentional properties. Not surprisingly, the effort to naturalize intentionality has focused on psychological properties – like that of being a mental representation with a certain content. By contrast, I think that attention to *nonpsychological* intentional properties is more instructive to one who hopes to naturalize intentionality.

Here is my argument that intentionality need not be naturalized:

(P*1) Artifactual properties are intentional properties.

(P*2) Artifactual properties do not require naturalization.

Therefore,

(C*1) Some intentional properties do not require naturalization.

(P*3) If some intentional properties do not require naturalization, then none does.

Therefore,

(C*2) Intentionality does not require naturalization.

When I say that artifactual properties are intentional properties, I mean this: For any kind of artifact *A,* the property of being an *A* is never determined wholly by local microstructure, but rather something is an *A* only in the context of particular practices, purposes, and uses – all of which are intentional. This is not to say that local microstructure is irrelevant to something's being an *A:* You couldn't make a spaceship out of mud, or a tractor out of jelly beans. The point that I shall defend is rather this: Artifactual properties are intentional (whether intentionality can be naturalized or not). Physical structure alone does not insure that something has the property of being an *A.*

In support of (P*1), let me offer a thought experiment. Suppose that what looks like a carburetor spontaneously coalesced in outer space. Is it a carburetor? I say no, the property of being a carburetor depends on more than local microstructure; it depends on our practices and intentions, the uses to which we put things; and these practices, intentions, and uses all presuppose propositional attitudes. So the spontaneously coalesced object in outer space, though physically indistinguishable from a carburetor, is not a carburetor. Consider some objections and replies.[3]

Objection 1: Given an analysis of the property of being a carburetor, we can see that the spontaneously coalesced object is a carburetor after all. We can eliminate the apparent intentionality of the property of being a carburetor (or any other artifact). Let M^* be the set of properties that define the physically possible structures that could be carburetors. Now the property of being a carburetor is the vastly disjunctive property of all the properties in M^*. So, for any possible x, x is a carburetor if and only if x has one of the properties in M^*. So, the spontaneously coalesced object in outer space is a carburetor. And we have got rid of all intentional presuppositions.

Reply 1: Not so fast. This is based on a faulty analysis of the property of being a carburetor.[4] To see this, suppose that we never had invented carburetors, but had instead constructed physical devices that were physically indistinguishable from carburetors. Suppose that these other devices mixed air and water and were used in the manufacture of soft drinks, and that they were called 'drinkalators'.[5] Following the preceding analysis, consider the set of properties that define the physically possible structures that could be drinkalators. Exactly the same set of structures – defined by properties in M^* – could be drinkalators as could be carburetors. Now the property of being a drinkalator is also the vastly disjunctive property of all the properties in M^*. So, for any possible x, x is a drinkalator if and only if x has one of the properties in M^*. It follows from these analyses that an actual or possible object has the property of being a carburetor if and only if it has the property of being a drinkalator. Indeed, on the objector's analysis, the property of being a carburetor would be identical to the property of being a drinkalator.

---

3 Some of the objections have affinities with theses about mental states that David Lewis has espoused. See, for example, "Psychophysical and Theoretical Identifications" in *Readings in the Philosophy of Psychology,* vol. 1, ed. Ned Block, (Cambridge, MA: Harvard University Press, 1980), 207–15.

4 For what it is worth, a carburetor is defined as "a device that vaporizes a liquid fuel such as gasoline and mixes it with air in the proper ratio for combustion in an internal-combusion engine, such as the gasoline engine that powers most automobiles." *Academic American Encyclopedia,* vol. 4 (Danbury, CT: Grolier, 1989), 141.

5 I am grateful to Ed Weirenga for discussion of this point and for suggesting the term 'drinkalator.'

But that is false: My car's carburetor has the property of being a carburetor, not of being a drinkalator. Carburetors are not drinkalators even if they are physically indistinguishable from drinkalators – any more than a "yes" vote is a "no" vote even if the bodily movements by which the votes could be cast were physically indistinguishable. Carburetors are what they are in virtue of their place in one set of practices (practices that include design, manufacture, distribution, advertising, sales, and use of automobiles); drinkalators are what they are in virtue of their place in a different set of practices (practices that include worldwide sugar sales, taste tests, recipe fixing, production, advertising, distribution, sale, and consumption of soft drinks). Since carburetors are not drinkalators, the objector's analysis of the property of being a carburetor is incorrect, and the spontaneously coalesced object is not a carburetor.

Objection 2: OK, then being a carburetor is a hybrid property, composed of two kinds of properties: nonintentional (a carburetor has one of the properties in M^*), and intentional (a carburetor is a device made and used for a certain purpose). Then, a drinkalator would also be a hybrid, but one that shares the nonintentional component of the carburetor.[6]

Reply 2(a): I have two replies. First, in general, the (putative) components of artifactual properties that are nonintentional are too unconstrained to play any theoretical role in understanding the properties in question. Hardly any physical property would fail to be in the set that defines possible physical structures that could be, say, a sculpture, or a doorstop.

Reply 2(b): Second, even if this decomposition of artifactual properties could be sustained, the original point of the example would remain untouched. The original point was to show that artifactual properties have intentional presuppositions, that nothing is a carburetor (or a drinkalator or a sculpture) apart from intentional presuppositions. By holding that the property of being a carburetor is decomposable into intentional and nonintentional

6 The analogy between the physical property and the (putative) narrow content of a belief is intended. The strategy of decomposing artifactual properties works better than the strategy for decomposing content into wide and narrow, because in the case of artifactual properties, there is an artifact that can be located apart from its artifactual properties – as 'the thing in the corner', for example. In the case of belief, without a type-type identity theory, there is no way to locate something (e.g., a brain state) as a belief other than by content.

properties, this version of the objection concedes that point, and then goes on to add that we can shear off a nonintentional property. But of course, the property in question is the property of being a carburetor, now understood as a hybrid property that has an intentional as well as a nonintentional component. So, on the current objection, being a carburetor remains a property with intentional presuppositions, which, if the naturalization project has any merit, must be discharged.

Objection 3: This just shows that we should distinguish between properties and the words with which we pick them out. When we say that something is a carburetor, we use the English predicate 'is a carburetor' to pick out the set of physical properties M^*. 'Is a carburetor' means 'has one of the properties in M^*'. M^* could equally be picked out by the predicate 'is a drinkalator'. So, the problem you cite is only a linguistic infelicity – a problem about the *appropriateness* of using the predicates 'is a carburetor' and 'is a drinkalator', not a problem about the property of being a carburetor or the property of being a drinkalator. There is no property of being a carburetor (or a drinkalator) per se, but there is an underlying physical property – the disjunction of the members of M^* – shared by both carburetors and drinkalators, that we can pick out equally by the term 'carburetor' or 'drinkalator.' Whether it is felicitous to use the word 'carburetor' or 'drinkalator' to pick out a member of M^* depends on a variety of contextual features, such as the purpose of the device. But the underlying (and vastly disjunctive) physical property expressed either of these terms has no intentional presuppositions.

Reply 3(a): On this line, there is no semantic difference between calling something a carburetor and calling it a drinkalator. 'X is a carburetor' and X is a drinkalator' have the same truth conditions: Each is true if and only if X has a structure determined by a member of M^*. Let a be a spontaneously coalesced object in outer space, whose structure is determined by a member of M^*. Then, on the current line, it is true of a that it is a carburetor and it is true of a that it is a drinkalator – although it would be infelicitous to say so. It is strained and unnatural to suppose that it is true to say of any carburetor that it is a drinkalator.

Reply 3(b): Moreover, consider the Tupperware bowl on my shelf; call it 'b'. On the current line, 'b is a carburetor' and 'b is a drinkalator' are both true. For suppose that, as it happens, my

Tupperware bowl has a hole in the bottom. And if it were placed under the air filter of my car, and I sat on the edge with an egg beater and furiously mixed the air and gasoline, the Tupperware-bowl-cum-egg-beater would make the car run in the same way as the carburetor does. Therefore, a member of M^* determines the structure of the Tupperware bowl. So, if having a structure determined by a member of M^* made 'is a carburetor' and 'is a drinkalator' true of an object, it would be true of my Tupperware bowl that it is a carburetor and that it is a drinkalator. But surely the bare (and remote) possibility of putting my unsullied Tupperware bowl to such use does *not* make it true (albeit odd) to say that it is a carburetor or a drinkalator.

So, the objector's shift from properties (e.g., being a carburetor) to predicates (e.g., 'is a carburetor') nets him no gain. For it is just as bizarre to suppose that 'X is a carburetor' and 'X is a drinkalator' have the same truth conditions (though they differ in "felicity conditions") as it is to suppose that the property of being a carburetor is identical to the property of being a drinkalator.

I conclude that 'is a carburetor' and 'is a drinkalator' are not just two ways to pick out a single complex physical property; rather, they express different *intentionally specified functional* properties, which are not identical to the disjunction of physical properties that determine structures that can serve the functions in question. A carburetor occupies a different functional role from a drinkalator: The function of assisting combustion in an automobile engine is different from the function of producing soft drinks.

It is simply a physical accident – one that has no bearing on the meanings of the predicates or on the identity of properties – that things that are carburetors could have been used as drinkalators and vice versa. Words like 'carburetor' and 'drinkalator' get their meanings from their place in our linguistic practices, which are wholly integrated into all manner of practice – from the practices surrounding automobile manufacture to junk-food consumption. These practices are through and through intentional.

In short, we do not use a term like 'is a carburetor' to pick out a range of physical properties at all (any more than we use 'is a "yes" vote' to pick out a range of physical properties), but rather to pick out the intentional property of functioning in a certain way in accordance with our purposes.

Objection 4: You are focusing too narrowly on a physical struc-

ture in isolation. Suppose that the object *a* had spontaneously coalesced inside a larger structure (that also had spontaneously coalesced) that was physically indistinguishable from a whole engine
inside a whole car, together with gas and air, in an atmospheric
bubble that allowed combustion. Surely, now *a* would be a carburetor. And its being a carburetor would have no intentional presuppositions.

Reply 4(a): Whether *a* in these circumstances is a carburetor or
not depends on how broadly we understand the functional property
in question. If something is a carburetor only if it has a certain role
in our automotive practices (as I think), then *a* is still not a carburetor. But if (as others may think) assisting combustion in a certain
way in an internal–combustion engine suffices to make something a
carburetor, then *a* may be claimed to be a carburetor. But even
under the narrower definition of function, such a claim would be
dubious, for to suppose that the larger structure is an internal-
combustion engine just raises the same questions about the artifactual property of being an engine that we already had about being a
carburetor.

Reply 4(b): In any case, another example will show that the "embedding" strategy – the strategy of taking *a* to be a carburetor if
embedded in a spontaneously coalesced larger structure – cannot be
generalized to all artifacts. A bushing tool is a steel cylinder with an
array of small steel pyramids on top that is used to shape stone for
making sculptures or building stones. Suppose that something
physically indistinguishable from a bushing tool spontaneously coalesced in outer space: Would it be a bushing tool – even if also
hunks of marble also spontaneously coalesced alongside it? No.
The "embedding" strategy does not work at all for a bushing tool,
unless the larger structure contains individuals with attitudes. For a
bushing tool must be wielded by an individual with attitudes in
order to serve its function. What makes something a bushing tool is
its use in the thoroughly intentional practices of shaping stones for
building and sculpture.

Thus, the "embedding" strategy for arguing that artifactual
properties are nonintentional is faced with a dilemma: Let *C* be a
larger context in which the object alleged to have an artifactual
property is placed. Then, either *C* itself has intentional presuppositions or the object fails to have the artifactual property.

Objection 5: Your claim is too strong. Even if being a carburetor or a bushing tool has intentional presuppositions, other kinds of artifactual properties resist such treatment. For example, what is produced by recombinant DNA has a good claim to being artifactual, but we do not want to say that such artifactual properties are intentional. To see this, suppose that geneticists have developed DNA for a juiceless tomato, with structure 123. Now compare the artificially produced 123 with some natural 123, that resulted from a mutation of ordinary tomato DNA. There is here a single property: being DNA with structure 123, regardless of how it came to be instantiated. So, assuming that the property of being 123 has no intentional presuppositions in the case of mutation, it also has no intentional presuppositions in the case of recombinant DNA.

Reply 5(a): Although I think that all artifactual properties are intentional, I do not need that claim for my argument. My argument will go through if I've made the case that the property of being a carburetor is intentional.

Reply 5(b): I agree that there is a property of being DNA with structure 123 and that that property has no intentional presuppositions, regardless of its manner of production. But that property is not the artifactual property in question; being DNA with structure 123 is not an artifactual property at all. If there is an artifactual property lurking here, it is the property of being *artificially produced* 123, and that property does have intentional presuppositions. For that property is defined in part in terms of its causal history, where that causal history is intentionally specified.

Indeed, this is not an isolated case. Intentional causal histories often contribute to important properties of a thing. For example, artificial diamonds are molecularly like natural diamonds, but worth far less; the property of being a diamond has no intentional presuppositions but the property of being an artificial diamond does – and if you are considering what price to pay, the difference is important. (Examples could be multiplied.)

The upshot of this discussion is that artifactual properties are intentional, as premise (P*1) asserts.[7]

---

7 There are deep issues here that are beyond the scope of this project. I am indebted to Katherine Sonderegger for patient and acute discussion of the drinkalator example, and for pointing me to the deeper issues.

Premise (P*2) asserts that artifactual properties need not be naturalized.[8] Here is my argument for (P*2): Suppose that some artifactual properties elude our best efforts to come up with nonintentional and nonsemantic conditions for their instantiation. (As far as I know, no specification of nonintentional and nonsemantic conditions for the *practices* in virtue of which something is a carburetor is on the horizon.) In that case, we must choose: Either give up the claim that artifactual properties need to be naturalized, or give up the claim that there are carburetors. Since the claim that there are carburetors is much better founded than the claim that artifactual properties need to be naturalized, we should give up the claim that artifactual properties need to be naturalized.

To see that the prospects for naturalizing artifactual properties really are slim, ask: How could nointentional and nonsemantic conditions be specified for artifactual properties? I can think of three strategies, the first two of which are kinds of individualism, the third an "ecological" approach. The first strategy is to try to naturalize artifactual properties directly.[9] First, show how nonpsychological intentional properties (such as being a carburetor) supervene on psychological intentional properties (such as representing something as a carburetor); then naturalize the psychological intentional properties. That is, first determine an "intermediate" supervenience base for the property of being a carburetor (still intentional, but psychological), and then naturalize the properties in the intermediate supervenience base of the artifactual property.[10] The second strategy is to naturalize nonpsychological intentional properties indirectly by reducing the special sciences in which they are taxonomic to psychological sciences (e.g., by reducing macro-

8 In "Computation, Naturalization and Psychological Explanation," presented at the Boston Colloquium for the Philosophy of Science, November 1, 1993, Steven Horst argued that scientific psychology does not and need not naturalize intentionality.
9 For example, Dan Sperber holds an individualistic view that might be adapted for this purpose. See "The Epidemiology of Beliefs," in *The Social Psychological Study of Widespread Beliefs,* ed. Colin Fraser and George Gaskell (Oxford: Clarendon Press, 1990), 25–44.
10 Notice that this kind of individualism (a reduction of the social to the psychological) does not entail "individualism" in the sense made famous by Tyler Burge (mental properties as supervenient on *intrinsic* nonmental properties). The kind of individualism at issue here is compatible with denial of individualism in Burge's sense. For example, suppose that the social were reducible to psychological properties that were nonintentional but still relational.

economics to microeconomics to decision theory), and then to naturalize psychology. The second strategy, however, is not independent of the first; for regardless of the success of reductions of social sciences to psychology, sooner or later the naturalizer will have to give a naturalistic account of the property of representing intentional properties. Moreover, not all artifactual properties are taxonomic in some science. So, even if the social sciences were reduced to psychology, naturalization of psychology would still require naturalization of the property of representing something as an F, where being an F is itself an intentional property. I see no way for the naturalizer to avoid giving a naturalistic account of representing intentional properties. (As far as I know, those undertaking the naturalization project have never even tried to naturalize the [doubly intentional] property of representing an intentional property; this is an important omission since many of our attitudes are directed toward intentional [with a 't'] states of affairs – for example, Jane hopes that her child will make good grades.)

Let us see how a naturalizer might set about giving a naturalistic account of an intentional property by naturalizing the property of representing an intentional property. What psychological properties are candidates for the intermediate supervenience base for an artifactual property? Perhaps the intermediate supervenience base would include the property of representing something as having the artifactual property in question – as, perhaps, Jack's being handsome supervenes on the property of Jack's being represented as handsome. So, letting 'F' range over artifactual properties, the first suggestion is this:

(a) a is an F only if someone represents a as an F.

Now as an individualistic reduction, (a) is circular unless we can naturalize the property of representing something as an F without appealing to the property of being an F. That is, on pain of vicious circularity, we must naturalize the property of representing something as an F without either presupposing that we have already naturalized the property of being an F or employing an unnaturalized property of being an F. For we cannot presuppose that we have already naturalized the property of being an F in the very naturalization of that property; and an unnaturalized property of being an F (or any other intentional property) cannot remain at the end of a successful naturalization. So, as it stands, (a) will not do.

For we first have to find some kind of decomposition of the property of being F into other properties. Then, perhaps we could say that a is an F only if someone represents something as having the properties into which F is decomposed. In that case, the property of representing the properties in the decomposition of F would be the intermediate supervenience base for the property of being an F.

Perhaps the property of being an F has a decomposition that includes the property of representing something as having some other intentional property besides the property of being an F. For example, the intermediate supervenience base for the property of being a carburetor may include the property of representing something, not directly as a carburetor, but as, say, a piece of equipment, or the property of representing something else as an engine. Letting F^* range over intentional properties, the suggestion now is this:

(b) a is an F only if someone represents something as an F^* (where being an F^* is an intentional property distinct from being an F).

But representing something as a piece of equipment or as an engine is doubly intentional: not only is representing something as an engine intentional in virtue of being the property of *representing* something; but also (by P*1) the property *represented* is itself intentional. So, on proposal (b), the naturalizer will have to naturalize the property of representing something as an F^*, where F^* is itself an intentional property.

The standard approaches to naturalization attempt to give nonintentional conditions for representing nonintentional properties. In the standard targets of naturalization, the intentionality resides, so to speak, only in the representing, not in the property represented. The standard strategy is to appeal to causal or explanatory relations between the property represented and the representation of it. For example, philosophers have tried to naturalize the property of representing something as a cat in various ways: An internal state represents a cat if it is of a type caused by cats in normal conditions; or an internal state represents a cat if its tokening is asymmetrically dependent on cats; or an internal state represents a cat if the proper functioning of the organism (or its ancestors) is explained by a correlation between the presence of cats and internal states of this

204

type.[11] All of these proposals appeal to the (nonintentional) property of being a cat in order to naturalize the (intentional) property of *representing* something as a cat. But these standard approaches to naturalization are blocked when the property represented is itself an intentional property. In naturalizing the property of representing an F^*, where being an F^* is an intentional property, one cannot stop at appeal to the property of being an F^*: One cannot claim to have naturalized one intentional property by invoking another.

Now either every intentional property has intentional presuppositions or else there are primitive intentional properties, in terms of which all the other intentional properties may be defined. If every intentional property has intentional presuppositions, naturalization cannot be carried out. If there are primitive intentional properties, then the naturalizer has a twofold task: first, to naturalize the primitive intentional properties without invoking the properties themselves; and second, to show how all other intentional properties – such as the property of being a carburetor – are definable partly in terms of the primitive intentional properties. Although I am dubious about both aspects of the task, consider here only the difficulty of showing how nonprimitive intentional properties are definable in terms of primitive intentional properties.

Suppose that among the primitive intentional properties are properties of representing nonintentional properties; and suppose that we had a naturalization for representing being a G, where being a G is a nonintentional property. Then, could we simply iterate the naturalization so that we get a naturalization for the property representing a representation of G?[12] If so, we would have a naturalization of at least one doubly intentional property. However, this strategy for reducing double intentionality to single intentionality (even if it were to work) would be of only limited use. For example, it would seem unavailable for naturalizing the property of being a carburetor. Even if we had a naturalization of the property of representing a representation of G (where G is a nonintentional property), it is difficult to see how we could know which nonintentional properties must be represented as part of a sufficient condition for instantiation of the property of being a carburetor – unless

11 See, for example, Dretske, Fodor, Millikan.
12 This strategy was suggested by Charles Parsons.

we already had a naturalistic reduction of the property of being a carburetor.

Alternatively, suppose that among the primitive intentional properties are properties of intending to X, where X is specified nonintentionally, and suppose that we had a naturalization of these intentional properties. Then, could we take a step toward naturalizing at least some artifactual properties – the property of being a knife, say – in terms of use, where use is understood as something like this: 'intending for x to cause rupture of a surface'?[13] If so, perhaps we could naturalize at least one artifactual property, the property of being a knife. I see two problems here.

1. The current strategy assumes both (i) that 'x's causing rupture of a surface' is a nonintentional description and (ii) that being intended to cause rupture of a surface is the defining property of a knife. I doubt that (i) and (ii) are both true. If being intended to cause rupture of a surface is the defining property of a knife, then 'causing rupture of a surface' is itself intentional. Not just anything that causes rupture of a surface is a knife; knives cause surface ruptures in some ways and not in others. Dynamite and ice picks rupture surfaces, but are not knives. It is not obvious how the way in which something is intended to cause rupture of a surface may be specified nonintentionally and still be the defining property of a knife.[14]

2. Even if this strategy were to succeed in reducing the double intentionality of representing something as a knife to the intentionality of intending to cause rupture of a surface, it has the same problem as the preceding one: It seems not to be generalizable to other intentional properties, such as the property of being a carburetor (still less to the property of being a driver's license). For each kind of artifact, we would have to enumerate properties, $P_1, \ldots P_n$, such that having intentions toward states of affairs in which $P_1, \ldots P_n$ were instantiated would suffice for something's being that kind of artifact. For more complicated artifactual properties, we have no idea how to enumerate the relevant nonintentional properties.

Both of the preceding strategies concern reducing the double intentionality of artifactual properties to single intentionality. Even

13 This strategy was suggested by Hilary Putnam.
14 I am grateful to Alan Berger for discussion of this point.

if one or the other were successful, we would still have the problem of naturalizing the (allegedly) primitive intentional properties. For reasons given in Chapter 2, as well as for those given in *Saving Belief*, I do not think that we are close to having a naturalization of properties like representing being a G (where being a G is a nonintentional property). Thus, I am not optimistic about either step in the two-step process of eliminating the double intentionality of many intentional properties – not just artifactual properties, but the property of having any attitude at all whose content mentions an intentional property.

The third strategy for naturalizing artifactual properties would simply bypass the problem of representing artifactual properties altogether. For example, following Ruth Millikan's teleofunctional approach to biology and psychology, perhaps the property of being a carburetor could be understood as a device that mixes air and gasoline under normal conditions.[15] But, as we saw in the discussion of (P*1), being a carburetor is an intentional property, and on the current approach to naturalizing intentionality, the normal conditions are themselves intentionally specified. They include, for example, the device's being part of a system that makes a certain kind of automobile run, where being an automobile is as much an intentional property as being a carburetor. This "ecological" approach to naturalizing intentionality is not satisfactory until nonintentional conditions are specified for the complex practices in virtue of which something is an automobile. Remember that the naturalizers' claim is that intentional properties stand in need of vindication in the following strong sense: For each intentional property, we must be able to specify nonintentional and nonsemantic conditions that are sufficient for the instantiation of the intentional property. I do not believe that anyone has given even the outlines of a story that would make such naturalization of artifactual properties remotely plausible. Although I have not proved that artifactual properties will not be naturalized, I hope that I have cast doubt on the prospects for naturalization of artifactual properties.

By virtue of what, then, one may ask, is something a particular kind of artifact, then? Not just its structural properties (drinkalators are not carburetors), not someone's having some attitude toward it

---

15 Ruth Garrett Millikan, *Language, Thought and Other Biological Categories: New Foundations for Realism* (Cambridge, MA: MIT/Bradford, 1984).

(there may well be carburetors whose existence is unknown to anyone), not its origin (a piece of driftwood [a natural object] becomes a sculpture [an artifact] when placed in a certain setting), not just the existence of practices in the same possible worlds as the artifact (practices on earth do not make a spontaneously coalesced carburetorlike object in outer space a carburetor). Rather, something is the kind of artifact that it is in virtue of being incorporated into our practices in many complex ways – ways perhaps impossible to specify with any generality, either intentionally or nonintentionally.

Thus, I think that the prospect for naturalization of artifactual properties is nil. This is no cause for alarm, however. For there is no good reason to undertake naturalization in the first place. There is nothing fishy about artifactual properties: The property of being a carburetor is not in any way unreal. Carburetors populate the world "out there," and no naturalization is required to safeguard their explanatory power or material reality. So, unless commitment to carburetors is ontologically risky, there is no need to naturalize artifactual properties. In that case, premise (P*2) is true.

What about premise (P*3)? It is difficult to see any principled motivation for requiring naturalization of some intentional properties and exempting other intentional properties. I have just suggested that the approaches to naturalizing the property of representing a nonintentional property may be ineffective for naturalizing the properties of representing an intentional property; so, I do not see how the approaches to naturalization so far (even assuming that they had been successful) could be adequate even for all psychological intentional properties. Moreover, even naturalization of all psychological intentional properties would fall seriously short of naturalizing intentionality in the absence of a reduction of social properties to psychological properties. So, if – as I think unlikely – we succeeded in naturalizing psychological properties, Fodor's worry, with which I began, would simply arise again for artifacts. But if the worry is misplaced for artifacts, it is equally misplaced for psychological properties. Thus, (P*3) seems acceptable. Therefore, intentionality need not be naturalized.

To sum up: Intentionality abounds, and the significance of the distinction between what is intentional and what is not intentional has been overblown: The fact that being a carburetor has intentional presuppositions has no bearing on the objectivity of carburetors, or on automotive engineering, or on our explanatory practices. *Pace* Quine, there is no a priori reason to be suspicious of a science whose domain is defined in part by intentional properties. On the contrary, the very successes of unnaturalized technology give a posteriori reason to insist on the objectivity of intentionality, without concern for naturalization.

How, then, should we respond to Fodor's remarks about reduction that motivate the attempts to naturalize intentionality? On the one hand, we could reject the metaphysical background picture, according to which physics is the sole arbiter of what there is. If I am right, then the metaphor of "depth" that generates the demand for naturalization is misleading. Locomotion does not go "all the way down" any more than intentionality does; but I doubt that anyone would say that if locomotion "is real, it must really be something else." On the other hand, we could turn the worry around: In light of the obvious reality of carburetors and other artifacts, we could say that intentional properties (like that of being a carburetor) must supervene on fundamental physical properties, though we cannot and need not say how. That is, we could just declare victory and go home.

UNREIFIED BELIEF AND SCIENTIFIC PSYCHOLOGY

The second objection concerns the relationship between a Practical Realist view of attitudes and scientific psychology. The objection has two parts. First, one may object that, since Practical Realism makes no effort to understand attitudes in nonintentional terms, beliefs can play no theoretical role in science. Since I have just argued that intentionality cannot and need not be naturalized, I agree with the premise. But the objection is a non sequitur. To say that intentionality cannot be naturalized is to say that there are intentional states for which we cannot specify metaphysically sufficient conditions in nonsemantic and nonintentional terms. If failure of naturalization made properties suspect for theoretical sciences, then we should be as dubious about properties mentioned by the so-called engineering sciences as about attitudes. So, if engineering is scientific, the failure of the naturalization project with respect to intentionality does not ipso facto put the attitudes beyond the reach of science.

Whether attitudes will play a theoretical role in scientific psychology is in part an empirical question and in part a question about what will be counted as a scientific theory. For example, attitudes play a prominent role in social psychology, but some philosophers may doubt that social psychology is really scientific. Such philosophers may require that, in order for a body of (putative) knowledge to count as a science, there must be a kind of "fit" between it and the physical sciences, and that social psychology is insufficiently integrated with the physical sciences to count as a science.

Such a requirement seems otiose. For the requirement is either that the "fit" be ascertainable or that it need not be ascertainable. If the requirement is that the "fit" be ascertainable, then the requirement is too stringent to allow, for example, engineering or economics to count as a science. If the requirement allows that the "fit" may be beyond human discovery, then any time we have an otherwise successful theory (i.e., it makes successful predictions, it generates research problems, and so on), we may simply declare the "fit" to exist even if we do not know just how. This alternative should be treated in the way that I treated the naturalization project for intentionality: Even though we cannot in general specify nonsemantic and nonintentional conditions for having a given attitude, when we are confident that a person has an attitude, we may just assume that the conditions needed for having the attitude must obtain. But if the requirement may simply be assumed to be met, then it is useless as a requirement. If we allow, say, current social psychology to count as a science, then attitudes also pass theoretical muster.

In any case, I take no stand one way or another on the use of the attitudes in scientific theories, except to urge two points: (1) Unreified attitudes are not precluded a priori from playing a theoretical role in science, and (2) the cognitive merit of the attitudes does not depend on their integration into theoretical psychology anyway. Their cognitive credentials – as I argue in Chapters 3 and 8 – are certified by their systematic and ineliminable role in our successful explanatory and descriptive practices.

The second part of the objection about scientific psychology is that in some areas the supposition that there are mental representations in the brain has borne fruit. In particular, the notion that believing that p is a matter of tokening mental representations, or sentences-in-the-brain, may seem entrenched in parts of psychology. In light of this consideration, it may seem idle to reject the

Standard View on philosophical grounds. I have a series of replies to this objection.

First, however useful it is to posit sentences-in-the-brain in psychology, it remains an empirical matter whether the brain is organized along lines compatible with beliefs as construed by the Standard View. (On this point, I think that the eliminativists are dead right.) From the mental representationalist's perspective, neuroscience should trump, say, developmental psychology. Suppose that the brain is not organized in such a way that it makes sense to suppose that there are brain states (discrete or distributed) that are "isomorphic" to intuitively correct attributions of belief. In that case, mental representationalists should conclude that there are no beliefs – since, according to their theory, if there are beliefs, they are constituted by brain states. But to conclude that there are no beliefs in light of disconfirmation of theories of mental representations would be on a par with concluding that there are no human memories if theories seeking a "trace" in the brain for each memory report are unsuccessful. Or worse, as I mention in Chapter 3, to conclude that there are no beliefs would be on a par with concluding that there is no motion in light of disconfirmation of the impetus theory. Surely, the proper conclusion would be, not that there are no beliefs, but that beliefs are not constituted by brain states. This conclusion is all the more obvious when we recognize that the causal explanatoriness of beliefs does not depend on their being constituted by brain states.

Second, I would predict that, even if mental-representation theories were to be disconfirmed by neuroscience, there would continue to be psychological interest in the phenomena that these theories are supposed to explain – for example, a child's capacity to pretend.[16] Children would still pretend even if neurophysiologists found no brain states that constituted beliefs. But it is difficult to see how even to understand pretense without presupposing belief. To pretend that this empty cup contains water seems to entail believing that it does not. Now, if (1) neuroscience fails to find brain states that can be described as beliefs, and (2) pretense is still possible, and (3) a capacity to pretend entails a capacity to believe, then it follows

16 See Alan M. Leslie, "Some Implications of Pretense for Mechanisms Underlying the Child's Theory of Mind" in *Developing Theories of Mind,* ed. Janet W. Astington, Paul L. Harris, and David R. Olson (Cambridge: Cambridge University Press, 1988), 19–46.

that defeat of the Standard View is not defeat of belief. Psychologists may well take heart in this conclusion.

My third point is a conjecture about why (some) psychologists seem confident that neuroscience will not disconfirm mental-representation theory. Here I tread lightly, but it seems to me that psychologists simply read the mental representation theory into the *data*. For example, the editors of *Developing Theories of Mind* say in their introduction that between learning to talk and beginning formal schooling, children "begin to recognize themselves and others as 'things which think,' as things which *believe, doubt, wonder, imagine,* and *pretend.*" This is fine, so far, as a description of the data; but then they go on, as if merely continuing to describe the data, to say that children's new recognition "marks their coming to make a systematic distinction between the world and *mental representations* of the world,*" where by 'mental representations' they mean sentences-in-the-brain.[17] Examples could be multiplied, but this suffices to suggest that the Standard View seems required by the psychological phenomena under investigation simply because of tendentious and unnecessarily theory-laden descriptions of the data. (The term 'representation' seems to invite a slide from 'representation' in an ordinary sense, in which beliefs represent or misrepresent the way things are, to 'representation' in a technical sense, in which mental representations are particular entities in the brain.)

Finally, the Standard View does not provide the only approach to the data. For example, we might think of pretense as requiring a child to have mastered enough of the language to understand counterfactuals. How mastery of counterfactuals is related to neural processes is no doubt a difficult question; but there is such a thing as mastery of counterfactuals, and psychologists already rely on such mastery in collecting data: The *evidence* for their theories (of meta-representations and the like) comes from asking questions such as, If John came in the room, where would he look for the candy? So, counterfactuals are in the theoretical picture anyway. For these reasons, I think that psychology could get along fine (and remain comfortably materialistic) without commitment to the Standard View.

17 Janet W. Astington, Paul L. Harris, and David R. Olson, eds., *Developing Theories of Mind* (Cambridge: Cambridge University Press, 1988), 1. Emphases in the original.

The third objection is that Practical Realism is at odds with materialism. More than one thesis travels under the banner of materialism. A minimal materialism would be the view that all that exists are physical particles and constructions out of physical particles: Take away all the atoms and nothing is left. Such a view is indeed minimal; for it says nothing about how the world is organized. Minimal materialism serves only to rule out the existence of an immaterial God and an immaterial soul – without any indication of any relation of dependence of "higher level" properties on microphysical properties. For example, minimal materialism is compatible with there being two possible worlds just alike physically, with the single exception that one has an extra hydrogen atom that the other lacks, yet the two worlds still differ in all their mental and social properties.[18] Since minimal materialism provides no clue about how microphysical properties *determine* all other properties, minimal materialism would not satisfy many contemporary materialists.[19]

The more adequate theses of materialism rely on the idea of supervenience. (See Chapter 5.) Define 'strong supervenience' as follows.[20] Let A and B be families of properties.

> A strongly supervenes on B just in case necessarily for each x and each property F in A, if x has F, then there exists a property G in B such that x has G, and necessarily if any y has G it has F.

18 In "The Myth of Nonreductive Materialism," *American Philosophical Association Proceedings and Addresses* 63 (1989), Jaegwon Kim argued that this possibility is allowed by global supervenience, and hence that global supervenience is too weak a materialistic thesis. However, in "In Defense of Global Supervenience," *Philosophy and Phenomenological Research* 52 (1992): 833–54, R. Cranston Paull and Theodore Sider argue that global supervenience entails a dependence relation analogous to the dependence entailed by strong supervenience. If they are right, we can define a materialistic thesis weaker than global supervenience, which has no implications about the way that physical properties determine all properties. I am calling that weaker thesis 'minimal materialism'.
19 After reading Paull and Sider, I think minimal materialism is the surer target of Kim's critique of global supervenience.
20 Jaegwon Kim, "Supervenience and Supervenient Causation," in *Spindel Conference 1983: Supervenience*, ed. Terence Horgan (*Southern Journal of Philosophy* 22, suppl. [1984]), 49.

Then, reductive materialism may be understood as (SS):

(SS) All properties strongly supervene on microphysical properties.

Nonreductive materialists, by contrast, make no claims about the properties of particular objects, but about distribution of properties in whole worlds. Define 'global supervenience' as follows:

A globally supervenes on B just in case any two worlds with the same distribution of B properties have the same distribution of A properties,

where sameness of distribution of properties "means roughly 'sameness of distribution throughout time and space among the objects of that world'."[21] Then, nonreductive materialism may be understood (GS):

(GS) All properties globally supervene on microphysical properties.

Is Practical Realism compatible with materialism? The answer is surely yes with respect to minimal materialism, which many materialists would regard as too weak for comfort. Practical Realism is also compatible with (GS), without entailing it. Practical Realism and (GS) may both be true, and Practical Realism may still be true even if (GS) is false. Suppose that (GS) is true. Then, since any two worlds with the same distribution of microphysical properties will be the same in all other respects, any world microphysically indiscernible from the actual world will be indiscernible from the actual world with respect to practices and indiscernible with respect to degrees of success of the practices. According to Practical Realism,

---

21 Paull and Sider, "In Defense of Global Supervenience," 834. Paull and Sider invoke the notion of *sameness of distribution* of properties in worlds, because the properties at issue are not properties of worlds but properties of objects in the worlds. For other defenses of nonreductive materialism, see Robert van Gulick, "Nonreductive Materialism and the Nature of Intertheoretical Constraint," in *Emergence or Reduction: Essays on the Prospects of Nonreductive Materialism,* ed. Ansgar Beckermann, Hans Flohr, and Jaegwon Kim (Berlin: Walter de Gruyter, 1992), 157–79; John Post, *The Faces of Existence: An Essay in Nonreductive Metaphysics* (Ithaca, NY: Cornell University Press, 1987); and Derk Pereboom and Hilary Kornblith, "The Metaphysics of Irreducibility," *Philosophical Studies* 63 (1991): 125–46. For a discussion of relations between intuitions about supervenience and various supervenience theses, see John Heil, *The Nature of True Minds* (Cambridge: Cambridge University Press, 1992).

successful practice is the best guide to ontology. So, if (GS) is true, Practical Realism will not distinguish between worlds deemed indiscernible by (GS). Thus, Practical Realism is compatible with (GS). On the other hand, suppose that (GS) is false. Practical Realism may still be true: The existence of chairs, artworks, and persons would not be thrown into doubt by supposing that there are two possible worlds with the same distribution of microphysical properties but which are discernible in some other respect. Therefore, the truth of Practical Realism is independent of the truth of (GS).

Practical Realism, however, is not compatible with (SS), on its standard interpretation. On the standard interpretation of (SS), the B properties are intrinsic properties of x. As we saw in Chapter 2, two individuals may be the same in all their intrinsic properties and differ in their relational properties. But according to Practical Realism, the property of believing that p is a relational property for most p. So, for example, the following is possible according to Practical Realism but not according to (SS) on its usual interpretation: Two people have all their (intrinsic) microphysical properties in common, but one believes that water is wet and the other does not. (One lives in a world in which there is water, and the other lives in a world with a superficially similar substance that is not H_2O but XYZ.)[22] Practical Realism would be compatible with a latitudinarian reinterpretation of (SS) – one that allowed the B properties to be relational properties, such as being in a world in which there is H_2O or one that allowed "scattered objects" to be individuals. But on such a reinterpretation, (SS) would be equivalent to (GS), contrary to the spirit of (SS).

So, Practical Realism is compatible with minimal materialism and with (GS). Nevertheless, I do not urge adoption of either. At this point, my quarrel with materialism is more methodological than ontological. Either materialism plays a role in inquiry or it does not. If it does, it leads to sterile research projects; if it does not, it is idle. Let me explain.

Minimal materialism plays no role in inquiry. As long as the minimal materialist makes no appeal to immaterial entities, she is free to pursue her investigations without any regard to materialism, and then to declare that whatever she turns up actually conforms to

22 Such Twin Earth cases have been thoroughly discussed in the literature. See Putnam, Burge, Baker.

minimal materialism. A thesis that functions in this way – as an "I know not what" – is idle.

(GS), as defended recently,[23] does entail a dependence relation of "higher level" properties on properties of microphysical particles, but I see no compelling reason to endorse (GS) either. Proponents of (GS), like Practical Realists generally, accept the apparent variety of properties (psychological, social, and so on) as genuine variety, but they retain the conviction that there is a single metaphysically interesting relation (supervenience) between these familiar properties and fundamental physical properties. It seems clear that only in special cases are supervenience relations discoverable. Proponents of (GS), I think, have generalized too liberally from a handful of successful reductions: lightning to electrical discharge, water to H_2O, genes to strands of DNA molecules. In cases of relational properties, in which the microphysical properties of constituent elements manifestly fail to determine the "higher level" properties (of living in a democracy, or of being prosperous, say), no such reductions are forthcoming. Indeed, there is no saying even in a particular case, on what nonintentional properties (micro- or macrophysical) Jones's property of having tenure supervenes. Our grounds for believing that some things are worth a hundred dollars or that arsenic is a poison (and for disbelieving that Rebecca is a witch) have nothing to do with any grand thesis like (GS). In general, we do not appeal to overarching metaphysical theses to decide what there is. Thus, as a comprehensive thesis, (GS) is as idle as minimal materialism.

Moreover, when materialism is imported to guide inquiry, it leads us astray. Materialists have us all barking up the wrong tree – as if to understand the nature of something, we must look to its (putative) physical constitution; as if causal powers supervened on intrinsic properties of physical constituents; as if what a thing really is is determined by its nonrelational properties; as if our philosophical task were to understand what is relational in terms of what is nonrelational. This emphasis on physical constitution is no doubt useful in the physical sciences, but, as I have tried to show, it is out of place in the social and behavioral sciences that describe and explain ordinary macroscopic phenomena.

So, when (GS) is taken to have epistemic import, its effects in

<hr>

23 See references in n. 18.

some areas are unfortunate; but when it is taken as a bare metaphysical thesis, it is idle. Indeed, if – as proponents of (GS) would have it – microphysical particles did organize themselves (over vast reaches of space and time) so as to constitute the British Constitution, say, it would be amazing that materialism would be *nonreductive*.

THE REALITY OF BELIEF

From the perspective of the Standard View, Practical Realism may seem to be no kind of realism at all. For Practical Realism does not require beliefs to be spatiotemporal entities (at least not in any sense that requires entities to have constituents). Nevertheless, I claim to be a realist about belief and protest the appropriation of the terms 'realism' and 'irrealism' by partisans who equate being real with being a physical entity. There are many things that are not entities in the ordinary sense of having particular spatiotemporal locations to which one can literally point:[24] the Fifth Amendment, the office of attorney general (even when it is not filled), Charles Keating's guilt, marriage vows, stock options, hiring practices, bigotry, atonal music. About all of these things, I am a realist. (Certainly, none of these things is just a "useful fiction.") Proponents of the Standard View tend to recognize *F*s only if there are sets of spatially contiguous particles that have the property of being *F*. But I am not prepared to cede the term 'realism' to such a partisan view, any more than I am prepared to cede the term 'metaphysics' to Hegelians (or worse, the term 'morality' to the Moral Majority).

Well, one may wonder, what does it mean to be a realist about belief if not that beliefs are brain states?[25] Although I cannot give an analysis of what it means to be real, I can note some marks of the real: What is causally explanatory is real. In Chapter 5, I argue that beliefs may be causally explanatory in the same sense that investments may be causally explanatory – and as anybody with a retirement account knows, this is a robust sense of 'causally explana-

24 Some entities, like oceans, do not have sharp boundaries; from a microphysical point of view, perhaps no observable entities have sharp boundaries. But this consideration is irrelevant here.
25 Although recent discussions of realism simply presuppose materialism, I take the question What is real? to be prior to the question What is material? (whether materialism is true or not).

tory'. A sufficient condition for being real in a nonpartisan sense is to have an effect, to make a difference in what happens, where what happens is often characterized in intentional terms – such as accumulating enough money to retire.

A second mark of the real is that reality has room for error. One may be justified in thinking that p even when p is false. If I sent you my travel schedule, I may be justified in thinking that you believe that my plane arrives at noon; yet, if the letter had not arrived, I may be mistaken. What makes it the case that I am wrong, according to Practical Realism, is the absence of relevant counterfactuals true of you. For example, there are no true counterfactuals like this one: If you planned to pick me up and were not delayed, then you would be at the airport at noon or soon thereafter. If no such counterfactuals are true, then my belief attribution is straightforwardly false.[26]

Moreover, having a belief, on the Practical Realist view, is observer-independent. S believes that p if there are relevant counterfactuals true of S for p – whether any human observer, including the believer, knows that there are or not. Assume that an Ideal Observer would know all the counterfactuals true of S that do not mention any attitude that either entails or precludes S's believing that p (e.g., do not mention attitudes like regretting that p). Let C^* be such a set. Then, someone who knew C^*, but who had no access at all to S's internal states, would know whether S believes that p. On the other hand, someone who knew all of S's internal states, but did not know S's relational properties, would not know what S believed. This appeal to C^* is here an idealization of the way that we know of our own and each other's beliefs – not by knowing anything about internal states but by knowing the relevant counterfactuals. Ordinary human attributors of belief may be straightforwardly mistaken – either in identifying relevant counterfactuals or in assessing their truth value. So, belief is observer-independent.

So, according to Practical Realism, beliefs are causally explanatory; they admit of a distinction between belief attributions that are true and belief attributions that are justified but false; and they are observer-independent. Finally, as I argue in Chapter 8, beliefs are thoroughly integrated into a comprehensive and indispensable

---

26 In Chapter 8, I discuss more generally the notion of objectivity, a notion that requires a distinction between being correct and seeming to be correct.

picture of reality. I know of no better marks of what is real than these.

In this chapter, I have tried to keep the bogey of "immaterialism" at bay, without endorsing materialism – all the while maintaining realism about belief. Attitudes no more need to be "naturalized" than do artifacts, nor does lack of naturalization bar attitudes from a theoretical role in scientific psychology.

Although Practical Realism is compatible with some forms of materialism, a Practical Realist impressed with the richness of reality may well eschew materialism in favor of a wildly pluralistic ontology – one that includes guilty verdicts, carburetors, war memorials, doctoral dissertations, rock concerts, and presidential elections – without adding any materialistic thesis, such as that all of these are constituted by physical particles. Finally, I defended the reality of belief as construed by Practical Realism. Practical Realism really is realism.

8

Practical Realism writ large

Part of the power of the Standard View of the attitudes is that it seems the inevitable result of a particular well-entrenched metaphysical outlook that takes science as the arbiter of knowable reality. In challenging the Standard View, I have also challenged some of the background assumptions about the nature of reality and knowledge that generate it. Now I want to locate the conception of unreified belief in an equally comprehensive metaphysics – one importantly different from the metaphysics of proponents of the Standard View but still compatible with various forms of materialism – in which the alternative conception of belief finds a natural home.

Practical Realist metaphysics differs from Standard View metaphysics primarily in its assessment of the cognitive status of what I shall call the 'commonsense conception of reality'. According to Standard View metaphysics, common sense is a patchwork of folk theories in potential competition with scientific theories. As we saw in Chapter 3, one prominent proponent of the Standard View, Paul Churchland, put it this way: "[T]he network of principles and assumptions constitutive of our commonsense conceptual framework can be seen to be as speculative and as artificial as any overtly theoretical system."[1] According to Practical Realist metaphysics, the commonsense conception is not theoretical in the same way that the sciences are; yet it is a reliable source of truth. A key feature of Practical Realism is that it strongly resists devaluation of reality as disclosed by everyday life.

After characterizing the commonsense conception of reality and contrasting it with Standard View versions of reality, I criticize a basic metaphysical distinction – between what is "mind-independent" and what is "mind-dependent" – that underlies Standard View ac-

1 Paul M. Churchland, *Scientific Realism and the Plasticity of Mind* (Cambridge: Cambridge University Press, 1979), 2.

counts of reality, and urge its replacement. Finally, I argue for the objectivity of the world as understood by Practical Realism.

A commonsense conception is a conception of reality that one learns in learning a natural language. It reflects the world as encountered – the world of medium-sized objects, artifacts as well as natural objects; of persons with propositional attitudes and various character traits; and of conventions and obligations. I use the term 'commonsense framework' to refer to any set of concepts expressed by nonlogical terms occurring in sentences understood by almost everybody in a linguistic community. I use the term 'commonsense conception' to refer to the sentences containing terms expressing those concepts. To ascertain a community's "thick" conception of common sense, find the utterances whose truth or explanatoriness is taken for granted by most members in ordinary commerce and daily life. Then, the nonlogical terms that occur in the sentences so uttered express the concepts of their commonsense framework – a thick conception. For example, most of us unhesitatingly assent to sentences (in appropriate contexts) that contain terms expressing concepts of computers, legislators, airliners, toys, optimists, benevolent people, dinner parties, tenure, unpaid bills, promises, trees, and surgeons. These are the concepts that we use to make judgments that facilitate our interactions – in our households, marketplaces, lawcourts, and voluntary associations.

A community's thick commonsense conception is the set of statements or propositions expressed by the sentences that are almost universally assented to, in context, by members of the community. For example, almost everyone in the United States would assent to 'Telephones are a good way to communicate with relatives overseas', and this sentence has a number of presuppositions – not only about telephones, but also about the physical world (overseas is out of shouting distance) and family obligations (there are some relatives with whom you ought to keep in touch) and even other minds (your speaking into a little machine will be understood and maybe even appreciated by a person on the other end of the line). Sentences expressing these presuppositions would also command assent.

The things that satisfy the concepts of our thick commonsense framework have (what might be called) second-order properties: The concepts of telephones, trees, and toys are concepts of medium-sized objects; the concepts of family members, surgeons, and optimists are concepts of persons with propositional attitudes; the concepts of dinner parties and tenure are concepts of sets of convention (with presuppositions about obligations); the concepts of promises and unpaid bills are concepts of obligations. If I am right, then every thick commonsense framework prominently includes concepts of things that have the second-order properties of being medium-sized objects, of being persons with propositional attitudes, and so on. If we abstract away from thick commonsense frameworks, we may take it as a mark of common sense in a thin sense to include concepts of medium-sized objects, of persons with propositional attitudes, of conventions, and of obligations.

In the broadest terms, the thin commonsense framework is not restricted to some particular outlook that may vary from culture to culture. Rather, it provides a common background against which differences among cultures become visible. If an anthropologist, for example, claims that a particular culture lacks a concept of belief,[2] that culture still will share the commonsense conception (in a suitably thin sense) if its members describe and explain phenomena in terms of medium-sized objects and of persons with propositional attitudes. Different cultures, of course, have different thick conceptions of common sense and perhaps explain behavior on the basis of motivation that we do not all share. (For example, the explanation of Antigone's disobeying Creon's order to leave Polyneices unburied may be quite foreign to us.) But cultural differences in motivation are irrelevant to the points that I want to make. What matters with respect to the commonsense framework is, rather, the propriety of describing behavior in intentional ways ('disobeying an order') and explaining it in terms of attitudes at all.

At a first approximation, the commonsense conception functions

2 For example, Rodney Needham, who is sometimes cited in this regard, has no qualms about reporting "the received ideas to which a people subscribed," where it is difficult to understand "received ideas" without attributions of attitudes with propositional content. His doubts about belief concern an ethnographer's saying "that people believed something when he did not actually know what was going on inside them" (*Belief, Language, and Experience* [Oxford: Basil Blackwell, 1972], 2). But the commonsense conception – if it is to be useful – does not require access to what is going on inside of people.

as cognitive background for our practical affairs, from formulating and pursuing personal ambitions, to explaining and predicting behavior, to developing laws and institutions, to devising theories. Although common sense makes many claims that purport to be true, its point is to direct action, and, ultimately, to allow us to flourish as human beings. (As almost everybody knows, flourishing is not guaranteed by the amassing of theoretical knowledge.) Embodied in natural language, common sense is the sea in which we all swim – scientists and nonscientists alike.

In Chapter 3, I gave reasons to reject the following thesis, which is the hallmark of Standard View metaphysics:

(MT) Reality, insofar as it is knowable, is knowable exclusively by means of science.

Here, although I can only be programmatic, I want to sketch an alternative to (MT) – an alternative that neither retreats into instrumentalism nor leaps into any rationalistic a priori understanding of reality.

Let me set out Practical Realism by contrasting it with Quine's scientific pragmatism. Quine's rejection of the analytic-synthetic distinction leads to the metaphor of a web of belief. As Quine develops the idea of a web of belief, however, the web is exhausted by science; that is, Quine is committed to (MT). Quine's famous dictum "The unit of empirical significance is the whole of science" really comprises two doctrines, which Practical Realism takes apart.[3] One doctrine is holism: Any statement may turn out to be relevant to the confirmation or disconfirmation of any other statement. In the face of recalcitrant experience, we may make adjustments in our beliefs in any number of ways. This doctrine is captured by the metaphor of the web of belief. The other doctrine, logically distinct from the first, is that the web of belief is exhausted by science.

Practical Realism accepts the metaphor of a web of belief, with its rejection of the analytic-synthetic distinction, and with the rejection of associated doctrines like a language-fact distinction, a scheme-content distinction, and with rejection of foundationalism

---

3 W. V. O. Quine, "Two Dogmas of Empiricism," in *From a Logical Point of View* (New York: Harper Torchbook, 1963), 42.

and the idea of the "given." Where Practical Realism departs from scientific pragmatism is in not accepting Quine's other doctrine that, cognitively speaking, "total science" is all there is.

According to Practical Realism, total science is only a proper part of total knowledge, which includes knowledge of homely truths (e.g., "If you want to get through customs quickly, you ought to wear decent clothes"), knowledge of social and political institutions (e.g., "If you are a registered voter, you are liable to be called for jury duty"), and knowledge in countless other areas – knowledge that is not scientific or theoretical knowledge in any constrained sense of those terms. It would be a senseless pruning of reality to confine cognition to science.

Assuming that empirical beliefs are those revisable on the basis of experience, Practical Realism (unlike scientific pragmatism) does not take responsiveness to new information to be enough to make a belief theoretical. Consider: "I was going to give the speed-demon a ticket; but when I discovered that he was the mayor's son, I decided to let him off with a warning." Or: "I believed that the progressive candidate was going to win until I saw the negative advertising of the opposition; now I'm not so sure." These are both cases of revising opinion on the basis of new information. But there is no reason to suppose that either opinion is part of any scientific theory.

Thus, according to Practical Realism, the fabric of cognition extends far beyond science (in any constrained sense of 'science'). Art and law, along with common sense, contribute to our understanding of reality and thus find their place in the web as well. By endorsing the web metaphor, I am agreeing that the parts of the web that are not science are susceptible to change prompted by results of science – and conversely, that science is susceptible to change prompted by results of nonscience. In this sense, the position that I am calling 'Practical Realism' is within the pragmatic tradition.

Indeed, in one respect, Practical Realism is more pragmatic than Quine's scientific pragmatism. On scientific pragmatism, any putative phenomenon that resists theoretical explanation is thereby eliminated as a phenomenon. On Practical Realism, we are not forced to infer nonexistence of phenomena from invisibility to scientific theory. Sometimes we do infer nonexistence (as when we declare astrological phenomena nonexistent on the grounds that

224

there are no laws governing such putative phenomena); and sometimes we do not (as when we continue to accept commonsense
explanations with little prospect of finding a scientific law – e.g.,
'The officers fired because they thought the suspect was armed').
The Practical Realist is not committed in advance to denying existence to phenomena that resist subsumption under scientific law.[4]

Of course, a Practical Realist, like a scientific pragmatist, will
look to science for illumination of the commonsense conception.
For example, we may expect evolutionary theory to explain the
origin of the commonsense conception. Indeed, from a broadly
evolutionary point of view, the commonsense conception looks
like a well-established means of coping with the physical and social
environments that have been encountered by our species.[5] If common sense arose in response to environmental need – as bee dances
did – then there is no reason to think that the commonsense conception has anything like the organization of a theory in any constrained sense of that term. Although the commonsense conception
is cognitive in that it enables us to make claims that are true or false,
its function is largely practical. And there is no reason to think that
the cognitive ground of practice is a theory.

From the point of view of the individual, the commonsense
conception is likewise indispensable. In learning a native language,
a child does not learn just a set of generalizations but learns how to
get along, and what to do when, along with a welter of particular
and general facts – intentional, nonintentional, and mixed, willy-
nilly. The commonsense conception encompasses platitudes about
behavior of persons and of medium-sized material objects, for example, that fire burns, that dinner tastes better than dirt, that insults

4 What the Practical Realist is committed to are the commonsense categories of
persons and middle-sized objects. The validity of these categories may be susceptible to a kind of "empirical" transcendental argument: Our knowledge of these
categories can be justified on the basis of any (reasonably long) experience that is
possible for us. This conception of transcendental justification – as dependent on
experience only to the extent that it appeals to information derivable from any
possible human perception, while it is independent of any more particular or
special experiences – is found in Derk Pereboom, "Kant on the Justification of
Transcendental Philosophy," *Synthese* 85 (1990): 25–54; and in his "Is Kant's
Transcendental Philosophy Inconsistent?" *History of Philosophy Quarterly* 8 (1991):
337–72.
5 I have been influenced here by Ruth Garrett Millikan, "Biosemantics," *Journal of
Philosophy* 86 (1989): 281–97, and by George Graham, "The Origins of Folk
Psychology," *Inquiry* 30 (1987): 357–79.

make people mad. Pretheoretically, there is a more or less unified conception that enables us to get on in the world. Although different natural languages embody different thick conceptions of common sense, they all share a thin conception of reality in terms of persons and medium-sized objects.

To doubt that there are attitudes is to doubt common facts of everyday life. For example, that there are presidential elections or that there has been recent publicity about scientific fraud are intentional facts: They could not obtain in worlds without attitudes. Therefore, if there are such things as presidential elections and scientific fraud, there are attitudes. The mistake of the Standard View is to suppose that if there are attitudes, they must be in some sense mirrored in particular brain states. But once we are relieved of thinking of beliefs as brain states, we can see that attitudes are unproblematic. (That is, some sentences of the form 'S believes that p' are unproblematically true.) Since many of the facts that are humanly significant are intentional facts – there are no tenure-track positions available this year; Michael Milkin served some time in prison – facts that presuppose that there are attitudes, denial of attitudes is denial of the everyday "life world."

The interwoven commonsense conception of persons and medium-sized objects categorizes actions and events in the terms that interest us. Common sense gets the explananda right. To suppose that common sense is wrong in a wholesale way about persons and medium-sized objects is to suppose that the commonsense conception of *behavior* (e.g., behavior like voting for the school budget or driving while drunk) is suspect. It is difficult to see how a scientific theory that did not permit prediction and explanation of behavior as ordinarily described could replace the commonsense conception that classifies behavior in the familiar ways. Such a scientific theory just would not serve the explanatory and predictive purposes that are part and parcel of recognizably human life.

Someone may object that the psychological theories that replaced theories of witchcraft had different explananda and did not serve the same purposes as theories of witchcraft; but that reluctance to change explananda would have been no reason to hang on to theories of witchcraft. By way of reply, I would agree with the point about witchcraft, but urge that the analogy between explanation in terms of witchcraft and explanation in terms of commonsense categories is misplaced. The (pernicious) purposes served by theories of witchcraft were "local" in that they could be abandoned and human life could still continue; but the purposes served by the common-sense framework are those without which there would be no recognizably human life. The purposes served by intentional classification of behavior are themselves indispensable: *all* social, political, and legal institutions, anywhere and everywhere, embody the commonsense framework. We could not exchange our categories of medium-sized objects and persons with intentional states for categories of fundamental physics (or even for categories of gross bodily movements) and still retain the practices, rules, and conventions that are constitutive of everyday life. It is not just prescientific ignorance that leads us to categorize reality in terms of persons and medium-sized objects. These commonsense categories are the categories that serve basic human interests of coping with our gross physical environments and of interacting with each other.

That we conceive of reality in this way is not a matter of choice. There are universal human interests – such as an interest in having satisfying relationships with others, or an interest in having a measure of control over one's own life and environment – that are intelligible only in terms of the commonsense conception. Explanation and prediction on the basis of commonsense categories serve these interests. At bottom, the commonsense conception is not expendable because such interests are not optional.[6]

Speaking for myself, I will not endorse in philosophy what I can not hold outside of my study. This is not to say that a Practical Realist should be oblivious to purely abstract matters. A Practical Realist may believe that the square root of two is irrational; she may even be able to prove it. But holding that the square root of two is irrational does not make the activity of balancing one's checkbook incoherent in the way that holding that there are no persons with attitudes does. A Practical Realist may even believe in the reality of nonactual possible worlds: Such belief is no impediment to understanding what it means to have driven to work safely last Thursday; if Thursday's drive had been particularly harrowing, one may even think that there was a very nearby possible world in which one did

---

6 If, by some series of mutations, our fundamental interests were to change, our successors may abandon the commonsense conception. Just as there is a sense in which human beings are continuous with tadpoles, there is a sense in which such successors would be continuous with us. But that continuity would no more make them human than it would make us tadpoles.

not make it to work last Thursday. And, I want to emphasize, a Practical Realist may be a realist about theoretical entities. I believe that my desk is constituted by fundamental particles like electrons, but my expectations about the behavior of my desk would be largely unaffected if theoretical physics turned out to be wildly mistaken.

According to Practical Realism, the world of human affairs – the world in which some professors have tenure, Germany is reunified, recycling centers are opened, budgets are cut, and all the rest – this world is no less real, no less noble, than the austere world of basic particles whose duration is too short to be measured. We have intimate knowledge of the human world, knowledge whose untidy nature invites proponents of (MT) to relegate it to second-class or purely instrumental status. But, according to Practical Realists, there is no better mark of reality than the utility, reliability, and indispensability of the commonsense conception.[7]

THE IDEA OF MIND INDEPENDENCE

Practical Realism differs significantly in metaphysical outlook from the Standard View. Whereas Practical Realism makes no effort at all to isolate any realm that is what it is apart from our concepts, many proponents of the Standard View take there to be a fundamental distinction between what is mind-independent and what is mind-dependent, and declare ultimate reality to be what is mind-independent.[8] Roughly, what is mind-independent is what there would be if there had never been any human concepts. Rocks, di-

---

7 Of course, a framework may be useful, reliable, and (in some sense) indispensable, yet false; for example, we may continue to navigate on the basis of a celestial sphere whose reality we deny. Suffice it to note that the case of the celestial sphere (like that of witches) is local. We could give up talk of the celestial sphere (indeed, we could give up navigation altogether) and still satisfy fundamental human interests. Such is not the case with respect to medium-sized objects and persons with intentional states.

8 A metaphysics based on a distinction between mind independence and mind dependence is an ontological analogue of foundationalism in epistemology. According to foundationalism, knowledge is partitioned into a foundation that needs no further justification, and a superstructure that requires justification ultimately in the foundation. According to the metaphysics of mind independence, reality is partitioned into a physical foundation that is independent of human thought and activity and a superstructure that is wholly determined by elements of the foundation, with ontological honors going to the foundation.

nosaurs, H_2O, and black holes would still exist even if there had never been any concepts of anything. Thus, rocks, dinosaurs, H_2O, and black holes are thus mind-independent. Contrast social things like money and carburetors; although there may have been dollar bill–like molecular configurations in the absence of human concepts, those configurations would not have had the property of being dollar bills. Thus, such social entities as dollar bills are mind-dependent. Proponents of the Standard View take the mind-independent–mind-dependent distinction to be of great metaphysical importance: What is ontologically basic, according to the Standard View, is what is mind-independent, what there would have been – what would have had the "nature" that it actually has – in the absence of all intentional activity.[9]

But Practical Realism is cavalier about "mind-independent" reality. Practical Realism looks to successful human practices – in science and in everyday life – for clues to what there is. Complex human practices, which would be impossible in the absence of concepts, are what proponents of the Standard View would call "mind-dependent," and hence, according to the Standard View, are ontologically derivative from what is "mind-independent."[10] Therefore, it will be charged, Practical Realism does not isolate the sphere of genuine reality – what there would have been had we never evolved to have concepts and practices.

I plead guilty. From the perspective of Practical Realism, the distinction between mind independence and mind dependence is ontologically irrelevant. While not denying that rocks and dinosaurs are mind-independent in an obvious sense, I shall argue that the mind-independent–mind-dependent distinction has next to no metaphysical significance. In particular, it marks no important boundary between what is real (or genuinely real) and what is not. Moreover, the distinction has set for philosophy a false agenda: It has led philosophers to seek to show how what is mind-dependent is determined by what is mind-independent. The project of "natu-

9 I am not saying that something is mind-independent if it is "unconceptualized"; I am saying, rather, that the thing is what it is independent of our concepts of it.
10 Believers in the Big Bang, or in natural selection, will take what is "mind-independent" to be temporally prior to what is "mind-dependent"; but what is at issue for metaphysics is not temporal priority, but ontological priority. I think that much contemporary philosophy is vitiated by what used to be called 'the genetic fallacy'.

ralizing" intentionality discussed in Chapter 7 is just one instance of a general pattern of trying (futilely, I think) to understand all that there is in terms only of what there would have been had there been no minds. Finally, the distinction is not needed to preserve objectivity. As is explained in the next section, objectivity does not rest on any distinction between (mind-dependent) social reality and (mind-independent) physical reality anyway.

My case against endorsement of the mind-independent–mind-dependent distinction, however, does not rest solely on pointing out that it leads to futile projects like the naturalization project or that the distinction is unnecessary as a shield against challenges to objectivity. Rather, I want to show that if the distinction is taken to be comprehensive (as it must be for the metaphysical purposes to which it is put), it does not partition reality in the needed way. To see this, let me try to be more precise about just what the distinction is. Here is a stab at a definition of 'mind independence':

(MI) x's are mind-independent if and only if x's exist in some possible world in which there are no concepts of anything.

But (MI) fails to make the needed distinction. For instance, portraits could not exist without human practices, practices in which mindless beings could not engage. Yet, according to (MI), portraits turn out to be mind-independent: Each portrait is identical with a particular group of molecules (namely, the molecules that constitute the canvas or whatever that it is painted or printed on), and each such molecular configuration exists in a possible world in which there are no concepts of portraits, or of anything else. A particular molecular configuration is the configuration that it is independent of anyone's having concepts. Hence, portraits satisfy the definition of 'mind independence' given by (MI).

The trouble with (MI) is that it construes 'mind independence' as pertaining to objects "transparently." If, as many materialists hold, everything that exists is identical with some particular subatomic configuration, then the point about portraits generalizes in an unfortunate way: Since, on such views, each thing is identical to some subatomic configuration, and each such subatomic configuration is mind-independent, then each thing that exists is mind-independent, according to (MI). Everything turns out to be mind-independent on (MI) – by definition, so to speak. The consequence of this is that (MI) cannot underwrite a metaphysically significant distinction between mind dependence and mind independence. So, we must look elsewhere to find any basis for the allegedly important distinction. Here is another attempt to define 'mind independence' in a way suitable to underwrite the Standard View:

(MI*) F's are mind-independent if and only if F's exist in some possible world in which there are no concepts of anything.

(MI*) does generate a distinction according to which some kinds of things are mind-independent and some are not. Its consequences are difficult to swallow, however. Carburetors and other kinds of artifacts turn out to be mind-dependent on (MI*). As I argue in Chapter 7, there would be no carburetors in a world without certain practices, which practices have intentional presuppositions. I simply see no good reason to suppose that computers and screwdrivers have any less ontological status than do trees and rocks. Thus, (MI*) seems inadequate as a basis for metaphysics.

Moreover, although the mind-independent–mind-dependent distinction generated by (MI*) is compatible with materialism, it has a consequence at odds with the spirit of many versions of materialism. For many materialists identify an object with its physical structure, in which case molecular duplicates are, one might say, maximally similar. But, according to (MI*), there could be molecular duplicates, one of which is mind-independent and the other of which is mind-dependent. For example, a statue and a molecularly identical, but naturally occurring, hunk of rock would be accorded different ontological status by (MI*): The hunk of rock would be mind-independent, whereas the statue would be mind-dependent; nothing is a statue in a world without concepts. So, if mind independence as defined by (MI*) is used to assign ontological status, then the materialist's intuition about molecular duplicates is misguided.[11]

Since I cannot think of any more plausible ways to define 'mind independence' than those I have surveyed, I submit tentatively that it is safe to deny the metaphysical significance of the distinction

11 Apart from doubts about the metaphysical significance of any distinction between mind-independent and mind-dependent, I think that the materialist intuition about microphysical duplicates is misguided. Artifacts may have a different ontological status from natural objects like rocks, but not because they are microphysically different; there may be no difference between artifacts and natural objects in terms of constitution.

between what is and what is not mind-independent.[12] The purpose of the discussion of mind independence is not to prove that there is no distinction between what is mind-independent and what is not; rather, its purpose is to blunt the force of a Standard View objection that Practical Realism fails to honor the distinction. For it is not clear just what the distinction is, or why it should be honored by a realist or anyone else. In that case, objections to Practical Realism based on the mind-independent–mind-dependent distinction can be simply put aside, and, indeed, Standard View metaphysics is on shaky ground.

OBJECTIVITY

Many philosophers take objective phenomena to be mind-independent. Without belaboring the point, this understanding of objectivity would make it a *nonobjective* (i.e., subjective) matter that you were short-changed. But if you asked me to change a U.S. quarter and I gave you two dimes and a penny, I short-changed you: and that's an objective fact. A machine that made change and returned two dimes and a penny would likewise have short-changed you. There is nothing subjective about either fact. So, it seems unhelpful to use the idea of mind independence (even if we could make it out in a metaphysically significant way) to understand objectivity anyway.

To ground the notion of objectivity, what is needed is not an idea of mind independence but of recognition independence. The idea behind recognition independence is that a property can be instantiated independently of anyone's awareness of it. This is *not* to say that recognition properties can be instantiated in worlds without minds, but only that particular instantiations do not depend on anyone's attitudes toward them. More precisely,

> (RI) A property P is recognition-independent if and only if it is possible that: For some x, x has P, and there is no S such that S is aware that x has P.

Carburetors, as I argue in Chapter 7, cannot be instantiated in worlds without minds, yet the property of being a carburetor is

12 I hereby recant the view I held in "Temporal Becoming: The Argument from Physics," *Philosophical Forum* 6 (1974–5): 218–36.

recognition-independent. Something may be a carburetor even if no one is ever aware that it is. Consider an automated factory that produced carburetors for years; then one night, at the end of a run with no humans present, an explosion destroyed the factory. The things that had rolled off the line were carburetors, even though no one had been aware of them and even though they never functioned as carburetors. They were carburetors because of their place in automotive practice, and things can have that place without anyone's being aware that they do.

Many social, legal, political, and economic properties are recognition-independent: A person may commit a felony without anyone's realizing that she has; a person may be the rightful heir to the throne without being so recognized. Having a belief that p is recognition-independent: For whether one has the belief depends on whether there are relevant counterfactuals true of the subject – whether anyone (including the believer) knows that there are such true counterfactuals or not. Many of the properties that matter to us are recognition-independent in this sense.

Intuitively, what is objective is what is not "a matter of opinion." In objective matters, one stands subject to correction: There is a difference between one's being right and one's seeming to be right. ("Oh! That's a dirty nickel, not a penny? Then, I wasn't short-changed after all.") As Tyler Burge has argued, objectivity is closely connected to the possibility of error.[13] But there can be straightforward errors about whether you were short-changed or whether Al is a felon or whether Frank failed French – all states of affairs that are recognition-independent but not mind-independent: In the absence of human concepts, there would be no felons or people failing French. Therefore, I think that the idea of recognition independence better captures the intuitive idea of objectivity than would an idea of mind independence. (It is difficult to deny that it is an objective fact that something is a dirty nickel and not a penny.) The commonsense conception, including belief and the other attitudes, is marked by recognition independence, and hence is objective. So, we need no recourse to a mind-independent–mind-dependent distinction to secure the objectivity of belief.

13 Compare Tyler Burge, "Cartesian Error and the Objectivity of Perception," in *Contents of Thought,* ed. Robert H. Grimm and Daniel D. Merrill (Tucson: University of Arizona Press, 1988), 62–76.

In sum: The idea of mind independence is not needed for objectivity, which is grounded in recognition independence.[14] Linguistic and other social practices require a publicly accessible world, and whatever is recognition-independent is publicly accessible. Many of the phenomena that matter to us – many of the states of affairs that we make sacrifices to bring about or to avoid – are recognition-independent but not mind-independent. Such meaningful phenomena involve having properties like these: being employed, living in Connecticut, going to a concert, playing softball, giving lectures, dining in an Ethiopian restaurant, running for the state senate, reporting a burglary, committing a burglary, putting money in a retirement account, going to the dentist, and so on.

In our efforts to understand the world and what happens in it, the mind-independent–mind-dependent distinction cuts no ice. Recall this memorable passage from Hume:

A prisoner . . . when conducted to the scaffold, foresees his death as certainly from the constancy and fidelity of his guards, as from the operation of the ax or wheel. His mind runs along a certain train of ideas: The refusal of the soldiers to consent to his escape; the action of the executioner; the separation of the head and body; bleeding, convulsive motions, and death. Here is a connected chain of natural causes and voluntary actions; but the mind feels no difference between them, in passing from one link to another.[15]

Here we have a "connected chain" of mind-independent and mind-dependent properties, all of them causally explanatory. The chain is forged by our embodied practices, which have no respect for the distinction between mind independence and mind dependence.

Nevertheless, one may object that successful practice provides no basis for understanding things as they really are; the commitments that underwrite our practices may be useful but false. How can we be sure that the ontological commitments of our explanatory practices are correct and not just heuristically acceptable? There are two ways to interpret this question. One way is to take the question to be internal to inquiry; the other way is to take the question to raise a general skeptical doubt. If the question, How can we be sure that the ontological commitments of our explanatory practices are not

14 For an argument that our practices require "external realism" – a form of mind independence – see John Searle's forthcoming book on social reality.
15 David Hume, *An Enquiry concerning Human Understanding* (Indianapolis: Hackett, 1977), 60.

just "useful but false"? is taken to be internal to inquiry, then we have familiar resources (i.e., the whole body of knowledge) for dealing with it. Although medieval scientists were justified in taking the impetus theory to explain motion, they turned out to be wrong. There are simply no metaphysical guarantees against error. But, after a putative explanatory property has been finally defeated – as impetus was by the seventeenth century – we may still find it useful to advert to it in practice.

If, say, navigating by the stars as if the night sky were a celestial sphere is the simplest way to get sailors where they want to go, then they are justified in treating the night sky as a celestial sphere for heuristic purposes – even though they know better. Before they knew better, they would have been justified, but wrong, to think that the night sky really was a celestial sphere.[16] So, understood piecemeal, the ontological commitments of practice are revisable and replaceable; if a commitment is revised, but continues to be a heuristically valuable assumption, then we discover that it is useful but false. At that point, and only at that point, we withdraw ontological commitment to the (putative) property.

It is difficult to imagine what evidence, or scientific advances, would lead us to conclude that attributions of properties like being a convicted felon, being married, making bad investments, or being counterfeit should be regarded as useful but false. If attributions of these properties are all false, imponderable questions arise: What truths would replace them? How would such truths serve our explanatory purposes? It is difficult to imagine developments internal to scientific practice that would lead to the verdict that attributions of such properties are "useful but false."

On the other hand, taken as raising a general skeptical doubt, the question, How can we be sure that the ontological commitments of our explanatory practices are not just useful but false? has no answer – any more than does the parallel question, How can we be sure that the ontological commitments of the sciences (or of metaphysics, for that matter) are not just useful but false? *Pace* Descartes, it seems to me to be useless to seek a hedge against global skepti-

---

16 If being a realist means that you may be justified in believing that *p,* even though you turn out to be wrong, then I'm a realist; if being a realist means that you can ponder the nature of reality as a whole from a hypothetical omega point beyond all inquiry, then I am not a realist.

cism. If the commonsense conception were mistaken – if there really were no presidential elections, or Hepplewhite furniture, or cases of scientific fraud, or parking tickets, or hiring freezes, and so on – then our mistakes would be so systematic as to leave no room for detection. If the commonsense conception were wrong in any wholesale way, it is difficult to see how we could have any plausible grounds for thinking it so. In order to explain the fact that our "mistakes" are such reliable predictors, we would need, implausibly, an "error theory" of everything – perhaps invocation of something like Descartes's Evil Genius.

In short, given the systematic reliability of everyday and scientific claims that presuppose everyday claims, we would need some powerful special reason to doubt them in toto. And in the absence of such special reason, we are justified in continuing to regard the commitments of explanatory practice as real, not just as useful for heuristic purposes.

THE OVERALL ARGUMENT

The structure of my defense of a Practical Realist construal of the attitudes is this: The Standard View of the attitudes has severe difficulties. A serious "internal" problem for the Standard View is to develop a suitable idea of content assignable to internal states (Chapter 2); serious "external" problems for the Standard View include miconstrual of commonsense psychology (Chapter 3) and adherence to far too restrictive a notion of causal explanation (Chapter 4). So, with the development of a better interpretation of causal explanation (Chapter 5), the way is paved for an alternative to the Standard View. I set out the alternative – the Practical Realist view of attitudes (Chapter 6). Next, I show that although Practical Realism holds out no prospects for "naturalizing" intentionality, it does not render belief unsuitable for psychology. The naturalization project is ill-motivated anyway. I argue that Practical Realism is compatible with a suitably relaxed materialism (Chapter 7). Finally (in this chapter), I locate the Practical Realist view of attitudes in a full-blown metaphysics of practice, into which it is thoroughly interwoven. Thus, there is nothing ad hoc about Practical Realism.

I want to conclude by distinguishing Practical Realism from several well-known views with which it has significant affinities. Perhaps I need not add that I admire a great deal of the work by each of the philosophers – Gilbert Ryle, Daniel Dennett, Richard Rorty, John Searle, and Hilary Putnam.

First, Practical Realism is non-Rylean in its understanding of causal explanation. According to Ryle, "Motives are not happenings and are not therefore of the right type to be causes," and "Roughly, 'believe' is of the same family as motive words."[17] Such statements at least suggest that, whereas I regard belief explanations typically to be causal explanations, Ryle would not. (It is difficult to be precise here since Ryle's style of philosophical argument differs from mine.)

Second, Practical Realism does not adopt Daniel Dennett's notion of an intentional stance. However Dennett finally understands the intentional stance – either instrumentalistically or as discerning "real patterns" – an intentional truth (such as a correct belief attribution) is "a truth one must understand *with a grain of salt.*"[18] Dennett is firmly in the physicalist camp: Genuine reality is physical reality; genuine explanation is physical explanation. I heartily dissent from any view that takes intentional explanation to be inferior to physical explanation, or that takes intentional truth to be second-class truth.[19]

Third, Practical Realism has no truck with Richard Rorty's relativism. Rorty holds that there are no privileged vocabularies: Our concepts, our vocabularies, are freely chosen. We are "free to shift vocabularies for the sake of convenience."[20] If I am right, then our everyday conception in terms of medium-sized objects, persons with intentional states, and so on is a privileged vocabulary – a vocabulary nonoptional for beings like us, "minded" as we are.[21]

17 Gilbert Ryle, *The Concept of Mind* (New York: Barnes and Noble, 1945), 113, 134.
18 Daniel C. Dennett, *The Intentional Stance* (Cambridge, MA: MIT/Bradford, 1987), 72–3. Emphasis in original.
19 Moreover, I think that taking intentional features to be less "real" than physical features makes for an incoherence in theories that aspire to be scientific. See my "Content Meets Consciousness," *Philosophical Topics,* forthcoming.
20 Richard Rorty, "Comment on Dennett," *Synthese* 53 (1982): 186. I think that Rorty takes "the premise that we have intuitive knowledge, knowledge which is prelinguistic and which thus serves as a test for the adequacy of languages" to be the only possible basis for a privileged vocabulary. See his "Contemporary Philosophy of Mind," *Synthese* 53 (1982): 336. For further discussion, see my "On the Very Idea of a Form of Life," *Inquiry* 27 (1984): 277–89.
21 'Minded' is Jonathan Lear's term. See his "Leaving the World Alone," *Journal of Philosophy* 79 (1982): 382–403.

Moreover, unlike the Practical Realist, Rorty seems ready to replace objectivity by solidarity.[22]

Fourth, Practical Realism rejects John Searle's global distinction between properties that are observer-relative and properties that are intrinsic.[23] According to this distinction, on the one hand, intentionality turns out to be intrinsic; on the other hand, social properties like receiving a death sentence turn out to be observer-relative. Since I take intentionality to be relational, and since I think that the sense in which the property of, say, receiving a death sentence is observer-relative is Pickwickian, I do not want to import Searle's distinction. Indeed, in the (Pickwickian) sense in which Searle intends 'observer-relative', his distinction parallels the mind-dependent–mind-independent distinction that I have just tried to undercut.

Fifth, Practical Realism differs from Hilary Putnam's "internal realism." As I understand it, internal realism entails the view that truth is relative to a conceptual scheme. Recently, Putnam has said:

Internal realism denies that there is a fact of the matter as to which of the conceptual schemes that serve us so well – the conceptual scheme of commonsense objects, with their vague identity conditions and their dispositional and counterfactual properties, or the scientific-philosophical scheme of fundamental particles and their "aggregations" (that is, their mereological sums) – is "really true."[24]

I have urged that, whatever one thinks of the reality of "fused objects" defined by mereological sums, the "conceptual scheme of commonsense objects" is "'really true.'"

CONCLUSION

In recent decades, appreciation of the theoretical achievements of science has turned into an attack on the commonsense conception of the world – not just an attack on "old wives' tales" or on snake-oil remedies, but an attack on the very conception of reality in

22 Richard Rorty, "Solidarity or Objectivity?" in *Objectivity, Relativism, and Truth* (Philosophical Papers 1) (Cambridge: Cambridge University Press, 1991), 21–34.

23 John Searle, *The Rediscovery of the Mind* (Cambridge, MA: MIT/Bradford, 1992), 211.

24 Hilary Putnam, *Realism with a Human Face* (Cambridge, MA: Harvard University Press, 1990), 96. Putnam makes many other remarks about internal realism that I would endorse.

terms of medium-sized objects (artifactual and natural) and of persons with morally significant properties such as interests, duties, feelings, and attitudes. The target of the attack is the conception of reality that is not proprietary to any disciplinary elite but is the common property of all. Philosophers do not dispute that we have such a conception. Rather, heirs to Descartes, they see it either as lacking cognitive legitimacy – good enough for practical affairs but not genuinely revelatory; at best, they see it as dependent on its relation to microphysical reality, in wholly unspecifiable ways, for whatever cognitive legitimacy it has.

Despite enormous substantive differences between contemporary materialism and logical positivism, these two philosophical movements are parallel in structure. Whereas logical positivism took all cognitively meaningful statements to bear a single relation (translation) to a set of privileged statements (protocol sentences, or sense-data statements), contemporary materialism takes everything that there is to bear a single relation (constitution) to a set of privileged objects (fundamental microphysical particles). Thus, contemporary materialism may be seen as a metaphysical analogue of logical positivism.

What I advocate is a kind of "one worldism." There are not two distinct realms, or two distinct kinds of properties, but a single world of practices with indefinitely many kinds of properties.[25] Our posits (as Quine would call them) are what are required to understand our practices and their cognitive success. The sciences are preeminent examples of cognitively successful practices, but so is common sense – the knowing-that that underlies the knowing-how in a language-using community. Thus, I see nothing fishy about saying that there are electrons and there are chairs. And I see no competition between electrons and chairs, or between brains and attitudes – whether chairs (or attitudes) are incorporated into any science or not. If we give up the scholastic notion that everything there is must be connected in a simple metaphysical way (constitution for objects and supervenience for properties) with some fundamental reality, we can get on with trying to understand

---

25 Although this position is not theistic, it is not atheistic either. A theist may see the area of investigation here as confined to the created order. From a theistic point of view, the position espoused here then is that there is a fundamental unity in creation.

the world in which we live and die – the world in which we send our children to school, take care of our aging parents, lose our jobs or move away from our friends, have trouble making ends meet, worry about illness – in short, the world that has meaning for us.

Contemporary materialists approach the *Lebenswelt* with an eye to understanding this world as nothing over and above inert physical elements – whence the "naturalization" project. Their aim is to show how what is meaningful may be understood in terms of what is meaningless. Whether materialism is true or not, the world that has meaning for us (the world in which one either does or does not commit suicide, the world in which some things are more important than others) deserves philosophical attention on its own terms.

According to the "scientistic" outlook behind the Standard View, the categories of common sense must be either incorporated into or superseded by scientific theory. On the contrary, I have argued that common sense is not in competition with scientific theories in any wholesale way: Although common sense may be corrected by science, scientific theories that do not recognize medium-sized objects and persons with intentional states cannot serve the explanatory and predictive purposes to which we put the commonsense conception. Whereas Practical Realism offers a way to do justice to common sense and science at the same time, the Standard View alternative, I believe, runs a serious risk of declaring nonexistent anything anyone has ever cared about.

The following, I submit, are important facts about human beings: Some like to read novels; many are afraid of getting cancer; almost all grieve over the death of a parent; some find fulfillment in scientific research, or in playing the violin; many are anxious about their careers or their personal relations; some wield language fraudulently; a few shape language into poetry; some want to be rich and famous. A psychology that cannot do justice to the fabric of life – no matter how well it is connected to the world as described by the physical sciences – falls short of a complete picture of human reality. Practical Realism need not deny the truth of any scientific theory, psychological or otherwise. Rather, it places scientific inquiry into a larger framework of reliable cognitive practice.

Practical Realism offers an answer to what seems to me to be a major challenge to philosophers: How can we take science seriously without lapsing into the permanent bad faith of refusing to accept the ontological commitments of the practices in terms of which the world makes sense? How can we understand mentality in a way that leaves room for serious moral concerns? The Practical Realist affirms as real such things as injustice, benevolence, and malice, and then goes on to join Dostoevsky in saying that life may be a messy affair, but at least it is life and not a series of extractions of square roots.[26]

26 Fyodor Dostoevsky, *Notes from Underground*, trans. Jesse Coulson (London: Penguin, 1988), 35.

Index

meanings of terms of, 80–2
as part of commonsense conception of reality, 75–6, 220
revisability of, 77–80
as would-be scientific theory, 70–4
constitution (material composition), 8–10, 132–3, 136–8, 182
counterfactuals
and nature of belief, 154–8
as necessary and sufficient for belief, 158–68
and realism about belief, 169–71
and sufficiency problem, 164–68
Cresswell, Max, 35n
Crimmins, Mark, 164n, 170n

Davidson, Donald, 8n, 86, 150n, 189
on explanation, 25, 27n, 97–8, 110–12
Dennett, Daniel C., 83n, 153n, 157n, 186n
on instrumentalism, 6n, 69n, 107, 237
on physicalism, 127n
"depth" metaphor, 126, 150, 181, 191, 209
Descartes, René, 3, 6, 12–13, 68
Devitt, Michael, 22n
Dostoyevsky, Fyodor, 241
Dretske, Fred, 29, 32, 205n
on beliefs as structuring causes, 57–62
Dreyfus, Hubert L., 41n

eliminative materialism, 11, 67–9, 90
explanation, 24–5
commonsense versus theoretical, 107
nonpsychological, 25, 98–101

physical-counterpart, 127
see also causal explanation
explanatory properties, 103–5, 135–6
"screening off," 106
see also causal explanation

Feit, Neil, 160n
Feldman, Fred, 176–8
Field, Hartry, 19n
Fodor, Jerry A., 9n, 11n, 12, 19n, 29, 32, 34, 94, 155n, 185n, 191
on causal explanation, 95–7, 109–10, 112–15
on causal generalizations, 172–5
and cross-context test, 52–6
on intentionality, 194, 205n, 208–9
on local supervenience of causal powers, 64–5
on narrow content, 42–4
and no-conceptual-connection test, 45–51, 117n
functionalism, 10–11

Garfield, Jay, 161n, 190n
Garon, Joseph, 73–77
Goddu, Geoffrey, 112n, 138n, 160n
Goldman, Alvin I., 69n, 72n
Gopnik, Alison, 71n
Gordon, Robert M., 69n
Graham, George, 68n, 69n, 225n
Gustafson, Don, 162n

Harman, Gilbert, 191n
Harris, Paul L., 212n
Haugeland, John, 41n, 122n
Heil, John, 214n
Horgan, Terence, 68n, 69n, 78n, 122n
Horst, Steven, 202n
Hume, David, 234

and science, 223–5
and supervenience, 214–17
Prieur, Annette, 161n
propositional attitudes, *see*
    attitudes
Putnam, Hilary, 8n, 86, 206n,
    215n, 238

Quine, W. V. O., 3, 135n
    on scientific theories, 71, 73, 77,
    79–80, 223–5

Ramsey, William, 73–7
realism
    counterfactuals and, 169–71
    of Practical Realist account of
    belief, 217–18
    of practice-based metaphysics,
    234–6
recognition independence, 232
relational properties, 11–12, 63–5,
    116–18
Rorty, Richard, 237
Ross, Lee, 79
Ryle, Gilbert, 27–8, 237

Sachs, Oliver, 149n
Salmon, Wesley C., 123n, 124–5,
    135n
science
    as only source of knowledge, 3,
    85–90
    and Practical Realism, 223–5
Searle, John R., 187n, 234n, 238
Sellars, Wilfrid, 3, 85–90, 190n
Sider, Theodore, 213n, 214n
Slovic, Paul, 79
Smolensky, Paul, 15n, 75n
Sperber, Dan, 202n
Stalnaker, Robert, 155n, 191n
Standard View of attitudes, 5–12
    and argument from causal ex-
    planation and rebuttal, 17–18,
    136–44

and argument from metaphysics
    and rebuttal, 12–14, 153–4
and argument from science and
    rebuttal, 15–17, 210–12
criticisms of eliminativist ver-
    sion of, 68–9, 77–84
criticisms of noneliminativist
    versions of, 36–42, 45–62
    see also Practical Realism, con-
    trasts with Standard View
Stich, Stephen P., 11n, 15n, 19n,
    46, 94
    on causal explanation, 53, 95–6,
    106–9
    on folk psychology, 7n, 67n,
    73–7, 175n, 185
Stoutland, Frederick, 5n, 123n
supervenience
    definition of global, 214
    definition of strong, 213
    as opposed to constitution, 132,
    137–8, 182
    and Practical Realism, 214–17
    as relation between beliefs and
    brain states, 182–3

Tversky, Amos, 79

van Gulick, Robert, 43n, 137n,
    144n, 178–9, 180n
    on nonreductive materialism,
    8n, 141n, 142n, 214n

Webb, Mark, 193n
Wedin, Michael V., 141n
Weirenga, Ed, 196n
Wilkes, Kathleen, 26, 69n
Wittgenstein, Ludwig, 33n, 86,
    187n
Woodward, James, 68n, 78n

Yablo, Stephen, 144n
Yates, Frances, 89n